2—

1 – 17 – 93          4 – 1 – 92

– DAO –

# NEAR THE
# MAGICIAN

# NEAR THE MAGICIAN

A MEMOIR OF MY FATHER,
EDMUND WILSON

Rosalind Baker Wilson

GROVE WEIDENFELD
NEW YORK

Published by Grove Weidenfeld
A division of Wheatland Corporation
841 Broadway
New York, NY 10003-4793

Published in Canada by General Publishing Company, Ltd.

Grateful acknowledgment is made to the following: Stephen Spender for permission to reprint the poem which appears on p. ix; David Chavchavadze for permission to reprint his correspondence with Rosalind Baker Wilson; Jacqueline Miller Rice for permission to reprint material from Dawn Powell's correspondence with Rosalind Baker Wilson; and Sterling Lord Literistic, Inc. for permission to reprint material from *O'Neill: Son and Artist* by Louis Sheaffer.

Library of Congress Cataloging-in-Publication Data

Wilson, Rosalind Baker.
Near the magician : a memoir of my father, Edmund Wilson /
Rosalind Baker Wilson.
p.      cm.
Includes bibliographical references.
ISBN 1-55584-342-5
1. Wilson, Edmund, 1895–1972—Biography—Family.   2. Wilson,
Rosalind Baker.   3. Authors, American—20th century—Biography—
Family.   4. Fathers and daughters—United States—Biography.
I. Title.
PS3545.I6245Z94      1989
818'.5209—dc20                                                     89-22470
[B]                                                                         CIP

Manufactured in the United States of America
Printed on acid-free paper
Designed by Irving Perkins Associates
First Edition

1   3   5   7   9   10   8   6   4   2

*For the Memory*
*of*
*Helen Mather Kimball Wilson*
*and*
*Jennie Corbett*

I should like to thank the Beinecke Library
at Yale University for its courtesy in sending me
copies of my letters to my father.

RBW

I think continually of those who were truly great.
Who, from the womb, remembered the soul's history
Through corridors of light where the hours are suns,
Endless and singing. Whose lovely ambition
Was that their lips, still touched with fire,
Should tell of the Spirit, clothed from head to foot in song.
And who hoarded from the Spring branches
The desires falling across their bodies like blossoms.

What is precious, is never to forget
The essential delight of the blood drawn from ageless springs
Breaking through rocks in worlds before our earth.
Never to deny its pleasure in the morning simple light
Nor its grave evening demand for love.
Never to allow gradually the traffic to smother
With noise and fog, the flowering of the Spirit.

Near the snow, near the sun, in the highest fields,
See how these names are feted by the waving grass
And by the streamers of white cloud
And whispers of wind in the listening sky.
The names of those who in their lives fought for life,
Who wore at their hearts the fire's centre.
Born of the sun, they travelled a short while toward the sun,
And left the vivid air signed with their honour.

*Stephen Spender poem etched by him
with a diamond pencil on three
panes of glass in the window at the
top of the stairs in the stone house
looking out to the high fields. The
panes were later cracked by vandals
with stones.*

# PART
# I

# I

I WAS TAKEN FROM THE HOSPITAL where I was born down
to the home of my paternal grandmother, Helen Mather
Kimball Wilson, in Red Bank, New Jersey. My mother,
my father's first wife, the actress Mary Blair, had been weak-
ened by whooping cough and pleurisy, brought on partially
by the violent attack on her by the Ku Klux Klan, the Anti-
Vice League and the nationwide one by clubwomen such as
the DAR, when she was playing in Eugene O'Neill's *All God's
Chillun Got Wings* and kissed Paul Robeson's hand on stage.
She couldn't take care of me and meet her theatrical commit-
ments. Under "Occupation" on my birth certificate she listed
herself as "Housewife." My father, Edmund Wilson, then
managing editor of the *New Republic*, listed himself as
"Plant Manager." It was four months after my grandfather's
death on May 15, 1923. I stayed in Red Bank because my
mother became tubercular; my grandmother felt, "Rosalind
is my child."

For the next twenty-eight years, my father was to come

3

down to Red Bank almost every weekend and sometimes for longer periods of time to see his mother and me until I went out on my own, and even then we still met in Red Bank. I spent the summer months with him; between his marriages to Mary McCarthy and Margaret Canby, it was he and I alone during those months.

His trained nurse and I were with him when he died on June 12, 1972, in his mother's family house in the hamlet of Talcottville, town of Leyden, county of Lewis, in upper New York State.

His ambivalent relationship with his mother was a deep one, as mine was to be with him. Until my grandmother's death in 1951, Red Bank was his other home, as opposed to the ones he made elsewhere with his wives or for himself. I believe his fourth marriage survived, although often stormily, because of my grandmother's death four years into it. When he was about to marry Elena, he said to me, "Elena is a derivative of Helen, Mother's name. Perhaps it will bring me luck." And three-quarters of the way it did.

It lasted for twenty-six years, and for twenty-one of those years he spent four or five months alone in Talcottville, which adds up to eight years, more or less, when he and Elena weren't together. I was surprised when I moved upstate for good at how much of his life was up here.

As I was brought up totally by my father and my grandmother, except for two summers when I spent a month with my mother, it gave him and me a past and a frame of reference no one else ever quite understood. We were both molded by my grandmother's strong will and values, as well as by the difficulties in communicating with the most important person in our lives because of her deafness. As I grew older, he was sometimes jealous of me as if I were a sibling rival for her affections.

A lot of my information on life in Red Bank before I was born came from my grandmother and Jennie Corbett, her maid-companion, also various great-aunts and people who had known my grandmother and grandfather. They had a different view of the past and the then present than my father.

This memoir uses the Red Bank years, and my memories of my father as I dismantled the contents of the Talcottville house, as stepping-stones.

He had his own room in his mother's house. It was not a boyhood room as she had moved to a new house right after her husband's death, nor a guest room, but a room in command of the line: books on the shelves, letters and papers, clothes in the closet, the great four-poster bed his Aunt Addie (who lived in the Talcottville house I now occupy) left him, a table ready with yellow pads and No. 2 pencils, and objects he had brought back from various trips: a carved wooden beaver from New Mexico, gnawing at a fish, and screwed to the bookcase shelf, and next to it a gruesome reproduction of a Notre Dame gargoyle.

At any hour, he could call Red Bank, announce he was coming, be met by Oscar, the chauffeur, and have his every whim catered to by my grandmother, Jennie, and Gerta, the cook. As my grandfather had left all the money in my grandmother's hands to dole out to my father as she saw fit, he discussed most of his business transactions with her. In spite of the fact that Red Bank was easily reached from New York City by the North Jersey coast train, it had southern aspects. In the spring, old men would appear on the streets selling soft-shell crabs from baskets of seaweed. The summers were long and hot and full of mosquitoes, bred in the Jersey swamps. My father and I were referred to in the household as Mr. Edmund and Miss Rosalind, except by my grandmother, who called me "Petty Lamb." Her nickname for my father had been "Bunny," but he'd managed to squash her calling him that.

In the summers, my grandmother took off for Talcottville in her Cadillac with Oscar and Jennie. Her home there was the stone house which had been in her family and which my grandfather had bought because he was so crazy about it. She didn't want my father or me to come and visit her and so discouraged any such efforts. She kept up a beautiful garden in Talcottville with a local gardener and cook.

It was to this house my father had come in May 1972 to die. He had heart trouble and the doctors had told him two years before that it was a matter of time before his heart would slow down and he would die; he had refused a pacemaker.

Once in Talcottville, he had a trained nurse three hours every day and some nights. We spelled each other. She'd tell him she felt she was stealing, taking a trained nurse's fee. He'd say, "Well, would you take half?" She'd ask, "Would you?" And they'd laugh. The day before I was to take him to meet Elena in Cummington, Massachusetts, at his old friend Helen Muchnic's, on his way back to Wellfleet on Cape Cod, he had a run-of-the-mill last day, went for a ride with his buddy Glyn Morris, and bawled me out for not bringing *Time* magazine quickly enough. (For years, he wouldn't have *Time* magazine in the house because he disapproved of Henry Luce.) He was reading Housman's last poems from a book he'd given my Great-aunt Laura as a boy. In the afternoon, he had a glass of white wine and played Ravel on the phonograph. He had a good supper. When his cousins, the Munns, came in at seven, he had gone back to bed; when he had me get him up and take him to the chair by the window where he always sat, he said, "Oh, that I should have come to this." He brushed his hair, and I took him into the living room. It was twenty of eight. I told the Munns to stay until his nurse came. I said, "Goodbye, Father," and went to my house.

At six-twenty the next morning, the nurse called and said, "Your father is having a bad spell"; I went over in my night-clothes. He was in his chair and she was giving him oxygen. He had had two convulsions. I called the doctor. My father was dead when he arrived.

6

He was laid out in the white iron bed which had once been Jennie's, in the long room in the stone house. He had a bouquet of mock orange and lemon lilies I had picked for him the night before. A short service was conducted by Glyn Morris, an ordained Presbyterian minister. A few neighbors, some of whom had worked for him for years, were there, and a few friends. The coffin went to the crematorium, and Elena, who had flown up, took his ashes to Wellfleet.

The split between his two lives remained intact until the end.

An old friend called me that night and said, "Well, one of the last of the great dragons has gone."

Two days later, I went down to Wellfleet for the last time for the memorial service, taking with me the local woman who some years before had given him the lady-slippers he coveted in exchange for an autographed copy of one of his books for her doctor. She was with me to help with the driving. We took some of the wild orchids and planted them at the gravesite before they "went into shock" as she feared.

At the service were some old Cape Cod friends from my childhood, some people from New York whom I didn't know, such as Lillian Hellman, and some I did, such as Jason Epstein, sloppily dressed, slouched over the hole in which the urn was to go. His attitude was that of chief mourner.

My half sister, Helen, and her boyfriend had arranged that the grave diggers shouldn't fill in the grave, something my half brother, Reuel, and I didn't know. Suddenly, we were handed shovels and told to fill in the dirt—a nightmarish situation as we stomped the dirt on our father's grave. The grave diggers had to stand by anyway by law. Jason later wrote that "Edmund's children played like happy children in the sand."

Right after the service, I drove the long way back to Talcott-ville. Some of the lady-slippers around the stone house had already been dug up by souvenir hunters. Coming out of

Albany, I remembered trips when I had sometimes been my father's unwilling chauffeur and how he'd always say "How wonderful to have the country widen out after the cramped-ness of Massachusetts." And we'd sing, "Oh, the Erie is a-rising, the sun is a-settin' low. And we won't get another drink until we reach Buffalo." Once I missed the Utica-Rome exit and crossed the grass to go back the other way, which is illegal. Naturally, our New York State Thruway card showed the toll booth operator what we'd done. My father bellowed, "Look here, I'm Edmund Wilson from Talcottville!" and we drove off, leaving the man openmouthed. He had probably never heard of the tiny hamlet of Talcottville, thirty miles north, nor of my father. But he knew the person in that car was someone, with a capital S, who thought he owned wher-ever he was from. My father had once announced, "I *am* Talcottville," a fact disputed by some of his neighbors then and after his death.

I never returned to the Cape. The great Tug Hill plateau in back of Talcottville rolling off to Lake Ontario, and the Adirondacks looming up in front took the place of the Cape Cod dunes, drifting along the Black River instead of braving the ocean waves. I never saw my stepmother Elena again, a woman for whom I had respect and affection, although we did continue to salute each other on birthdays and holidays.

I had inherited the stone house in Talcottville and the contents thereof except for the books in foreign languages, which went to my brother, Reuel.

Once having moved upstate permanently in 1969, I had spent the first winter in the stone house and then moved to a house several houses south of it belonging to two old sisters who were remaining Talcotts. I eventually bought it from them. It was easy to heat in winter and had pleasant memories from when our cousins, the Sharps, had rented it in the summers. This was during a time when Malcolm Sharp, a brilliant lawyer married to my cousin Dorothy, had been

8

amicus curiae in the Rosenberg case and advisor for their children.

I steeled myself to go over to the stone house and begin the strangely emotional job of dismantling its contents. For years, my father had arranged things so that there were two sets of everything: one for Wellfleet, one for the stone house— puppets and puppet theaters, records and record collections, collections of his own books, collections of the classics, furniture and pieces of art. A group of stone sculptures cut by a Utica artist named Despirito stood huddled in the corner of one of the living rooms along with a stone bunny rabbit he had sent my grandmother from Europe during World War I.

It had been a famous house even before he had written about it in *Upstate* in 1970. There had been a giant picture of it on the wall of the New York pavilion of the 1939–40 World's Fair, and the local historical society had tried to buy it from my grandmother instead of the more beautifully landscaped Constable Hall, which is now Lewis County's answer to Charlottesville's Monticello.

June can be cold in Talcottville; the house was no longer heated after my father's death. My grandmother had always said the only way to go into a cold stone house and stay in it was to take a bottle of brandy with you. I put the bottle of Courvoisier on the mantelpiece of the long double room in which he had died, next to the picture of Grandmother taken in profile in her twenties, which had an oval gilt frame and pink taffeta matting. The picture had been on the bookcase in his study in Wellfleet for years, along with a picture of Edna St. Vincent Millay and one Elena had given him of herself in her twenties. He had brought the picture of my grandmother up recently.

Nothing was left of a house in which arrival is expected. The old Red Bank tray would never again be used for his meals; Jennie's white iron bed, which had been brought downstairs for the last two years, would never be made again.

In the desk of what had been my grandmother's bedroom, I found a valentine he had sent me that year. We were a family who sent valentines the way other people send Christmas cards. No matter how frightful the family relationship was at the moment, the annual valentine was posted. It was a two-foot red card with a large goofy-looking white bear on the outside and a gold heart over his head. Inside, in large black letters it announced: "OURS HAS BEEN A STRANGE AND WONDERFUL RELATIONSHIP." That bear said a mouthful.

I was driving past the stone house a few summers before and had seen him coming down the steps, anticipating a date, his small feet in their polished brown shoes pointed firmly toward the afternoon's enjoyment. It was like seeing a stranger. I thought, "Boy, you've really had a good time of it." A few minutes later, on my return trip from visiting an elderly connection up the road, there was an old man with a light straw hat on his head, carrying a cardboard suitcase, standing in front of Roch's store next to our house, begging a ride to the fair. I picked him up and he said, nodding toward the stone house, "He's a great man with the ladies."

I had also come across a postcard with a fine print of a very disagreeable fish on it, a toothy pickerel. I had received it from my father during a year when I had simply refused to see him. The card asked, in his meticulous handwriting, "Whatever happened to you?" I had framed it in a small dime store frame.

He had called me one day in Boston and demanded I come up to Talcottville. I was then working and there had been a series of threats when I didn't toe the line of "Then I won't leave you Talcottville." Naturally, I had said, "For heaven's sake, don't," and rather unnaturally hung up for a year. I had called him up a year later and he said, "I was just thinking about you"; it was the one dereliction of mine he never mentioned again.

He also had a habit of mentioning in a similar vein his

diaries, "which will make a lot of people mad," and "from which you will all be living," which made me say, "Shove them." Happily, I never did have anything to do with my father's literary remains. When I did get around to looking in the diaries, my reaction was to be amazed sometimes at his view of things, which goes under the heading of "which side of the fence were you sitting on?" The picture of the pickerel brought back memories of some minor matters he left out of his forties diaries.

The unconscious is a convoluted affair; my father's was more intricate than most. The popular writer Phyllis Duganne had had a coolness with him, and had suddenly received a playing card he'd taken from her deck during a magic trick five years before. Being a New Englander, the only true-born Cape Codder in the literary set, she'd kept the deck and was glad to get the card back and resumed amenities with him. "What can you do with a man like that?" was her comment.

# II

I BELIEVE THE POSTCARD with the spiteful pickerel on it stemmed from some far-off association in my father's mind with the summer I was twenty-three and my fishing quests with the pianist George Chavchavadze.

That summer of 1946 had found me in the Wellfleet house. As I have said, when my grandfather died, he left everything to my grandmother; because she controlled the finances of my father, she also was in charge of mine. One of the reasons I was home at twenty-three was because my grandmother had bought the Wellfleet house when my father was married to Mary McCarthy as a place for me and Mary's son Reuel to go. When my grandmother had gone to the Cape to look at the house before buying it, she stayed at the local inn, the Holiday House, and paid a visit to Father and Mary, who were staying at a rented house in Truro. When they saw her coming, they slipped their drinks under the chairs. Why? I don't know, as she had every sort of cocktail shaker and glass and liquor in the Red Bank house. She sat and talked with them for a while, and as she went out the door, she said, "You can bring your drinks out now."

I had left Bennington at the end of my junior year, taking quite a few other restless students with me. I was heady with successful winter work periods and the feeling of restlessness generated by the war. I had had an apartment in New York City and worked for the *New York Post*. After his tumultuous divorce from Mary McCarthy, which more or less coincided with my leaving Bennington, my father had pressured me into coming back and keeping house for him.

Most of the men I knew were on the GI Bill of Rights at Ivy League colleges, freshmen in their middle twenties. The atmosphere on the Cape was one of happy beaches, perpetual parties and some very magical people.

My father loved his children and his animals but often forgot about them for long periods of time; and when he looked around again, after skipping several chapters, was confused by the scenario. Anyone closely connected with him was likely to develop a helter-skelter way of life. He would want me around when it was convenient and turn me out when it wasn't. My grandmother's way of dealing with this was to say she didn't want me out on the streets and to curtail his finances. And I was not above playing the situation.

Also, I could be very indolent. I was, after all, named after my Great-great-aunt Rosalind Baker of Talcottville, who rose from her chair only once a year to make a little apple jelly. It was said things had skipped a generation, and so I was like my grandfather, a trial lawyer, who would get out of bed and take a case only when the money ran out.

That summer my father and his fourth wife, Elena, wanted to go to Europe, and it was convenient to have me there while they were away to run the house for my baby half sister born in February and her nurse, Miss Carver, an adorable pink and white dumpling of a woman who looked like a baby herself.

The summer when I was sixteen, my father had taught at the University of Chicago. I had had a room in a dormitory until Mary (McCarthy) had taken Reuel out to see her grandmother in Seattle. Then I moved into their apartment, and my father and I did a lot of moviegoing. One night, as we watched a scene in which a cad plied Simone Simon with champagne, he leaned over and bellowed in his resonant voice, trained by speaking to my deaf grandmother, "Never let anyone do that to you." Mademoiselle Simon was propped up on a Madame Récamier divan and the man in a tuxedo was leaning over, proffering her the bubbly liquid with ardor in his eyes. It all looked delightful.

I didn't start to drink until I was twenty, but when I did, it was champagne all the way. John Dos Passos dubbed me "Champagne Rosie" and, as his wife, Katy, leaned that way, they always had some on ice for me. I spent a lot of my time at their place if things got complicated at home. It was part of the whole never-never ambiance of my life then to sit with them, popping corks, looking out on Provincetown Harbor from their back garden.

Father and Elena were not leaving until July. (I was happily disposed toward her as her family had made Mumm's champagne.) But I deftly managed to savor the pleasures of a languid summer from May until September.

On a warm harmonious morning in mid-May, I was following my usual course of seeing the day in. I'd bicycled to town around eleven with our dog Wrecky and was sitting in the back of Newcomb's soda fountain, gossiping with its owner, my friend Elrie, a local Wellfleet beauty. We had discovered that a very good place to chill champagne fast was the ice-cream freezer. I had barely walked the bottles the few blocks from William's liquor store to Newcomb's when they were cold enough to drink, while she made the sandwiches people called for at lunchtime. As we progressed with the popping of corks and toasting, the westerners got a little confused with the peanut butter and grilled cheese. But Newcomb's was such an institution, no one complained. Wrecky, who had been given us by Elrie's father, an ex–circus man, went out and put his paws on the counter while the help gave him ice-cream cones.

I asked, "What's new on the Wellfleet riviera?" Elrie, who had a romantic streak, would sometimes wear English riding clothes and ride her horse over the dunes.

"Liz Freeman [Admiral Chester Nimitz's niece, who was the real estate agent in those days and would say, "And when Chet gets in with the fleet, they'll come and mess up the house"] says she's rented the Moran house to three bachelors, one of them a prince." The Moran house, a classic small Cape Cod house in a hollow, belonged to an old family and was just outside of town on Mill Hill Road.

Newcomb's was known for its attractive personnel, and occasionally one of the waitresses would come back, take a quick gulp of champagne and gossip en passant. The girls began planning ways to meet the three bachelors. Elrie thought she might pass by on her horse and faint or have the horse faint. Little did I think I would be the chosen one.

Shortly after, I went to dinner at Paul and Nina Chavchavadzes', who were intimate friends of my family's and mine. Nina's maiden name had been Romanov and she was a grand duchess of Russia. Her father, the tsar's uncle, had been shot by the Bolsheviks as he was leaving Russia. Her mother had been queen of Greece. Paul was a Georgian prince. Although Georgian princes are a dime a dozen, he came from a very distinguished family. On his maternal side, one of his uncles, General Radzianko, known en fa-mille as Uncle Horse, had been head of the Russian cavalry.

When Nina and Paul became American citizens, they dropped their titles. They moved to Wellfleet, where they took in paying guests. Nina, who had been brought up with enormous discipline and frugality as her father had seen what was coming, did all the work. Very often, their relatives would surface, all of whom seemed to have handled with panache the strange hand fate had dealt them. Their son David was a GI Yalie, now at summer school, and the friends he brought up on vacations had lightened the Wellfleet scene for me. The house was set off in the woods and although a small New England one, gave the illusion of being a palace, perhaps because every side looked out on a different garden and patio. Somehow when the Russian songs pealed out over the guitars and vodka, you felt it was the Summer Palace in the Crimea.

In England, Nina had, for a while, been in the position of being the poor relation of the British royal family and thought very little of their riding ability. She claimed they fell off all the time and couldn't hold a candle to the cossacks. She took a dim view of outcast European royalty who became American citizens and still insisted on using their titles.

That summer my wardrobe consisted of a blue-and-white-striped cotton Gibson Girl blouse for day wear and a violet linen blouse for evening wear and a navy blue broadcloth skirt run up by that great couturier, Louise Hazlett of Well-fleet. She would say, "If you don't have enough material, I'll insert a piece of my skin." The blouses were castoffs of my generous best friend, Jeannie Clymer, whose mother, the designer Gwenyth Waugh, had a shop in Dennis. Jeannie had solved her pin-money problems by selling Gertrude Lawrence, who was playing at the Dennis Playhouse, some dresses Jeannie had made for herself, so the blouses, though shabby, were well cut. With the money I was spending on champagne, I'd had to forget about clothes.

The night of my dinner with the Chavchavadzes, I tossed on my dinner blouse and cycled over to their house. When I arrived, they were having drinks on their patio with two gentlemen, while a third in a white coat hovered in the background. Paul introduced his brother, George, and George's secretary, Orlando, a handsome Mexican known as "the Puma." It turned out George was to be the tenant of the Moran house along with Puma and George's cook, Lorenzo, "the Magnificent," a blond Italian. Both Puma and Lorenzo exuded good looks and a light in their being. George looked like a brunet Leslie Howard and his manner was somewhat that of the Scarlet Pimpernel in his foppish phase. At dinner, cooked by Nina, we ate in the kitchen alcove, as was their custom, while Lorenzo ate in the dining room.

George was a concert pianist and had come to Wellfleet that summer to be near his brother and prepare for a concert in Europe that fall. He had been chosen to play at the Chopin festival. He suffered from the stigma of being a society pianist, although every important music critic had lauded him as otherwise. He said that as soon as he solved the problem of getting his piano into the Moran house, he intended to turn his attention to fishing. I said I enjoyed fishing the Wellfleet ponds with salt pork or live minnows; the catch was pickerel. This was before the days of massive trout stocking. George said, "Why don't we go out early tomorrow morning?"

I said, "Fine. I'll meet you anywhere on my bicycle," as he saw me to it.

"No, no, no, we'll pick you up in the Cadillac," which was a long black convertible.

At five the next morning, I was ready, but only Puma showed up. George was waiting for the piano movers. We stopped in town to pick up the minnows caught by young Alfred Pickard, my usual fishing companion, and set off for Higgins Pond. Never have I seen pickerel bite as they did that morning. They are a mean-looking fish with a lot of teeth and bones, but very good eating once you've managed to clean them. The fish seemed to fight each other to take our hooks. Usually, you sat for hours ruminating among the lily pads before you got a nibble. Within an hour, we'd caught sixteen large ones and decided we'd better stop.

I went home and at about ten o'clock George called. His voice exuded excitement. Would I come to dinner that night and eat the fish which even now Lorenzo was cleaning?

I said, "Sure."

He could kick himself for not having gone with us, etc. That was to be the first of many happy evenings at George's, sometimes with Paul and Nina or Jeannie or a few people he had in to play for, but very often just George, Puma, Lorenzo, me and, above all, the freshly caught fish.

George, unlike most of the people on the Cape, didn't drink, except perhaps a small Dubonnet before "din-din," but that was it. He practiced long hours and spent the rest of the time fishing. Lorenzo devised a way of pouring champagne into a thermos that had a faucet so it was "on tap."

Due to the fact we ate nothing but fish, which Lorenzo prepared in every possible way, it wasn't an extravagant household. Lorenzo did the shopping at the Prima Nazionale, as he called it, which evoked visions of great Italian markets. His English was mottled, to say the least, and he would hopefully slip in a few German words, which he had learned in order to survive during the war, when he became desperate to communicate. He was soon learning English with the village postmistress, whom he neglected to tell he was married and had several children. A lack of knowledge of the language was no excuse!

George himself had married a very rich woman, of French extraction. And they had a huge palazzo in Venice which was later used to film *Brideshead Revisited*, and a great place in Bernardsville, New Jersey, occupied by the Marquis de Cuevas and his ballet company that summer. Nina rather liked George's wife, Elizabeth, whom Nina said was perfectly beautiful except for a pathological weight problem which made her grotesquely fat. She said Elizabeth was deferential about George's music and had a lot on her side but certainly loved being called "Principessa" by the Italians. Since

George was a British citizen, where a prince was still a prince, Nina let his use of "prince" slip by; but I noticed none of the Moran house trio used it much when she was around. I gathered George and his wife had come to some arrangement about their lives, but as my relationship with George was purely that of a fishing companion and a comrade he liked to have around, the state of his marriage was of no importance.

George, who had been used to sport fishing with lures and flies and going off to Scotland to fish in a civilized way, would put his hand to his head, "How crude this is! What have I come to? Live minnows. Pieces of salt pork." Nevertheless, it became an obsession—like Captain Ahab and Moby Dick. But Captain Ahab seemed halfhearted in his pursuit of the great white whale compared to George in his frenzied search for the Wellfleet pickerel.

The first morning after Puma's and my success, we caught nothing, and on successive mornings we caught only one or two, and this drove George wild. He had been pictured in *The Tatler* in correct fishing apparel, his beautiful hands tying a fly, and now the mean, common, toothy pickerel had reduced him to a humble rowboat and his cook handing him hooks with live minnows on a handline he dropped straight into the water.

I had become an almost nightly fish-eating guest at George's. He would call my house at five or so in the morning and say to whoever answered, "I just bounced out of bed and want to speak to Rosalind." Unfortunately, several times he woke my father, who answered. I tried to explain how touchy my parent could be. But it would have done no good for Captain Ahab's first mate to complain he was being a bit of a nuisance about that white whale. And that was my situation.

My father never slept in just one room. He went to bed early with a glass of scotch, then woke up periodically during the night and wandered from room to room. He had long ago taken over the yellow room in the front of the house, which was supposed to be mine, but would sometimes go to the room in the back of the house over his study or to the one he and Elena shared. You could never tell where he was. I occupied a room on the third floor.

My evenings with George could go very late. He often played the piano for several hours; his playing was unspeakably beautiful. And it took a long time for Lorenzo to prepare our pickerel. It can take an hour just to clean and debone the fish, and if you're going to cook it haute cuisine—Milanese, Romano, or perhaps Française—as Lorenzo did, the night could wear itself away. Also, George loved elaborate charades with props that had to be tracked down, and everyone dressed up. (He also parodied the great operas in an amusing way, taking several parts, and if put to it could have gone the way of Victor Borge.)

Once, some time into the second week of my George saga, I had bicycled home (I didn't dare be dropped off, as our old dog, Wrecky, howled with delight when I got in). I met with an obstacle as I started in the front door. As I pushed a little farther, I recognized the leg of a rocker, on top of which was a Hitchcock chair, and on top of that a bread box, which came crashing down as per my father's plan. He had booby-trapped the door.

"Rosalind!" he bellowed as only he could pronounce that name disapprovingly. "Why are you making all that noise? What are you doing?"

"Getting in from George's."

"What's going on?"

"He played some music."

"You woke me up."

"Why did you put the chairs in front of the door?"

"I don't know what you're talking about."

The next night, I tried the back door and was met with a noise that sounded like the cymbal section of a seedy orchestra. He had piled up garbage cans on the inside of the door.

At this point, George said he would take things in hand, so he invited Father and Elena over one afternoon with me and played for us. As George had read only two books in his life, *Alice in Wonderland* and *Three Men in a Boat*, by Jerome K. Jerome, the conversation lagged when he wasn't playing. But no one could listen to him perform without coming away with a profound respect for his talent.

My father continued to build his booby traps. If it hadn't been that he didn't dare negate the fact I had been listening to a first-class musician and needed me to be in the house while they went to Europe, I would have been a dead duck. Also, there was the specter of my grandmother.

The carefully constructed booby traps, the nightly tirades, my father's paradoxical behavior in complaining that I made a noise and woke him up when the booby traps made it impossible for me not to, and his denial of their existence began to wear on me.

As a result, I disappeared from the family scene altogether except for coming home to sleep, a nerve-wracking nightly experience. We took our search to further ponds in Eastham, Dennis, Sandwich—although they didn't compare to the chain of Wellfleet ponds. George said mockingly that he didn't dare go fishing alone, for once a mammoth snapping turtle had "put its paws on the side of the boat" and tried to climb in.

My blue skirt was riddled with fishhook tears. We had inadvertently shifted to eels for several dinners, as George had caught some and nothing could be wasted. The first two nights, I held this delicacy in my cheeks so I wouldn't hurt Lorenzo's feelings. He had been so glad to lavish his talents on something different. Then I had to admit I hated it.

But the maddest coup of all was George's discovery of the solunar hour when the sun and the moon are just right for the fish to bite.

Occasionally, he would go fishing for sea bass on the ocean

side with lures and he met a man who gave him the solunar table. I didn't take part in the more elegant bass fishing except to go along once in a while and swim, often with my clothes on, as there was a group who went nude on the ocean beach; I took a perverse pleasure in shocking them.

With the solunar table in his hand, he rallied his entourage—Puma, me, Lorenzo. He gave us a pep talk, as a coach might to a losing team. Now everything would be all right; we would re-create that halcyon morning when Puma and I had caught sixteen great pickerel in an hour. The solunar hours came at very strange times, say, 3:23 in the morning, or 7:16 in the evening, which meant that we had dinner at midnight.

Not only was my father trying to monitor me, but there were people trying to get hold of George. His nephew, for instance, home from Yale summer school for the weekend; the Paul Chavchavadzes, who, though involved in the mad Wellfleet cocktail circuit of no interest to George, would have liked to see a bit more of him. One day his nephew called and pressed Lorenzo as to when we'd be back. Lorenzo, cornered, said simply over and over again, "Prince mit fish, Prince mit fish." Much as one might say, "Woman with child." At last, Lorenzo, who was left home to cook when not carrying the minnow pail, had discovered the all-purpose phrase which eliminated giving time of return, future plans, attempting explanations in English, etc. It stopped my father cold when he called with such questions as, "Don't you have any idea when they'll be back? Where are they?"

I had been too busy with George even to go into New-comb's, but word of my being seen in the Cadillac with the inhabitants of the Moran house had gotten back there via Alfred Pickard, our minnow procurer, as he spooned his chocolate sundae bought, no doubt, with his accelerated income. Other people had noticed the man who had been hired to drive a boat to Spectacle Ponds, two inaccessible little ponds which had never had a boat on them or, as it turned out, a pickerel in them. Acquaintances saw us as the big Cadillac hove into view on the small dirt roads going to the ponds.

With the advent of the solunar hour, people would come upon us late at night or early in the morning. George had a routine he'd do, an imitation of the leader of a bird-watching group. One night he was doing this by the light of the moon, "See the double-breasted, single-twitted tit hawk." And we looked up, pretending to be devout bird-watchers. Some people emerged from the woods, exiting from a party, and word was all over the next day that we'd been seen acting strangely. Gossip blazed. It would have been useless to explain that my relationship with George was based almost solely on fish because I would have had to explain George, his strong mystical streak, my own untethered spirit, the petty wish for revenge the crafty and elusive pickerel could engender. And we were too busy for explanations.

After my father and stepmother had gone to Europe—and Elena was glad to get off as the nightly noisy rows were making her hollow-eyed—the fish dinners switched to our house, and Puma and Lorenzo were free to pursue their various social lives among the local ladies. Miss Carver enjoyed the dinner parties, some of which were memorable. Usually the guests would be assembled and George would arrive solunarly late and stand for a minute in the doorway dressed impeccably in white flannels and navy blue blazer, holding a large dead bass, presenting it to the assembled dinner guests at large. It had to be stuffed and cooked. Having the whole dinner ready except for the main entrée made for some tense moments until George's arrival.

The days shortened and fall came and George began to make plans for a short stay at Bernardsville before his return to Europe. His nephew, David, had his eyes on a girl who was a succulent beauty and whom his parents weren't happy about.

(She later achieved fame by tangling with Humphrey Bogart in a nightclub, apparently trying to take his toy panda away from him.) George, in his role of guiding uncle—"Watch me handle this"—had conceived of the idea of a house party at Bernardsville with David and his friends, myself, and perhaps some extra girls to take David's mind off Miss X, whom Lauren Bacall referred to in her memoirs as "a young lady about town."

As I was going back to my grandmother's in Red Bank, I would go to the party from there. George wanted to drive to Red Bank from Bernardsville and pick me up, but I discouraged this. I didn't see how I was going to explain the nuances of George to my deaf grandmother. To her, he would have been a married man in a long car. She kept asking me if Nina Chavchavadze would be at the house party, and I assured her she would.

The party was from Thursday until Sunday after lunch. I took a series of trains from Red Bank on Thursday; George met me and explained the others had been delayed a night. The Bernardsville house was gigantic and rather ugly, with massive high-ceilinged rooms. Lorenzo was doing everything: cooking, turning down beds, serving. Puma, George and I stayed up all night as we invented a game, a poor variation on hockey using curtain rods as hockey sticks and ashtrays as pucks. We played on the Persian carpet in the great downstairs entrance hall.

David and his friends and Nina, Paul and their cousin Natalia appeared the next day, and Lorenzo continued his miraculous activities. George had planned a dinner party for Saturday. He announced this to us proudly during the soup course on Friday, which Lorenzo had served even as his foot was on the stair to rush up to turn down the beds, valet a few clothes, lady's maid a few, and be down in time for the next course. George said two girls from prep school were coming, chaperoned by a Mrs. Millicent Fenwick (who would later become a force in Jersey politics). I myself was wearing an old blue serge school uniform I had unearthed in Red Bank, with my blouses and an old silk kimono of my grandmother's sewn up the front for evening wear.

Saturday came, a stormy day. George and Puma, who had for some reason grown a beard, were rushing around making preparations for charades. Many of George's charades were real productions, elaborate and carefully rehearsed. He had one which involved himself sitting in a picture frame with a girl standing outside admiring him. He said to me, "Now, do you think you could possibly be the girl and say 'I'm madly in love with you' without bursting into laughter?" I couldn't.

The storm raged on and time sped by as Orlando ran around with props, vases, curtains torn down, pictures removed from their frames. There was a clap of thunder, a flash of lightning. Puma stepped on my toe as he bounced by in the hall with a large plaster cupid. I screamed and at that moment there were shadows on the glass at the front door, which Puma flung open. There were the girls and Mrs. Fenwick looking terrified. The driveway up to the house was very Gothic.

The girls were nice-looking but certainly not going to take a young man's mind off the spectacular charms of Miss X. I think they found the charades very exciting and probably had plenty to tell their friends when they went back to school.

The next day, we went our various ways, leaving George at the house, which was sold after that, preparing to return to Europe. He asked me to come and stay if I came to Venice, but I never called him. I felt there were no pickerel in the Venice canals. Pickerel was his nickname for me; I didn't think he could cope with Rosalind.

I'd hear about him occasionally from Paul and Nina. The news was always sad. George and his wife had gone to the great costume ball given by Charles Bestegni in Venice to which the superrich from all over the world had come.

George's wife had gone as Catherine the Great, with George as her weak tsar walking behind her, and a man dressed as a Russian priest walking before them sprinkling holy water. This, quite rightly, appalled the White Russian church-in-exile establishment, and showed what a pass George must have come to in his need for financial support from his wife, as he was partially supporting Aunt Mare and Uncle Horse, the Radziankos.

Several years later, I had gone to work as an editor at Houghton Mifflin in Boston and while on a business trip was walking in New York with Bertrand De Gafoy, a photographer with whom we were dealing. We were going down East Eighty-sixth Street in Yorkville late at night, taking in various drink and dance places when a voice yelled "Rosalinda." It was "the Puma." He invited us for champagne and said he was getting married the next day. When we congratulated him, he buried his head in his hands and said, "Maybe it's a mistake. She's got one big mind of her own." I asked about George, and he said, sadly, he'd heard nothing since he left his employ.

One night in Boston after the theater, I went with some people to a young couple's house. When the hostess said there was someone below who wanted to see me, I went down. There was Miss Carver sitting gloomily below the stairs. "I heard your voice," she said. "Oh, how I enjoyed that summer and the dinners with the prince."

The last I heard of George was a letter from Paul Chavchavadze saying George and his wife had been killed in a motor accident outside of Paris and that they had had a rapprochement the year before their deaths.

They were apparently killed immediately. George had been driving. I couldn't imagine George with his perfect timing and eagle eyes getting into an accident, but then neither had I been able to imagine him with the false Russian priest walking before him, unless it was a ghastly extension of his charades.

If anyone asked me what the most pleasant thing I've done in my life was—not the most romantic, exciting or fulfilling, merely the most pleasant—I would answer, "Sitting on the shabby sofa in the Moran house after a day or night outdoors, a glass of champagne in my hand, the smell of haute cuisine pickerel in the air, and listening to Prince George Chavchavadze play Chopin."

# III

I N JUNE OF 1972, I could come and go as I pleased; there was no one to booby-trap my movements.

Phyllis Duganne, to whom my father had returned the playing card, and whose off–*Saturday Evening Post* comments were of a different caliber than her best-selling stories, which radiated romance and light, had once said to me, "Your father is the most complicated person I have ever known. He has an almost homosexual perception." He did have an almost female radar, which enabled him to aim for people's soft spots and hurt them deeply, and which was parodoxically combined with having total blind spots about them. Yet he could also be generous, loyal and forgiving.

He had known what he wanted to do at an early age and never let anything divert him from his chosen path. He was a domestic tyrant who never presided over a household in which the occupants were comfortable. It seemed almost as though if they were comfortable, he was not. Somehow his fourth wife, Elena, managed to turn this around to a certain extent through goodness of character and the ability to be devious. She was three-quarters German and one-quarter Russian. The stolid Teutonic trait of imposing order, with a dash of the Russian soul, stood her in good stead.

But the truth of the matter was that he functioned best when he was alone in Talcottville with a housekeeper coming and his family a comfortable thought in the background. If he hadn't wanted children, seven daughters for whom he had picked names, he would have done very well with a household which didn't involve a wife, certainly in his early years.

Shortly after his divorce from my mother, he had a breakdown, which he described to me years later when I myself was having one, which he saw me through gallantly.

My mother had played in the early O'Neill plays at the Provincetown Playhouse in New York, where they often used just the harbor itself as a backdrop. She was one of the three original women members of the Theatre Guild. She and my father were married for seven years but separated after two. I was born during a play called *The Lullaby*. My mother contracted whooping cough, which eventually turned into pleurisy and did some permanent damage to her lungs. When I was eleven and went away to school, she went to stay in her hometown of Pittsburgh at the Tuberculosis League there.

But even after they were divorced, my mother and my father were always on good terms. Among the sculptures by the Utica stonecutter, Despirito, that I inherited with the stone house, was the head of a woman asleep, which he bought in 1965 because it reminded him of my mother.

In 1930 my mother married a well-off man, Constant Eakin, who was the New York manager of the Frigidaire Corporation. They lived in a duplex at 37 West Twelfth Street. The bedroom had been designed by Cleon Throckmorton, a famous set designer, with some help from Norman Bel Geddes, also a designer. There was a massive blond wood bed on a platform and a great bureau. In the living room was a huge portrait of my mother in costume painted by Djuna Barnes. In the summer, they lived in an old remodeled farmhouse with a swimming pool and tennis courts in Redding Ridge, Connecticut.

My mother's father had his own printing company in Pittsburgh at which her two brothers worked. They were Swedenborgians who interpreted the Bible through the writings of Swedenborg. She was one of five children and when she was very young, had begun ripping up the living room dividing curtain with dagger scenes from various plays. She was in the first graduating class from Carnegie Tech's dramatic school and had married a classmate, Charles Meredith. They did some exhibition dancing together at Bryn Athyn, Pennsylvania, a Swedenborg stronghold. Then she went into a play and he went out West to try and get a job in Hollywood. There he became the escort of an older lady; my mother went to Reno when her play was over. Her life was a tragic one, which I shall discuss later. Years later in a bar I met Sam Behrman, who told me what a good actress my mother was and that she was the sort of actress who should have belonged to the Abbey Theatre, which would have saved her.

She toured with John Barrymore in *Justice*. When she played with Paul Robeson, he had just graduated from Rutgers. Part of her obituary in the *New York Herald Tribune* follows, as well as a letter to me from her older sister, Lois Jansen. My mother died September 18, 1947. The obituary spoke of her being known as "the O'Neill Actress" and being one of the three original members of the Theatre Guild and of her role with Paul Robeson in *All God's Chillun Got Wings*.

In the face of threats of violence, Miss Blair continued to portray Ella and at each performance kissed the hand of her stage husband as called for in the scene. She held that the play was a work of art—and that art could brook no racial bias.

Other O'Neill plays in which Miss Blair appeared included "Desire Under the Elms," "The Hairy Ape," "Marco Millions," and the one-act monologue, "Before Breakfast." . . . Her last New York appearance was in "Lysistrata," a Norman Bel Geddes production.

Rosalind—To the best of my memory, Mary Blair was attending Tech Drama School when she was about 15. The students occasionally performed, for instance, on the lawn of Pittsburgh's Hotel Schenley. The first professional performance I saw her in was a one-act "Before Breakfast," by Eugene O'Neill, in which O'Neill played the only other character. Then she played the leading role in "All God's Chillun Got Wings," and at the finale she kissed the hand of black Paul Robeson, thus creating a furor in the audience. Mary played in "Desire Under the Elms." She toured in "Lysistrata" where I saw her in Philadelphia. She toured in "The Man from Home," I saw her in Pittsburgh in support of a then famous actor. I'm now reading "O'Neill, Son and Artist," by Sheaffer, in which O'Neill says, "I consider Mary Blair not as a good actress, but as a great actress."

Lots of love
Lois

During his breakdown, my father had thought there was a pencil writing for him all by itself. He was always very grateful to my mother for sticking with him through his breakdown, although they had separated, and credited her with having gotten him out of the upstate sanitorium he had settled into, which, in his words, was "full of attendants who couldn't quite make it in a Turkish bath." She repeatedly called him up and told him to stop goofing off and enriching the doctors.

He went to a psychiatrist in New York for a while, to whom he sent the son of one of his friends years later, and always referred to him as "that sort of a nerve doctor I went to when I had that sort of a breakdown. He tried to get me on the couch. But I wouldn't let him!" My mother said the doctor told her he had a mother complex and should never marry anyone.

Perhaps the doctor was partially trying to comfort my mother. But the escape route of the north Jersey coast train—Elizabeth, Rahway, Woodbridge, Perth Amboy, South Amboy, Matawan, Red Bank—to that comfortable feminine household with its eccentric communications because of my grandmother's deafness, was always there when his wives were coping with their difficulties, household and otherwise.

My grandmother had been dead opposed to my parents' marriage. But my grandfather put his foot down and said, "Any woman Edmund married would be accepted completely." Yet when things turned out badly, my grandmother loyally communicated with my mother about me for years.

My mother always told me it was not she who had wanted the divorce. Her story was that she was the breadwinner and would come home from the theater to find a DO NOT DISTURB sign on the door and that my father was still seeing Edna Millay, with whom he was in love for many years.

After my grandmother's death in 1951, my father inherited both the Red Bank and Talcottville houses. Talcottville was his now, but it was also still his mother's; when his wife, Elena, tried any redecorating on her own, he said, "That wasn't the way Mother had it." She soon refused to go there because of this and because she loathed the crudely beautiful countryside of Lewis County, with its large farm families. Talcottville replaced Red Bank as the other place with the other set of people who took care of him.

Elena, like most Europeans of her set, loved New York and the Cape, both of which had an international population.

Her reaction to Talcottville can only be described as phobic, which is what my father unconsciously wanted.

Although my grandmother and Elena were mountain ranges apart in character, temperament and approach to life, they had two things in common: They were not women of imagination, and any creativity they had was expressed in the running of their households.

Helen Mather Kimball, known all her life as Nelly, was the daughter of a well-known general practitioner in Lakehurst, New Jersey, who kept brown-bread pellets in his dispensary for hypochondriacal patients. She rode with him to the Phalanx commune the night he delivered Alexander Woollcott. She had two brothers who were doctors: Reuel, a famous diagnostician, for whom there is a plaque in St. Luke's Hospital in New York, and Paul, a society doctor who could sing "The Man Who Broke the Bank at Monte Carlo" with hat and cane and went with rich people on their yachts as ship's doctor.

Her youngest brother, Winfield, the only one alive when I was born, had gone into trade and divided his time between the Hotel Royalton in New York and his golf club on Staten Island, but would spend his holidays with us. Her two sisters, my Great-aunts Laura and Adeline, were very different types. Laura, tall, thin and aristocratic, had married Charley Corliss, a farmer, when she was forty. Everyone said my grandmother was the one who should have married the farmer, and Laura, the lawyer.

Adeline, called Addie, the oldest, had, to the consternation of her family, married Joe Stilwell, whose family ran a slaughterhouse. She was large and handsome. Joe would leave her sporadically when a child was on the way. Her oldest daughter, also Adeline, later known as Kim Moran (a combination of her middle name, Kimball, and one of her married names), would marry several millionaires, among them Bamberger (of the department store family) and Secretary of Housing Moffet; the second daughter, Dorothy, only one, Cecil Stewart, a marine insurer who handled Onassis' business. Dorothy was my grandmother's favorite until Stewart's penchant for other women hardened her. She came one day and talked in the harshest terms about the money she was going to demand during the divorce settlement from Stewart, who was dying of cancer at the time, and upset my grandmother so much they never saw each other again. Joe Stilwell had left the girls nothing but his beautiful greenish-blue eyes and quick wit and those, along with the luxurious Kimball auburn hair, carried them far.

One of the reasons I had been loath to have Prince George Chavchavadze pick me up in his long, low, opulent Cadillac convertible in Red Bank was that I didn't want grandmother and Jennie getting their hopes up that I was going the way of the Stilwell girls.

When Adeline came to Red Bank, she would often press a hundred dollars into Jennie's hand. According to Jennie, as a young married woman, my grandmother had often skimped on her own clothes to give Addie money toward Adeline's convent education. The Stilwell girls had all had to baby-sit my father at various times and regarded him as a spoiled brat.

Aunt Addie and my grandmother had their spats; but it was Addie who told my father off when she felt he was hurting his mother, which was fairly often. In typical fashion, he would launch a tirade against my grandmother over something he wanted, to the point where she felt she couldn't stand up against it, it was all on such a heroic scale. Then he'd snap out of it for a minute like someone out of a delirium and pat her hand as if to make it all right. It didn't because often she was really ill after the argument was over. Jennie would call Addie and she would appear and summon my father to her car. Speaking emphatically from amidst her furs, she would say, "Edmund, you aren't very nice to your mother. You ought to be whipped!" When my father would try to excuse his behavior, she would repeat, "You ought to be whipped, I say," and roll up the window.

My grandmother was the youngest in the family, and petite. She married my grandfather, Edmund Wilson, when she was thirty. He had been a chess partner of her father's for years and had sworn up and down Monmouth County that if he couldn't marry Nelly Kimball he'd be celibate.

She had great difficulty having her one child, my father.

My grandfather had gone to Andover Academy, Princeton University and Columbia Law School and had entered the bar as counselor in 1891 at the age of twenty-eight.

He had been attorney general of New Jersey and was a very successful lawyer. There was a great deal of entertaining and coming and going in their large gloomy house on the outskirts of Red Bank, with its small farm whose produce they used.

My grandfather didn't believe in insurance and he didn't believe in investing. He was a lawyer who lost only one case in his life, and a hypochondriac who retired to bed after each legal triumph until the money ran out. Then my grandmother would stand at the foot of his bed and say, "Enough now, there's no money in the bank." He would get up for as long as it took to take a case and then return to bed.

He was tall and dark with great dreamy brown eyes and always dressed very elegantly and was very attractive to women without expending much effort. Among his many lady admirers was a very pretty, rich widow who had gone to Abbott Academy with my grandmother. When she came to Red Bank for weekends from New York, she would sit up talking with my grandfather while my grandmother went to bed and read. The widow would say over and over again, "Ed, you are the sweetest thing." "Wasn't grandmother jealous?" I once asked Jennie. "Well, she went upstairs and read. That shows you how jealous she was."

When he thought of taking partnership offers from New York or Washington law firms, my grandmother dissuaded him, although it would have meant much more money, because she realized it would take an impossible toll on his nervous temperament. She would have liked to move the fifteen miles to Rumson, a community of rich stockbrokers, pretty estates and delightful houses. But as long as they were to live in those parts, he preferred the gloomy house they had moved into when first married.

My grandfather died at sixty. People came from all over New Jersey for the funeral. Following are some of the comments by the judges, Judge Kalisch and Judge Lawrence, who gave the eulogy and the memorial speech before the New Jersey bar, copied by my grandfather's sister-in-law, Mrs. John Wilson.

To me Mr. Wilson was a fascinating character, as I think he was to all the members of the bar with whom he came in contact. Notwithstanding his peculiar aptitude for eloquence, he was one of the most reticent men I ever knew in expressing that talent. I have often thought that if I had the ability to make the telling and captivating addresses that Mr. Wilson could I would do more of it. Not only were his speeches thoroughly prepared but they had a substance which expressed profound thought to all his hearers. He regarded law as a science and always came into court thoroughly prepared. I remember an experience of mine some years ago involving the trial of a libel suit. I was associated with Mr. Wilson. I went to his office. He had all the witnesses there; and it was a novel experience to me as to the manner in which he prepared that case to have him sit as judge, so to speak, and dissect the testimony of every witness, who was to appear subsequently in court.

Judge Kalisch's address, which he delivered at Freehold, New Jersey, in October 1923, speaks of my grandfather's magnetic eloquence. The judge mentions having appointed my grandfather as attorney general and the job he did in cleaning up Atlantic City, which "left his name etched in gold on the public records. His companionship was most extraordinary and exhilarating." They had probably made the tavern scene together.

The house my grandmother bought after he died was a large white wooden one at 36 Vista Place, Red Bank, very cheerful and bright with a view of the Shrewsbury River. There were four bedroom suites: my father's and mine next to each other in the middle of the house, my grandmother's and Jennie Corbett's at opposite ends. Gerta, the cook, Oscar, the chauffeur and gardener, and Joseph, the subgardener, came in during the day. My grandmother was almost totally deaf and could be reached only by ear trumpet or by speaking directly into her ear. There was a battery box she used when playing bridge, but the mechanics of that drove her crazy for everyday communication. She had become deaf suddenly on a European trip when her brother came into her stateroom on the boat and put the light on suddenly. There was talk of gout of the ear. Doctors I talked to did not believe it was psychosomatic. Until I was eight, my Jamaican nurse, Stella, was also a part of the household. When I was first brought down to Red Bank, my grandmother looked at me in my crib and said, "That baby is wild as a hawk."

Jennie Corbett, numero uno in the household after my grandmother and when my father wasn't there, had come over from Ireland when she was fifteen and gone directly to my grandparents' house. She remained with my grandmother fifty-five years and became my grandmother's ears. She was almost six feet tall, with thick wavy hair—white by the time I came along—beautiful Irish blue eyes and a perfect nose. She was on the order of Maud Gonne. She had the soul of a saint, and was high-strung and a severe asthmatic for most of her life. She had been trained as a witness by my grandfather, who after my grandmother became deaf tried his cases in dress rehearsal for her.

Occasionally, the Wilsons would ride her too hard and she would leave. My grandfather would go and retrieve her. He had bought her a house in Red Bank. My information of how things were comes both from Jennie and my great-aunts, but it tallies, and in spite of Jennie's occasional flights of Irish fancy, her view of people and what was going on was shrewd and accurate.

My grandmother and Jennie were a Mutt and Jeff combo. Jennie did the talking on telephone calls which took place in the downstairs hall. There was a balcony on the second floor and so anything said echoed in the house, which had unusually thin walls, as well as into the old-fashioned upright phone. My grandmother, sitting next to her, often made very insulting remarks in her loud voice. Jennie, who was always trying to be diplomatic, would have to stop and yell the conversation of the party at the other end of the line into my grandmother's ear. "Mr. Edmund, Mrs. Wilson says the house is being painted; although she'd be glad to see you, you'd better not come down this weekend." Then, into my grandmother's ear, "Mr. Edmund says he's coming down this weekend; he has to use some of his books here." Then my grandmother's loud, shrill, definite voice could be heard saying, "Oh, pshaw, he'll talk to me about money and tire me out. I don't want him." Then Jennie would stand in front of my grandmother expressing her sympathy for my father in pantomime. His need for his books, his possible loneliness, her own regret at delivering a negative message. She had become so adept at mime she could have joined the Chinese theater. "Why are you making faces at me? Stop it," my grandmother would scream. Sometimes Jennie would laugh ruefully and say, "Well, you hear *that*, Mr. Edmund." Of course, if he felt like coming down, he came; even while my

38

grandmother was denying him thrice, she was planning what she'd give him to eat.

My grandmother's deafness explained a lot in my father's life and in mine. It made a compulsive letter writer out of me, because the easiest way to communicate with her over any complicated matter was via a series of notes. (My tendency to reply on the spot via written missive instead of sleeping on it was to make some of my future romances nonnegotiable.) She voiced her innermost thoughts out loud, forgetting others could hear; my father unconsciously imitated his mother even though he could hear.

Whereas someone else might only think, "The child's so homely I don't know what to do with her" or "Edmund's so fat and disagreeable I wonder if he's having trouble with that no-account woman," she'd voice it. She wouldn't voice it directly to the person except in argumentative dialogue, but a thought would cross her mind while she was reading or eating or looking out the window and she'd think out loud so the verbalization would ricochet all over the house. In the summer, her thoughts would take flight off the back porch in the form of comments on her neighbors' gardens, physical failings or private affairs, which they could hear if passing by, hidden from my grandmother by the lilacs and climbing roses.

After my grandfather's death, she had no thoughts of remarrying and to a certain extent unsexed herself. She said, "I was a funny, fat little thing, who married the best man who ever lived." She wore no makeup except occasionally a little rouge, which she hid in her bureau. Her dresses were custom-made of the finest materials: cotton for morning, silk for evening, with lace insets at the neck. She wore beautiful slips and white cotton pants with a slit in the back which met her stockings. I would spend many hours in my twenties scouring stores, stubbornly facing incredulous saleswomen as these once standard undergarments became obsolete. She wore hats with a brim and if it was a sporting event, a feather stuck in the side.

In the morning, she got up and came down to a large breakfast during which she read the *Herald Tribune*. One day she looked up from it after reading about some labor brew John Dos Passos had been arrested in and said to my father, "Well, I see they caught your friend Dos Passos." In my teens, when the Dos Passoses' house was one of my surrogate homes, Dos would repeat this story to me time and again. He was delighted with this picture of himself as a desperado, and years later, when I saw him at a party in Boston, he suddenly made his nearsighted way across a great room and repeated the anecdote to me conspiratorially in his stuttering way. He had paid a visit to Red Bank one summer to see my father, who had come down to see me when my grandmother wasn't there, and had come down to breakfast with a terrible hangover. I was sitting in my high chair laughing and he kept saying, irritably, "Can't you stop that baby from laughing?"

# IV

MY GRANDMOTHER still had the air of a pretty woman who was used to being catered to by men. She had a fine mind and a good business head. She read an average of two books a day from the library: popular novels, biographies, travel books, mysteries. She hadn't gone to college. She might not be able to discuss existentialism with you, except if you'd demanded she read some books on the subject she might say, "Pshaw! What a waste of time!" But she would absorb them, although probably complaining, "This man goes around Robin Hood's barn and makes everything so difficult." She had an all-around point of view in spite of her Republican principles. She had read Shakespeare, Dickens, Sir Walter Scott and Jane Austen. Stanley Dell, one of my father's Princeton friends, said she was one of the prettiest, brightest women he'd ever met and was half in love with her himself, when he used to come over from college. Ted Parsons, a prominent lawyer whom my grandfather had helped through law school, said she had a better grasp of any legal problem than most lawyers. Men liked to do business with her.

After breakfast, she would turn out the icebox and plan the day's meals. Then shop. The big meal was in the middle of the day. In the afternoon, she took a nap until three, usually reading some. After that, a ride around the countryside, then supper (for which she changed), cards (a game called whiskey rummy with deuces wild), and then to bed at ten and reading until two or three in the morning. Her garden, her antique collecting, especially luster pitchers, and, in the fall, Princeton football games took up her life.

My father complained to his wives that his mother never kissed him—perhaps a half-truth and half a great line to use in conquests; but the people she loved were on her mind constantly. Although she might show her affection by worrying about what they ate or tugging at their clothes. She was so small it was hard for her to throw her arms around people.

Bill Wallace, my cousin Dorothy Stilwell's ex, who headed the Cadillac Division in Detroit and oversaw my grandmother's custom-made Cadillacs, always sent the message, "Tell Aunt Nelly she still served the best food I've ever had."

She was given great loyalty by the five people who worked for her in Red Bank. There was Oscar Breckinridge, the chauffeur and gardener, whose daughter was principal of the Red Bank High School. He made some of the finest applejack in Jersey, known as Jersey Lightning. Later in life, when a beau ordered some Calvados for us, warning me it was very, very strong, I thought, "This stuff is nothing but apple juice compared to what Oscar used to make."

He could have worked for many richer people in Rumson. Sometimes my grandmother drove him wild by telling him not to go so fast and at the same time to speed up or to make a sharp left when he was in the middle of the right turn she had advised; but he stuck with her. One day when my grandmother and he had been out in the country, they saw a man beating a woman outside a shack. She told Oscar to go for help and jumped out and began slapping the man in the face with her ear trumpet. He was so flabbergasted, he fled. Oscar was a master cabinetmaker who had had to give it up because he was allergic to sawdust. Still, he occasionally lavished himself on making extraordinarily fine pieces—boxes and birdhouses at Christmas; my playhouse was a work of art, perfectly scaled.

My father really demanded of any wife that she perform the same duties as my grandmother's staff, which is what he was used to.

The neighborhood she moved into after my grandfather's death was middle- and upper-middle class: some lawyers, some bank tellers, some representatives of large companies such as Pittsburgh Plate Glass. There were three and a half acres, which she had fenced from the outside world with trellises of twenty different climbing roses, pines, lilacs, rhododendrons and box bushes. The main rose garden was in the shape of a horseshoe and there were always a huge vegetable garden, a root cellar and a cold room for hanging fowl and meat. She had a few chickens, her own gas pump, and continued to be self-sufficient to a certain extent although there were no cows. The very rich lived across the Shrewsbury River, which is a tidal river. You could see their great houses set back with lawns going down to the water. Or they lived in Rumson. Some of the children I was to go to school with were very rich indeed; their homes would have given the prerevolutionary Russian nobility a run for their money.

My grandmother usually played bridge two afternoons a week, often as the partner of a bachelor, a maiden-uncle type, Mr. Vanderbilt. If the game was to be at our house, the preparations were intense: sandwiches covered with linen napkins wrung out in cold water, punches and cocktail glasses set out just in case. Otherwise, the high point of the day was the afternoon ride.

She had very short legs and the longest custom-built Cadillacs anywhere, not only encompassing jump seats but eight feet after that to the footrest in front of the backseat. Her initials were on the doors, flasks of brandy in the side pockets, fur lap robes on a rack and fresh flowers in the side vases.

During the afternoon rides, we drove around the countryside antique hunting or to favorite outside produce stands, or took the shore drive to Asbury Park with its fairy-tale summer houses on the Atlantic Ocean, with cupolas and turrets and every kind of gingerbread molding on their windows and box bushes boarded up against the North Atlantic gales. There was James Garfield's house. In the last gruesome stages of his illness after he was shot, Garfield was brought up from Washington to his home on the Jersey coast in a converted baggage car. Tracks were laid from the railroad station to his house. Remnants of the tracks remained. Very often we would go over to Eatontown where my Great-aunt Laura and her husband, Charley Corliss, lived. They had married in their forties; my grandfather, when they actually set the date, drove down the main street of Red Bank in his trap, waving his hat and cheering, offering champagne to anyone who turned around or popped their head out of a store.

My Aunt Laura was very delicate after unsuccessfully trying to have a child. The farmhouse had a cold country smell I loved which was absent in Red Bank. They had, unfortunately for Charley, some very fine antiques and silver from his family and some Laura had collected. Unfortunately, because after Laura's death, he was to be the target of every antique-mad widow. My grandmother's intentions, when she was kind to him, bringing food and meals, were genuinely honorable, but even she tried to rustle around. He hadn't changed a thing in the room he and Laura had used as a bedroom. The shades remained drawn, the clothes in the closet, as if he were a male Miss Havisham.

He was a nice-looking man with silky gray hair and a

mustache. He was the recipient of all sorts of provender—
jellies and pies—from various widows who would force
themselves into darkened rooms, exclaiming, "Oh, Charley,
you've got a Chippendale." "Oh, look at the dear little Dun-
can Phyfe." On several occasions, we found him hiding in
the barn literally under the hay. Several times he begged me
not to tell my grandmother he was there.

The people my grandmother saw after her husband's death
were of a very different kind than the ones she had seen when
he was alive, with the exception of a few old cronies. For the
most part, they were chosen for their bridge-playing ability.

She had spent her life surrounded by brilliant men. She
simply assumed that any man connected with her would be
brilliant and that her job was to take care of the mechanics of
the household. It would have been totally out of character for
her to congratulate her brothers, her husband or my father on
their success or to point it out. It would have been impossible
for her to say, as my father's fourth wife, Elena, often did,
"Oh, dearest, you're so brilliant." Certainly not in front of
people. Once when my cousin Dorothy Mendenhall, one of
the first women doctors, was making a dispassionate observation in disagreement with something her son Tom Mendenhall, then president of Smith College, thought, my father
said, "That's the sort of observation Elena would be incapable
of making about her son."

When I was trying to get a book from Wanda Landowska
for Houghton Mifflin, she gave me two tickets to a concert she
was giving at the Frick Museum. She was then in her middle
seventies; her hands were soft and small and very young, like a
child's. I took Elena backstage to see her after the concert.
After we left, Elena said, "But you didn't tell her she played
well." I couldn't imagine telling Landowska she played the
harpsichord well; my grandmother couldn't imagine telling
my father he wrote well.

She read the books of his which dealt with travel and the

Indians and his *New Yorker* reviews. She kept his books which he inscribed to her in the lower shelf of her bedroom bookshelf behind locked glass doors with her favorite books. Perhaps she regarded them as she did her husband's briefs. Her husband had often been involved in delicate cases, sometimes with unsavory people, especially while cleaning up Atlantic City. Her son had had the Ku Klux Klan after him. She had learned to keep her conversations to surface matters and dwell on where one could get the choicest meat or what fertilizer was best for the roses and other safe subjects or generalities.

She was highly amused at a conversation a friend overheard at a dinner party. The host said, "Mrs. Wilson was a very pretty woman with a very sweet smile." A woman remarked, "Yes, you can still see traces of it."

My grandmother wouldn't stand for tattletaling. It was a major crime—to the extent that both my father and I remained silent in office and business situations when we really should have gone to the boss or blown the problem wide open.

She also had a tough side, which was therapeutic in most cases, such as telling me I couldn't come into the house until I'd learned to ride my bike, which I had had plenty of time to do. It worked with me. But when she told my father more or less the same thing about his new motorcycle when he was in his late thirties, he came careening through the three curb-bordered, pine-tree-frilled islands in the middle of Vista Place, ending up in her rhododendrons and in Riverview Hospital with minor contusions.

When she got mad at you, she let fly and that was it. She never referred to the matter again. Unlike my father, who would hold things against you for years and never let go.

In 1935 when he went to Russia on a Guggenheim, he brought me back a hooked rug he had bought from an old man on the street for fifteen cents. It was a tiger chasing a butterfly. For years I had it on my wall in school and college. Finally, when I got an apartment, I put it on the floor. In 1968 he was still mad about that, although he had taken the rug back twenty-five years before and hung it on the wall at his Wellfleet house. After his death, my brother told me he had often spoken to him about my delinquency over the rug.

Sometimes I would complain to Jennie when my grandmother raised cain, ranting at me over some minor infraction, "She's so nervous and hysterical, Jennie!" Jennie would say, "As a young woman she didn't have a nerve in her body." Various relatives bore this out. Everyone laid it to my grandfather's hypochondria and strange working schedule and my grandmother's not being sure when he'd pull himself together and go out in the world again.

There was a very pretty inlaid box on one of the living-room tables. I asked her once where it came from. "One of your grandfather's doctors took it off his desk and gave it to me, he was so sorry for me."

Looking back, it was obvious that her nervousness had been superimposed on her nature by external stimuli and that it hadn't been built in from the beginning.

Unlike many widows, she was prepared to deal with business affairs and had been coached and kept informed about what was going on by my grandfather. He left her a rich woman, and eventually she augmented her wealth by investing, which of course he had refused to do. For this reason, the 1929 crash didn't affect her. But Roosevelt's bank holiday laid her out. The Monmouth County Bank in Red Bank was in big trouble, and in order for it to reopen and for her not to lose everything, she and a man named McCarter, who lived in a great imitation Spanish castle on a hill looming up in back of her old house, had to put the money in to reopen it, which they never got back. If her brother Winfield had not left her money when he died, things would have been very rough.

The household I came into, when my grandmother was

47

fifty-six, was a very different one from the one of the woman whose husband was attorney general of New Jersey (his picture hung and perhaps still does in the Freehold courthouse) and who had to be prepared for at least twenty people every night for dinner. My grandfather was likely to bring home anyone he met in the course of the day. He used to say that rather than ever eat alone he would pick up a strange bum off the street, which he often did.

There were remnants of that life in the new house my grandmother bought: the dozens of cream and gold oyster plates; the sherbet dishes with compartments for the cracked ice and the watermelon molds for ice cream; the separate sets of china for breakfast, lunch and dinner; the endless rows of wine, cocktail and highball glasses in the pantry. But the woman who had been married to a charismatic man, however difficult (Jennie had endless stories of his trained nurses' going quite mad, rushing downstairs to beat up sofa pillows or to scream uncontrollably), and who had driven the fastest set of matched grays in all of Red Bank, New Jersey, settled down to the single phase of her life. Except for Talcottville where she went from mid-June to mid-September, she no longer traveled.

There were no more trips to Europe with my grandfather's seeking a cure for his imaginary illnesses. The doctor who had had the most success with him was a German who told him he must take a cup of chamomile tea every night before retiring, that it must be made a certain way involving twelve steps and almost as many people. It made him feel a lot better. There were no more trips to Europe with her favorite sister-in-law to retrieve both my grandfather and Great-uncle Reuel, who occasionally left his practice and went on benders. Once, when Reuel was on deck with his practice, which was most of the time, and my grandfather was in decline, Reuel said, "Come away with me, Ed. I will take you to Europe to take the waters, to hear the birds sing, to hear the waltzes, to become yourself again." Off they went to some spa, where wine was served with meals; Reuel went off the wagon and my grandfather was indeed brought out of his nervous stage, having to take care of him.

My grandfather eventually died of a combination of appendicitis and pneumonia, which he caught when he went up to Talcottville in the early spring to the unheated stone house. He had cried wolf so often, it took people a while to realize how really sick he was. The local pharmacist, not knowing he had died that day, said to Jennie with a smirk, "Oh, he's off on one of his toots of hypochondria, he's not sick." Jennie replied, "He's dead; he can't be much sicker than that."

On the table of the house at 36 Vista Place, there was a tile with a picture of the Talcottville house—red roof, romantic balcony. One of the conditions when my grandfather had succeeded in buying the stone house was that his wife's Uncle Tom Baker, who had owned it, would live in the downstairs room. He was very waspish to my grandparents, refusing to speak to them and complaining about the quality of the meals which were sent in to him when they were there. Many times I heard my grandmother, in some frightful dispute with my father, say as a final insult, "Honestly, Edmund, you get more like your Uncle Tom Baker every day. You're so disagreeable to me." Their altercations were often about money. It was a sore point that his father had left him nothing outright; it was a neurotic situation in which he had to ask her for every single cent. Very often he would write bad checks knowing she would make them good at the bank, where there was some hanky-panky, as everyone was to find out when Roosevelt declared the bank holiday. The man who had handled the transactions of switching money from her account to my father's eventually committed suicide.

On the other hand, it was true my father had no idea about money. He didn't give a damn about it from the point of view of buying himself fancy clothes or living high. He didn't care anything for being fashionable or about rich people; but he did throw money around. Once when I was about eight and we were waiting at Penn Station in the waiting room, a man came up and said, "Brother, can you spare a dime?" My father, who was reading a book, felt around and said, "I have no change but take this ten and bring me back change." Naturally, he never came back, and as our train hadn't been called yet, we had no ticket. We had to take a cab to the *New Republic* and borrow it from Betty Huling, their great copy editor. Meanwhile, Oscar came back from the station at Red Bank empty-handed, Gerta's dinner grew cold, and my grandmother wailed to Jennie, quite correctly, "Edmund has no idea about money." In spite of the fact my father carried me under his arm like a book and often forgot me, and that there were incidents like the train ticket, I felt here was a force that, however unpleasant at times, wouldn't go away.

The only two old cronies of bright plumage my grandmother saw in her single life who were worthy of her, as opposed to her new bridge set, were her sister-in-law Caroline Kimball, who was always cheerful and moved in the worlds of New York and Rumson society and brought back stories of high-life doings, and Annie Edwards, a widow, who occupied a great house on the river. She always wore lively red clothes and told raunchy stories. When she came, the sun-parlor doors were closed because naturally the punch lines of these jokes had to be yelled through my grandmother's deafness. Occasionally, fragments would drift through the thin walls of the house—"And on their wedding night" or "Nelly, she was widow-nightgown-unmentionable disease"— followed by raucous laughter on Mrs. Edwards' part and "You don't say" by my grandmother.

Of paler plumage were Jessie Warner, a widow, and a couple, the Wrecklesses. Never were a couple more inappropriately named. Mrs. Warner spent July with my grandmother in Talcottville and the Wrecklesses, August. How I longed to go with them as I heard talk of trips to Canada and the cheese factories and the island my grandfather had bought for fishing in the Thousand Islands. When I was nine, I was allowed up there for two weeks. I think my father was in Russia on the Guggenheim he used to write *To the Finland Station*. The stone house seemed the most romantic place in the world; the trip to Canada to buy blankets was my first trip to a foreign country.

My grandmother had a beautiful garden in Talcottville cared for by Abijah Carpenter and sometimes Joe Maguire, and a cook named Cornelia Hubby, a tall, gaunt woman from Turin. The evening meal was exactly the same every night, tomatoes and corn picked while we were at the table. Oscar came along and sometimes his wife stayed at a house down the road. But because he was on semivacation, he only drove the car.

Abijah Carpenter, who lived across the road from the stone house, had two sisters, Carrie and Ann. Ann wore long filmy dresses and, like my grandmother, was deaf and had to use an ear trumpet. She was very possessive of Abijah, who asked Jennie to go to the fair with him in his buggy. Ann came over and said if my grandmother didn't send Jennie away, she wouldn't account for the terrible things she would do to my grandmother. My grandmother naturally replied that what Jennie did was Jennie's business and she had no intention of firing her.

The ear trumpet battle took place on the front porch of the Talcottville house, which is a very public place on the corner of a main road, with people passing by constantly. Ann persisted with her threats for several hours, with ear trumpets being extended and withdrawn and voices becoming louder. Word got around and people were coming from hamlets as far as Port Leyden, five miles away, to see what was considered one of the great sporting events in the county. It ended in a draw when my grandmother called Jennie out on the porch, who naturally said although she hadn't planned to go to the fair with Abijah, nothing would stop her now. Ann and my grandmother never spoke again. And Ann was to have her revenge when my father and Elena moved into the house.

My first trip to Talcottville was my last while my grandmother was alive. Joe Maguire's son and I found an old bow and arrow and inadvertently shot it through the dining-room window, where it lodged in the table at which my grandmother and the Wrecklesses had just sat down to supper, vibrating in front of Gillie Wreckless' plate. My grandmother said nothing, took the arrow and placed it beside her plate along with the place silver. Shortly after that, a distinguished hawk-nosed woman appeared. She ran a Camp Huckleberry in Norfolk, Connecticut, where I was soon enrolled for the following summer.

My grandmother didn't go to Talcottville the seven years before her death and although my father managed to stay there a few weeks when he was married to Mary McCarthy, my grandmother quite simply didn't want him there. He always felt that if she had turned Talcottville over to him, his life would have been different, as he could have gone there to live. It was a bone of contention between them. The last seven years of her life she always thought she'd make it up north again to these hills where we all felt the same sense of freedom Sicilian bandits must have had when they once again took refuge on their island.

# V

I N RED BANK, I went to school the first few years at Miss Hazard's. In the winter, my father came down every weekend, sometimes more often, and gave puppet shows in which the devil figured prominently. I had to call him *Father*, no *Dad* or *Pops*. We took walks, and he read out loud to me. After that, I went to Rumson School, a branch of the Buckley School in New York. The Rumson school building had been a church. "A little brown church on the corner stood somber, lone and bare, until they made it a schoolhouse and the children filled it there" went our school song. I felt very plebeian next to the truly rich Rumsonites, who included my cousins, the Hartshornes. Their mother was my Great-uncle Reuel's daughter. She had a brother, my father's first cousin Sandy, who was my father's closest friend and really his alter ego.

As children, my father and Sandy were inseparable. Sandy was always at my grandparents' house. My father lost his hair one Fourth of July when they were setting off firecrackers that exploded. Sandy and my father were both at Princeton when World War I was declared. Sandy was very handsome and brilliant and was taking premed courses. Of the two, he was pegged as the one who would be a success. They both wanted to enlist. My father did so, and although my grandmother protested, she and my grandfather gave in and signed the necessary papers. Sandy's mother would not, as she was set on his going to medical school. Sandy developed dementia praecox. One of the manifestations of his illness became apparent when he was staying with my grandparents. He drove back and forth all night from my grandparents' to the house of a girl across the river, back and forth, back and forth. Then he sat in the upstairs bathroom, eyes cast down, refusing to move in spite of Jennie's coaxing. He was to be entombed for the rest of his life. He cast a long shadow over my father, who I think felt part of himself had been sent away. Sandy's mother and sister couldn't bear it when the men came to take him away. They locked themselves in the bathroom. My grandmother had to handle it, saying, "Sandy, has your Aunt Nelly ever hurt you?" Thirty years later, she couldn't discuss it without bursting into tears.

Then there was his first cousin Susan Wilson, on his father's side, who was like a sister and remained his closest family tie aside from his parents and his children, until his death.

My classmates lived on huge estates in Rumson with long driveways, great houses, servants for every occasion, butlers, maids, cooks, nannies. I was never really part of all that, although I did go to the birthday parties, which were very elegant and always featured the same menu—creamed chicken and peas—until one madcap party when we all threw the peas at one another. After that, it was a mashed vegetable of some sort.

On Tuesdays, there was dancing class. A Mrs. Hubbell came down from New York, where she taught the likes of the

Bouviers, and instructed us in the imitation Elizabethan manor house of some very rich people who had Great Danes. We all had to wear white gloves, party dresses and patent leather pumps. There were long foot charts with black feet on them. Mrs. Hubbell was a portly woman with white kid gloves. It was awful. I was a wallflower except for one loyal boy, the only other student who lived in Red Bank. I could feel my nurse's humiliation. The nannies all sat and watched. One day Mrs. Hubbell announced we were to learn the tango. She was such an untango type and really could have substituted for Margaret Dumont with the Marx Brothers. (I lived in a fantasy world where George Raft was my real partner.) She singled me out as her partner but after a few steps cast me aside for one of the fashionable Haskell girls. I much preferred Mrs. Coleman's in Red Bank, where I took ballet and tap. She had a daughter who was a Rockette. The day Prohibition was repealed was a dancing-class day. The lady of the manor came cheering out onto the balcony of her long Elizabethan living room where we were dancing, then ran down the stairs off to New York to celebrate.

On weekends when my father didn't come down, my nurse would take me up to New York to stay with him or my mother. I hated staying at my mother's. I saw her act only once, in *Lysistrata* in which she was the leader of the old women who poured water on the heads of the men. She had a tremendous low-pitched voice. In a review of Eugene O'Neill's one-act play, "Before Breakfast," which was produced in New York in 1929, Brooks Atkinson wrote in the *New York Times* that the play "at least has the virtue of bringing Miss Blair to the stage again to make our protesting blood run cold with her piercing screams at the curtain."

After she married Constant Eakin, called Connie, who was very well off, she didn't act for a long spell, having rejected *Tobacco Road*, which she felt wouldn't be a success. She and Connie drank a lot; her thwarted acting and creative powers came out in the tremendous scenes she threw. I enjoyed being taken to the latest musical shows and speakeasies but hated everything that went on in between. We simply didn't get on together. I felt secure with my father, that somehow he'd continue to exist. Later the writer John Bowers was to tell me that when he was young his mother had taken him to see the barter players in Tennessee. A woman had come out on stage and said, "Damn, well goddamn"—lighting a cigarette— "well damn." The play was set in New York. At that instant, he planned to get to New York somehow. Well, having seen my mother's friends, lighting cigarettes and saying "Damn, well goddamn" in the flesh, my one idea was to get back to the country by the very next train.

The only times I ever saw my parents together were during the few minutes they visited when he dropped me off at her apartment. My father lived in an old rented brownstone house in the East Fifties. It had four floors. The first one had a double living room; the second, two bedrooms and bath; the top, two bedrooms and a bath, which were rented out to two teachers, I believe; and the basement had a kitchen and a room and bath, which were occupied off and on by various people. The one I remember the best was Griffin Barry, a pleasant man with white hair. Frank and Edith Shay at one point occupied the second floor, and Frank's very pretty daughter Jean, who was five years older than I, was around.

Connie Eakin was making a big salary. He had a Belgian cook, Louis, who would announce, "The soup be on the table." Among the people who came and went in my mother's social life were the Cleon Throckmortons. Mrs. Throckmorton was very pretty but always crying because "Throck doesn't think me pretty." There was always talk of Fitzi—M. Eleanor Fitzgerald—and the Theatre Guild. e. e. cummings and his wife came occasionally, and various young men to read my mother their plays. But the days with my mother and

Connie always ended in drunkenness and her tremendous theatrical scenes, which had Medea-like overtones when she threatened to throw me out the window. It was great acting, but as a child I just didn't see it that way. I didn't dislike Connie; he just made me very nervous. The one great loyalty in his life was to my mother, as it was to turn out.

It was my grandmother's habit to take me to Best and Company once a year and buy me two plaid skirts and two sweaters for the school year plus two pairs of brogues and a Sunday hat from Knox. My party dresses, which were sometimes very strange, were made by Mrs. Dobbs, a Belgian dressmaker in Red Bank; strange because they were likely to have leather Scotties appliquéd on them. Against Mrs. Dobbs' gentle pleas in fractured French, my mother tried to upset this sartorial applecart every time I came to see her, taking me to Hearn's and buying me more flamboyant outfits and having my hair bobbed. My grandmother's chief worry was that I'd end up wearing rhinestone buckles on my shoes as she had seen my mother do.

My father made scenes only when he came to Red Bank. When I went to New York, it was all very pleasant and we went out to dinner. On several occasions, he said he wasn't hungry and didn't want any dinner. Afterward, I realized he was too broke to order two dinners. He would take Jean Shay and me to Coney Island. Gilbert Seldes was around, talking about how television would some day come along and change the world. He was a great friend of Jimmy Durante's and he introduced him to us at the circus.

Muriel Draper and her son Paul, the dancer, lived next door; we would see them out in their garden. Muriel had a salon. She would sit in a huge gilt chair. I met Muriel years later during the intermission of some play and she said, "Your father and I were rowing down the Volga in Russia and he kept telling me you were troubled because you didn't understand

when he read you *Pickwick Papers* what Mr. Pickwick did."
Well, I never was sure what Muriel did. Everyone knew her
and she wore extraordinary hats.

In the winters, I went to school and dancing class and
riding lessons. On weekends when I didn't go to New York,
and very often in the middle of the week, my father came
down, always on a different train on Friday nights. His dinner
was held and no matter what it was, he complained about it.
The muffins were a few seconds late, the omelet was tough.
So supper was not a pleasant affair. My grandmother sat at the
foot of the table in a high-backed chair with arms. The
duplicate chair at the head of the table, which would have
been her husband's, remained empty. My father and I sat in
lesser chairs, I on her right, he on her left. The rest of the
evening was likely to be spent in a row over money with my
grandmother saying, "Honestly, Edmund, you upset me so
when you come down." After dinner, he would read Dickens
to me, or the Bible. The next day he would lock himself in his
room and write with occasional bellowing requests for quiet.

Often, as it held a fascination for him, we would walk over
to the old house in Red Bank, yellow and brown, with a
circular porch around it and a stained glass window in front,
right on the street, with several acres going up the side of a
hill behind it, the barns and coops and fences all unused now.
It had the same fascination for Jennie. My grandmother
wouldn't go near it. Time and again my father would say,
"You see, you see how cheerful she has everything in the new
house," but he and Jennie were homesick for the old house.

Another favorite walk was to a house almost in Rumson,
deserted and strange on a circular province on the river. You
walked along the driveway for a mile. There was a family
graveyard with bleeding hearts and honeysuckles and col-
umbine. The whole ambiance was much more southern than
northern. The house fascinated both of us. One day we
walked in and the owner was there, a man in a wheelchair.

My father asked if he wanted to sell it, which he didn't. The spell was broken as often happens when a real character enters a dream.

In the evenings, we would play whiskey rummy with my grandmother and Jennie. This was sometimes quite pleasant, with good-natured bantering. We played for small sums of money. My grandmother usually won; there were times when that was simply too much for my father and his resentment over her hold on his purse strings would intermingle with his resentment at her winning at cards. He would slam down his hand and retreat up to his room, his four-poster bed, his books, his gargoyle.

My father also came down for holidays; Christmas Eve we went to the Hartshornes' big house across the river with its sunken living room. My Great-uncle Winfield came down and my Great-aunt Addie came along. It was all very elegant. Esther Hartshorne had bright red hair and their three boys sang "We Three Kings of Orient Are." The Hartshornes raised Scotties on the side. Esther's husband, Bob, was a very pleasant man, a stockbroker. He had had a difficult time during the war. My grandmother loved Scotties; she and Bob would discuss dogs at length. A lifelong Republican and a fierce hater of Roosevelt, the only time she softened toward the president was when she read the "Fala" speech in the *Herald Tribune* in which he defended his Scottie, Fala, who was rumored to have traveled at vast expense subsidized by the American taxpayer. Roosevelt said that he didn't mind the attacks on himself, but Fala's Scottish soul was wounded at the suggestion he was transported in luxury. She went around all day saying, "That old political devil," almost fondly.

My father always came down for any activities I was connected with at school. He tried to encourage me, but my grandmother wouldn't let me be in a tap dance recital Mrs. Coleman put on at the Red Bank movie house. My grandmother was terrified I might end up an actress like my mother.

Jennie loved to sing "After the Ball," "My Gal's a Highborn Lady" and "Tessie"—"Tessie, you make me feel so badly, why won't you turn around?" And she clogged in a Bojangles way. I sang a song I'd picked up, "Hey Young Fellow, Won't You Put Down That Old Umbrella." Jennie thought I really should go on the stage and sat coaching and reacting as she had to my grandfather's rehearsals of his trials. With my grandmother afraid I might become an actress and Jennie coaching me to be another Shirley Temple, they added to my confusion.

One problem everyone tried to deal with was my right eye, which drifted outward. My father was always meeting some woman at a cocktail party who knew just the doctor to fix me up. I was dragged from office to office. In Red Bank, the doctor had told me I must never go without glasses and terrified me to the point where I slept with them on. Then some doctor in New York would say I should wear a black patch over the good eye. Luckily, I finally ended up with Alan Greenwood in Boston. My friend Jeannie's uncle, Coulton Waugh, who was doing the comic strip "Dickie Dare" at the time, recommended him. Coulton had lost one eye as a child in an accident.

Dr. Greenwood was a very famous surgeon who had made his great reputation during the war. He was well on in years, with a beautifully kept white mustache. His office was on the second floor of a house on Commonwealth Avenue in an enormous room. Unlike most eye doctors, he took only one patient at a time, and he had no professional examining chair. You sat in a regular chair. In front of him were rows and rows of wooden boxes with lenses in them, graduating upward like the keyboards of an organ. My father, who was a very good quick-card magician, said, "He works those lenses like magic." Dr. Greenwood was the only doctor who really fitted me with glasses. The others had been too worried about operating or black patches. They never dealt with the fundamentals. He said to wait until I was old enough to decide what I wanted to do, that I could go without my glasses except for reading.

It was all a tremendous relief, and even then I could see the difference between New York doctors and Boston doctors, between great doctors and pedestrian ones. The more rich and famous the Boston doctor, the shabbier his office (often with adhesive tape wound around a pipe leak), the quieter his manner. After I'd been examined, my father, with the air of a man who has held something in for a long time about which he is very worried, blurted out that he saw a white butterfly out of his left eye all the time. Greenwood said this was the sort of thing that might happen if you were very nervous, and to try and forget the whole thing.

There was no social life for my father when he came to Red Bank except with his relatives and in his mother's household. His great friends he had made at Princeton, and much of his childhood social life was with his cousins, mainly the tragic Sandy. One night Margaret Rullman, who was married to a successful surgeon, came over (my grandmother would have liked my father and her to marry), the only Red Bank friend left. It was pleasant for a while. She was a nice woman, but it became apparent she was frightfully anti-Semitic, referring to Jews as kikes, which he couldn't let pass; the evening ended badly. He tried to see something of the parents of my neighborhood friends, but he had nothing in common with them.

Once we went to see Agnes O'Neill, Eugene O'Neill's ex, at Point Pleasant, New Jersey, for the afternoon, and her daughter Oona came in from school, a pretty little girl with dark hair and rosy cheeks. They lived in a charming little house right on a sand dune. Agnes and my mother had shared an apartment after Agnes' divorce from O'Neill, and according to my mother she had cried for months.

I envied Oona's living right on the sea with a doting mother, and things seemed drab as we drove back to the well-ordered house in Red Bank on the quiet river and the weekly tension of my father's visits and the silent meals interrupted only by his criticism of the food. Occasionally, my grandmother would try to make a cheerful remark or he would try to tell her a story at the table; but it was hopeless and even if he were in a communicative mood, if he and I talked over the centerpiece, it left her out. She would smile at us indulgently as if to say, "Don't mind me, try to talk."

On the weekends when he didn't come down, we went to the movies: Grandmother, Jennie and I. Grandmother sat on the aisle in the second row of seats so she could hear, and Jennie and I sat back. Occasionally, she would yell back to us, and there were always people screaming at us to shut up. It was embarrassing, but I much preferred it to going to the movies with my father, who would always do a critique on the actors as I was being swept away by them in the love scenes, fight scenes, death scenes. I'd be in the midst of being transported away with the romance of it all when I'd hear, "My God, they've ruined the book" or "He's the worst actor the world has ever seen."

My grandmother's was a household in which the occupants spent a lot of time innocently in bed. When my father was there, Jennie took his breakfast up, and never throughout his life did I ever see him in any situation where he didn't have someone to bring him exactly what he ordered for breakfast. When Jennie made the beds she also turned them down. I never saw a bedspread on a bed until I went away to boarding school. They existed, beautiful patchwork ones, always folded over a chair or blanket rack. To have had them on the beds would have made us feel insecure. We had to know we could leap back under the covers at any time and continue reading whatever book was in hand at the moment. My grandfather, after all, had spent most of his life in bed. My Great-uncle Reuel Kimball, remarkable physician that he was, had said that anyone who had been ill should never get up early for at least a month after their malady. We were never quite really up and about in the sense that the bed was made and forgotten about until the long night's sleep.

My father read Dickens and Shakespeare out loud in a booming toneless voice, and I read and reread my grandmother's library: the Tish stories by Mary Roberts Rinehart, *Red Pepper Burns*, *The Trail of the Lonesome Pine* and *The Irish RM* by E. E. Somerville and Martin Ross. There were no Bibles in her bookshelf. I don't know what deal she had made between herself and the Supreme Being. I never heard her mention God. Thank Him. Beseech Him. Ask Him to make His face to shine upon her. Or use the expression, "Oh, my God." Late in her life, she did say she knew her favorite Scottie, Bobbie, named after Bob Hartshorne, would be waiting for her in heaven and that's the nearest I ever heard her come to a religious reference. She did send me to Presbyterian Sunday School, run by one of my grandfather's law partners, and the only Bible in the house was mine. My father refused to have me baptized, although they ended up sending me to a high Episcopal boarding school for five years.

After my father's death, I found all his children's books in the stone house including school books, ones he had never had in Wellfleet. Except for the Joseph Lincoln Cape Cod series. A lot of his childhood books had bookplates, which he never used as an adult. Coleridge's *Ancient Mariner* popped out at me one day. It said "EWJR" in large embroidered capital letters on it. Inside, in his handwriting, it had one of his typical line drawings of the mariner, labeled "Anchaunt Marinere." After he died, there were a lot of these drawings on the yellow foolscap he used for a telephone pad. On page 37, "Love of animals standing for the sacredness of life" is underlined and there is a note in his handwriting, which was much bigger and more generous than the careful, meticulous pen he perfected as an adult: "See Mr. Leicester about the sacredness of life."

He did see Mr. Leicester and wrote the following poem in his schoolbook, addressing the commentator on Coleridge as if he (EW) were Leicester.

> I question thee Mr. Woodberry
> I question thee sair.
> My name is John A. Leicester
> An wha' could you ask mair.
> I wish to have an argument
> (no combat feud or strife)
> About your stated sacredness
> Sacredness of all life,
> I can give you thirty reasons
> A monologue and a song,
> Which will prove to you conclusively
> That you are in the wrong.
> (A word to the wise, Mr. Woodberry)

Jennie felt that some terrible change had come over my father at Princeton, which she attributed to "some man under whose influence he fell. That dean," i.e., Christian Gauss. She said that's when he began becoming so disagreeable at times. Jennie was much too intelligent and sharp to be insecure because her Mr. Edmund had gone off to college and out into the world. She felt he had become dehumanized and arrogant in a way his father never was. She understood the fact that "his mind is working all the time in a world of its own," and admired the fact that "he cares nothing for things for himself such as clothes."

He never tried to make me read his books or even to interest me in them. I didn't want to read them, just as I didn't want to see my mother act. Things were complicated enough without this added dimension. Barry Callaghan once told me that his father, Morley, would have taken a strap to him if he hadn't read his books.

My favorite of my Red Bank relatives was my grandmother's older sister, Addie, mother-in-law of millionaires. She was quite the physical opposite of my grandmother. She lived at the other end of town opposite the Molly Pitcher Hotel. Molly was the Red Bank historical heroine who had taken over the firing of the cannon in the Battle of Monmouth when her husband was killed. The memorial cannon was pointed right at Aunt Addie's front windows.

Aunt Addie had a midget cook, Sylphie, and was not supposed to eat rich foods. She would invite me over to supper without my grandmother. She always said, "Rosalind, we aren't like the rest of them; we have a strange streak." I think she meant I wouldn't marry a millionaire. She would tell my palm and talk to me about books. Then we would go into the dining room. Sylphie would draw the two sets of heavy carpet curtains and like two Roman emperors, we would sit down to a feast of the richest possible foods: biscuits, potatoes in cream, creamed vegetables, great heavy corn fritters, rich pastries.

At home, the big meal was at midday except when my father was home. Supper was often hot cereal and toast. I was instructed not to actually lie about what Aunt Addie and I had eaten but when asked what I had, to say, "What Aunt Addie usually has for supper." Sometimes Dr. Lovett would have to be called to my aunt's after one of these clandestine orgies, as he had to be again and again for my grandmother during the soft-shell crab season. He once sat down wearily in the hall and said, "If she'd only eat them for breakfast, I wouldn't have to come out at night." Dr. Lovett was a very decent sort and was always good-natured about being called out by the Kimball girls (my grandmother and her sisters). If it were anything really serious, a doctor came down on the train from New York. Because of my Great-uncle Reuel's New York practice, all sorts of courtesies were still extended to his sisters.

My Aunt Addie had a chauffeur, Robert, and a La Salle that couldn't compete with my grandmother's Cadillacs. But her bejeweled hands, weighted down with heavy diamond rings her daughters had given her, which she rested casually on the edge of the rolled-down window for my grandmother's benefit when picking me up, far surpassed anything my grandmother had. My grandmother would try and retaliate occasionally by buying a diamond and sapphire bracelet, but Addie was always at least four handsome pieces of jewelry ahead of her.

Two of Addie's children had not walked the path of big money: George, her son, an actor with traveling stock companies, who died of pneumonia; and Helen, who married cartoonist Gene Carr, then separated from him and lived in an apartment in New York with a lot of chow dogs. She made some of my grandmother's hats. My grandmother would return from hat-negotiating trips to New York, totally bemused by Helen's way of life, with stories of hat accessories all over the place amid the dogs and sitting on the sofa next to a cold cooked pork chop which the dogs had somehow overlooked.

When Aunt Addie died, she left me five hundred dollars, with which I bought my first car, a cream-colored deluxe Ford convertible, known as the "Cream Dream." It would become one of the instruments that held me in my on-and-off-again bondage to my father's life, as it was the only transportation his household had.

When I was nine or ten, on one of our New York weekends, my father took me to a party at the Chelsea Hotel featuring Margaret Mead. When we went home on the train to Red Bank, he said to me, "You didn't know it, but Miss Mead, who is very famous, was observing you and she thought you were fine." Great anthropologist though she may have been, she was no good as a child psychologist because I was a mess. She may have known all about coming of age in Samoa, but not doing the same in Red Bank, New Jersey. I had developed five sets of fictions: one for my grandmother, one for my mother, one for my father, one for my Rumson peers and one for the Red Bank ones. I had a high scholastic aptitude but was terrible in my day-to-day work. My energy was being sapped by telling five sets of people what they wanted to hear.

The winters, as I have noted, were pretty much weekends with my father in Red Bank or up in New York with him or my mother, Friday night movies with Grandmother and Jennie, school and dancing classes, the occasional Roman orgy with Aunt Addie, and rides around the Jersey countryside and shore. The summers were wild and unpredictable, except for the one and a half seasons when they managed to incarcerate me in Huckleberry Camp.

# VI

THE TIME I SPENT with the Eakins, my mother and Connie, at Redding Ridge was very different. My mother wouldn't put up with a nurse. There was Connie's son Elliott, but we weren't close. There was a swimming pool and a girl down the road who came from a very classy conservative family with station wagons, who spelled security to me. We imitated my mother making theatrical speeches. We pretended to commit suicide by jumping into the swimming pool.

My mother was totally out of her element in the Connecticut countryside, except she loved to swim in the swimming pool. Louis, the Belgian cook-valet, ran the house, and the caretaker, Mac, ran the place. And in the afternoons a man named Tony came to teach her how to drive in Connie's red La Salle. It was hopeless. She never did learn. Every afternoon we would sit on the porch, watching the La Salle take a series of leaps, eventually hitting a tree or the barn, and my mother emerge near hysteria. Late afternoons we set off with

Tony to meet Connie at the Stamford station. Connie would drive home. One night he yelled, "Hello, you niggers," to some children playing by the roadside. I said, "You shouldn't do that," and Connie said, "Rosalind is right, you shouldn't call people names they don't like," which in a nutshell was everything good and bad about Connie Eakin.

The everyday drinking was on a grand scale; one night, when someone hid the liquor from Connie, he said, "If I can't have a drink, I'll drink ink," and proceeded to down a bottle of Waterman, with resulting doctors, emergency measures and excitement.

Connie's Fourth of July parties had been famous before he married my mother and continued to be so. He spent vast sums on fireworks and two or three hundred people came on this glorious day. The Fourth parties had a wild name and my conservative little friend's parents down the road wouldn't let her come. A lot of it was actors and actresses drinking and reciting great speeches as they fell into the swimming pool. There was a long steep hill rising up almost right behind the main porch of the house, which made the perfect setting as a spot for the firework display extravaganza.

The cummingses came. Djuna Barnes and her brother usually surfaced looking very handsome in a mammoth convertible. William McFee, a sea writer who lived nearby, and Stark Young, and Peggy Bacon and Alexander Brook, who were prominent artists and married to each other. The Brooks always seemed to enjoy themselves and do as much falling into the swimming pool as anyone else and cavorting with the actors and actresses. Peggy always dressed in Victorian clothes.

At that stage in my life, I was terrified by my mother and Connie's parties. I didn't understand that her life was acting, which she was not doing except for the benefit of those around her. She would mix me up with my father's "Mr. Edmund" side and resent what suddenly seemed to her a spoiled fat child brought up to be a useless snob. She was given to declaring in her terrifying thunderous voice, "I am your mother, Rosalind." One night there was a terrible scene when she wanted me to scrub the kitchen floor. Had I been older than seven I probably would have done it. It was two in the morning. My mother was no child abuser; it was all part of the act and the fact that actresses in those days had to scrub for it to make it big. When I read Christina Crawford's book, *Mommie Dearest,* I wondered if some of the scenes which seemed so awful to her didn't come from that same theater philosophy. But she had no solid grandmother in her background as I did.

I saw little of my mother after I was eight. The year I was eleven and went away to school, she went to Pittsburgh to the tuberculosis sanitorium. Her family came and got her. She had nursed Connie through a nervous breakdown. She was literally out in the street. They said they thought they'd never see Connie again. He had drunk himself out of his lucrative job. But they did. He followed my mother out to Pittsburgh and for the next twelve years held down a job at Gimbels selling refrigerators. He had a room sometimes at her sister's. His life was his little job and going up every night to the hospital to see my mother.

I was to see more of my parents together after I was twelve when my father and I visited her than I ever had in my life.

During my years at school, my mother's letters were always brave and cheerful and full of good advice: "When in Rome, do as the Romans do." I adored her family, especially her older sister, Lois, who was married to a successful newspaperman, Roy Jansen. My Aunt Venita, the youngest of the sisters, had come along, as my father explained to me, when things were more settled, and was a family woman. My mother and Lois had left the Swedenborgian church, although my mother said she had continued to see visions until she was in her twenties. My grandmother Blair had corresponded with Henry James, Sr., who was very interested in Swedenborg.

Although I enjoyed my Pittsburgh relatives and the trips when my father was with me, my relations with my mother didn't really improve. It was better seeing her under controlled circumstances when no liquor was involved. I felt desperately sorry for her, but for weeks she'd look forward to my visit and then haul off and fight with me, saying I knew which side my bread was buttered on and making cracks about the luxurious Red Bank life. She was still the actress who wasn't acting and no matter how much I understood that, it did seem unfair to be ranted at for a situation I hadn't made and wasn't able to change.

When my father came along, it was embarrassing for Connie, who behaved very well considering his wife's ex-husband, whom, she told me, she was still in love with, was bouncing around demanding to see the doctors and taking her out to dinner and the theater and things he could not afford. We would take my mother, who weighed only seventy pounds, to our rooms at the hotel, where she would lie on the bed and order up a big meal which she never touched. My father said that's what she had always done.

He and I went to the theater one afternoon in Pittsburgh to see Katharine Hepburn in *Jane Eyre*. My father kept commenting that Miss Hepburn had reversed the roles and was throwing Rochester around the stage. I could see this was true when he pointed it out but would have preferred to remain caught up in the performance. He would try to tell my mother choice bits about people they had known. The dinners with the two of them in the hotel rooms were really the best times I ever had with her except when we would eat lunch at the Algonquin in New York and people would come up and greet my mother.

Of my mother's theater friends, the one who remained the most loyal was Tallulah Bankhead, who, if she was on the road, would try to route herself through Pittsburgh and go to the sanitorium. They loved having her come because some of the male patients who hadn't shaved in months would pull themselves together. I once took a school friend backstage to see Miss Bankhead during the run of *The Little Foxes*, and she made us feel enchanted. Sophie Tucker visited my mother steadfastly too.

When I was seven, my father married Margaret Canby, whom I adored. The first summer of the marriage, my father and I took the train to New Mexico and met Margaret and her son Jimmy, and we all stayed at Boyd's Ranch. Jimmy, whose hero was Tom Mix, toted a holster with two large cap pistols on all occasions. He had been happy at the thought of a sister but had hoped for one who knew more about the ways of the West than I did.

We had a magical time riding and roaming the countryside. My father was writing about the Indians, and we went to the Pueblo towns and ate their Indian bread, which was like brown paper. There was one beautiful Indian girl one of the men connected with the ranch would stop to see. She still seems to me the most beautiful person I ever saw as she stood in the door of her house with her turquoise jewelry. Then we met my nurse and got ready to go to Santa Barbara, where Margaret had a house. As the train pulled out of Kansas City, at one point on our trip, my father didn't show up. My nurse and I had no cash. He'd missed the train browsing in a bookstore in Kansas City. Santa Barbara was heaven. Margaret's house was Spanish with a walled courtyard and avocado trees and the mountains rising beyond it.

Margaret was always thinking up treats for Jimmy and me. One wonderful evening, we went to a Wild West show with a couple who worked for Jimmy's father, who lived up in the mountains. We actually met Tom Mix. Father and Margaret would give dinner parties with very hot Spanish food, and Jimmy and I would hide under the table pinching the guests' legs. We had some extracurricular activities. The walled courtyard made it very easy to sneak out at night when my darling nurse was asleep. You walked along the wall, cap pistols in place in case of marauders. Using a garden fountain spout as a foothold, we made our escape. At that time, there was no age requirement for obtaining a California driver's license and Jimmy, who was twelve, drove Margaret's rumble-seater with the top down. We drove all over Santa Barbara until one night a friend of Margaret's coming along saw Margaret's car with what appeared to be no driver, as Jimmy couldn't be seen above the steering wheel. After that, things tightened up. But we still spent a lot of our time at the Belmont Club on the ocean, in a cabana ordering anything from cabana service which struck our fancy.

Margaret had some very rich friends, the Chancellors, who had a crippled son who was a friend of Jimmy's. They gave a birthday party which was so lavish it made my Rumson ones look drab. I got a real gold miniature luster tea service as a place present, and there were wonderful toy cars which the children drove over a wide mall that extended in front of the mansion.

One night Margaret went to a dance and a man stepped on her evening dress. He gave her fifteen dollars and she bet him fifty dollars she could get three evening dresses for that, which she did. She and two of her friends wore them to a ball, identical styles of different pastel organdies. I never remember my father and Margaret quarreling, except he naturally thought she was spoiling Jimmy. One morning after a disagreement which none of us heard, my father left, driving to Hollywood. As far as I know, it was the only time he ever drove a car. I think Ted Paramore, an old friend of my father's, a westerner and writer who had gone to Hollywood, and who was supposed to be my godfather although I'd never been baptized, drove him back.

Another summer during the time he was married to Margaret, we stayed in the old Coast Guard station at Peaked Hill Bars on the Cape, which had belonged to O'Neill after it was condemned by the Coast Guard. We had a pony named Betsy. It was before the days of dune buggies, and we had to walk the hour and a half into town, with mosquito nets wrung out in citronella over our heads, then bring our groceries back in knapsacks. On Saturdays, Jimmy and I would go into town to the movies and be given money to load up on ice cream at Adam's Pharmacy and soda pop at Peter's gasoline station. The owner was an amateur magician and occasionally my father and he would trade card tricks.

The old Coast Guard station itself was partially buried in the sand, so you could slide down the roof from the watch-tower right to the sand. Grown-ups often did it after a few drinks in the lookout. The bathroom didn't work. Everything had become filled with sand, but there was an outhouse and a hand pump. My nurse, Stella, was miserable. People would come out from Provincetown to see Father and Margaret and a few people had shacks around us. The new Coast Guard station was a quarter mile away with its trusty boats ever ready, and at night Coast Guard personnel walked up and down the beach patrolling with giant flashlights. They would stop at our beach picnics, which were held practically every night, and have a drink of the dynamite which was working away in the bathtub of our hors-de-combat bathroom. In return, the Coast Guard cook was always giving Jimmy and me cakes and cookies. Up and down the beach were remains of shipwrecks, a reminder of the Coast Guard's purpose. The liquid in the bathtub was a brilliant lime green color. There was a ladle hung over the side of the tub. People, the Dos Passoses for instance, would come visit and change their suits in the bathroom to swim. They were always much more talkative and animated when they came out of the bathroom.

There were dishes with fish on them on the walls and a Victrola with all the Frank Crumit songs: "My Uncle Jack was what some people call a lucky tar. Jack was every inch a sailor, five and twenty years a whaler, sailing on the bright blue sea." My nurse did the best she could, but it wasn't her thing and, as she didn't swim, there was nothing for her to do. We were at close quarters, she and Jimmy and I, in the old Coast Guard dormitory with its ladder going up to the tower.

One night there was a dreadful scene when my father in the middle of the night demanded she make him a fried-egg sandwich, a great standby of his through his whole life. She demurred and he bellowed at her. She must have put up with a lot for fear of upsetting me. She was a wonderful woman, well educated, with beautiful clear handwriting. Most of her family were still in Jamaica. That's really the only unpleasantness I remember during my father's marriage to Margaret. Perhaps arguments went on behind closed doors or I was too young to remember or Jimmy and I had our own balance and played outdoors so much I wasn't around.

Two great dune people were Hazel Hawthorne, a writer with a lot of children by her ex-husband, a minister (the oldest, Jane, was a great friend of mine), and a man named Harry Kemp, who was to go on for years in his role of Bohemian, dune poet, and great lover. He was keen on having séances and Father and Margaret were all for it, much as they might be for a game of cards. Jimmy and I went through elaborate preparations to get a long rope and tie a log on it and drop it down the chimney during one of these spirit meetings, hoping the grown-ups, mainly Harry, would think it was a message from a ghost. But it didn't create any stir at all. Harry, according to my mother, had locked up his first wife, a beautiful redhead, for long periods of time with nothing but bananas.

In my freshman year at college, a friend and I spent a few days in Hazel's shack on the dunes. Harry was there, playing the part of the romantic poet with us, referring to my friend's "wild, winsome, eerie look." For years I would see him in various Provincetown haunts, surrounded by young lady disciples. He became a travesty of himself, a Provincetown landmark with a great black cape, proclaiming himself "the dune poet." Old Provincetown friends would have him for Christmas dinner. I never was quite sure who he was; he was simply there, a leftover from a childhood scene in which all the other grown-up characters had moved on.

The summer after our charmed one at the O'Neill house, Jimmy's only summer at Peaked Hill, and my second, Margaret stayed out West. When my father and I returned from the Cape, my mother met us, which was unusual. She gave us the horrible news of Margaret's death. We returned to my mother's apartment at 37 West Twelfth Street and Margaret's family called from Santa Barbara with the details. She had gone to a party in a Spanish-style apartment house with steep outside steps. When she left, she tripped and fell, fatally injuring herself.

My father spent the night in the guest room at my mother and Connie's. It was next to mine and I could hear him sobbing, the only time I ever heard him cry, and the only night I ever remember staying under the same roof as my parents.

# VII

ONE SUMMER AFTER MARGARET'S DEATH we spent at
Susan Glaspell's house on Commercial Street opposite the Dos Passoses' house: Father, my nurse Stella
and myself. It was a nondescript summer. Father and I occupied the two big upstairs bedrooms while Stella had a horrible
little closet downstairs. In those days, when you rented a
house in Provincetown, you usually took on the Portuguese
maid who came with it. In this case, she was a little doll of a
young woman who lived in a little house like a doll's house.
Entertaining wasn't easy in Susan's house, as the bathroom
was off the dining room and the house didn't then, or at any
time I went there afterward, lend itself to any sort of jolly
socializing.

Stella was asked to watch the still at the Dos Passoses' house
across the street occasionally. She was so terrified of it, she
couldn't relax and read a book. She would watch every slow,
steady drop, feeling that if her eyes strayed the still would
blow to kingdom come. Eventually, she broke like a prisoner

under the Chinese water torture, becoming hysterical for the first time and refusing to "still" sit.

Susan's house was smack up to the house next door. The roofs touched. A sailing family named Foster lived there with three sons, one of them my age. We talked all night through the bedroom screens, so I slept all day. There was some talk of sleeping sickness until Mrs. Foster discovered what was going on.

The next summer, we rented Frank and Edie Shays' house on Pleasant Street in Provincetown, which was high on a hill overlooking the harbor. The theater next door was doing *Hamlet*; the actress who was playing Ophelia would sit on the Shays' front lawn doing the flower speech over and over again, going mad. Stella had been let go and was working for an aristocratic Russian family, the Eristoffs, and Jennie was with us. The entire U.S. Navy fleet was spending the summer in Provincetown Harbor. Jennie and I occupied the two upstairs rooms with the usual one-bathroom-downstairs situation which curtailed my father's entertaining of the ladies. Jennie, always a severe asthmatic, had one attack after the other, and then when she returned to Red Bank, never had one in her life again. I think the summer, the only one she'd ever spent away from Red Bank, was a shock to her whole system.

My father decided I must learn a poem a day and couldn't go out until I did so. This was awful on hangover mornings when he didn't get up until late. But every day we went through the tortuous order of "Tiger, Tiger, Burning Bright," or "Behold her single in the field yon solitary highland lass," or Shakespeare, "There is a place where the wild thyme grows," and many more. He was not a good teacher where one of his own was concerned and it was emotional, with a great deal of shouting and stubborn resistance from me. The rest of the time, Jennie and I played hearts upstairs until the advent into my life of Jeannie Clymer, who would remain my best friend until our early twenties, when my job and her marriage separated us geographically. She was the grand-daughter of the famous marine painter, Frederick Waugh.

She lived at the far end of Provincetown, which in those days was known as Waughsville because it was dominated by the charming Waugh family. Jeannie's grandparents, Jean and Fred—known as Wizard Waugh for good reason—lived in the house later bought by Hans Hoffman. It was a beautiful house surrounded by gardens and fantastic courtyards with fountains, opposite the old Wharf Theater where the some-time director George Cram (Jig) Cook had chased my mother around, while my father was chasing Edna Millay in Truro, before my mother and father met. Jig was a Grecophile married to Susan Glaspell at the time. The Waugh house looked out over Provincetown Harbor and was occupied by the Wizard, who did great marine paintings which sold for thousands of dollars as fast as he could get them off the easel. He said he hadn't seen the sea in twenty years, and the Wizard's wife, an adorable woman with a tiny waist, who had gone to a dentist when she was forty and had all her teeth pulled, acquiring false ones because she was tired of having her teeth filled. They were in their seventies. The house was furnished with beautiful antiques. The other occupants were their son's mother-in-law, Mrs. Jenkins, who was paralyzed from the waist down and occupied a downstairs room, and Jeannie. Across the street lived Jeannie's father, a very good artist, Floyd Clymer, and Jeannie's mother, Gwenyth, a fa-mous dress designer who lived in New York. She and Floyd, although not legally separated, led separate lives. Next to Jeannie's father lived Jeannie's one-eyed uncle, Coulton, and his wife, Elizabeth. Next to Jean and Fred's was the oldest house in Provincetown, where Elizabeth and Coulton ran their hooked-rug shop. The Waughs also owned several other houses in the area. They were unworldly people with a capac-ity for making money. My father had a crush on Elizabeth, who was his kind of woman—pretty, neurotic, difficult, bright and amusing. She had red hair and brown eyes. She had nose problems, so she talked strangely. She had back problems. She had psychological problems, and she was faithful to her husband, who was eight years younger than she. And she was full of nutty ideas about how to bring up her niece, Jeannie. In looks, Jeannie was totally different from me, a slim blonde with long curly hair and a lithe figure. Even then she made her own beautiful clothes and was later to design for Gertrude Lawrence. Waughsville was totally art-oriented, not a literary one in the lot. Elizabeth brought Jeannie up to see me. We walked down to the ice-cream store and Jeannie confided she always kept an emergency five-dollar bill in her espadrille for bus rides, extra Popsicles and such. Elizabeth had talked my father into sending me to the school she had chosen for Jeannie, Wykeham Rise in Washington, Connecticut, the following year.

The Waughs provided my other home until I was in my early twenties. I didn't see much of Elizabeth but Jeannie's father and the older Waughs made up the most delightful households, free of strife. Jeannie and I started spending as much time as possible together. We loved walking from one house to the other. We were totally innocent, but it was fun having the sailors who were jamming the streets whistle at us. One day we decided to meet at Adams pharmacy in the center of town for a sundae, dressing up as older women. I put on rouge, a pair of Jennie's shoes and one of the Shays' curtains, and started off. When Jeannie and I were coming back, we were suddenly accosted by two shore patrol types whose aid Jennie had enlisted, and a little later my father was wiping my makeup off with one of the large white linen handkerchiefs he always carried, and returning me to William Blake and his damned tiger. Not a thing had happened. Not a sailor had even whistled at us, especially me, in our strange getups.

I was furious at Jennie, who said she didn't care. But it may have been what shocked her permanently out of her asthma. Jennie was no alcoholic but followed the rule laid down by my great-uncle that there should always be a good bottle of whiskey in the bedroom closet. She may have had a snort that day because she was quite flirtatious with the shore patrol, asking them to come up and have a beer, telling them what nice boys they were. They took her up on it and were soon cavorting with the *Hamlet* cast and the actress playing Ophelia doing her mad scene for them. While my father bellowed for *quiet*!

That was the summer ladies first began to confide in me about my father. A woman named Jean Corman complained to me he had hit her. Actually, I never saw him hit anyone, including Mary McCarthy. He would occasionally raise his hand in an ineffectual way as if he were going to, and perhaps these ladies were so upset they thought he had. My own feeling was that if anyone hit me, I'd hit them back, and probably harder. Mary was more than a physical match for my father. Miss Corman was very eloquent on the subject and I said I couldn't do anything about it.

My cousin Helen Augur showed up with her rich husband, Warren. I adored her. She was small and blond and blue-eyed and they drove me to all the beaches in a convertible with lots of ice cream thrown in. Helen was a journalist. My grandmother couldn't stand her for some reason. My father took the reverse position and was really rather in love with her until he turned on her years later in the most unfair way. It was in Talcottville, where he had asked her to be caretaker of the house for him, but he grew to resent her as he did any woman who wasn't his mother but was living in his mother's house.

In my father's fifties' diaries, when he gives the account of the disappearance of some Boston rockers, he leaves the impression that Helen might have stolen them, which was characteristic of the way he could turn on people, a trait which, according to Jennie, had been with him since childhood. I had been there that Fourth of July. The state troopers were called. They found the missing rockers within the hour in an antique store and discovered who had sold them to the store. It was not Helen Augur. It was clear she had not taken them. My father had adored Helen, her looks, her company, but when he turned, he turned viciously and usually on the wrong person. As Leon Edel was working from the original diaries, it can only have been a distorted image from my father's angry inner world.

My father worked and slept in Frank Shay's downstairs study the whole summer. No matter what happened anywhere, anytime, he always had a big breakfast and he always worked. And he always brushed his teeth with a washcloth instead of a toothbrush.

My favorite couples to whose homes he took me for visits were the two childless ones, Betty and Niles Spencer and the Dos Passoses. I spent a great deal of time in my late teens and early twenties at the Dosses. Perhaps it was because there was no competition in the form of their own children and they always rushed around making horse's necks, a fruit-juice drink with lots of cherries and citrus peel. There were pets. Betty Spencer loved to talk about their cat, "a very fine cat." The Dosses had very smart poodles as well as cats. The Dosses were often away as Dos was a traveler. He once said to me, "Some people like to travel rather than feel deep emotion."

The summer we were in the Shay house, we often went to the Spencers' in the evening. They had a home-brew whiskey known as "Tiger Cat" to which my father was devoted. Elated by the Tiger Cat, my father would walk back on Bradford Street with me humming along, singing the two popular songs of the summer, "I'll String Along With You" and "Cocktails for Two," with various people popping their heads out the window along the way begging us to shut up.

The next two summers my father and I spent alone in the Dos Passoses' house. They were exciting, enchanting summers for me, but obviously not for him, according to a letter to my mother written at the end of the second summer, which follows. *

September 19, 1936
571 Commercial Street
Provincetown, Mass.

From Edmund Wilson
To Mary Blair
in the Tuberculosis League Hospital Pittsburgh

Dear Mary: We are leaving here next Wednesday. Betty Huling's sister is coming up to drive us down. We will stop over in Boston and Rosalind will go to the oculist Thursday morning, and I hope I'll get her down to Red Bank Thursday night. Her eyes seem to be much better than they were. Certainly they look much better and do not turn out unless she gets tired. In general, she has improved enormously during this last year: people who come here remark on how well she behaves. And her observations on the people she meets are quite penetrating. I have had a very good time with her— really, the best summer we have ever spent up here. Her grandmother is making so much fuss now about bringing her back to have some new dresses made for her by the dressmaker that I guess I'll have to take her down there. Christmas I'll bring her to Pittsburgh.

I'm sick of Provincetown for myself—sick of all the people and tired of seeing the tide go in and out. And during August and early September, when you live down this end of town, great quantities of people who have come up here for brief vacations and to whom it is a matter of great indifference that

* When my mother died, she left her correspondence to her oldest sister, Lois, with a letter from my father giving specific permission to do as she liked with it. Lois destroyed a lot of my father's letters to my mother, as she thought they should be destroyed. Perhaps she thought some of it might embarrass me. This letter was written by my father to my mother on my thirteenth birthday, a fact of which he is obviously unaware.

you have come up to work, barge in on you in a gala spirit and expect to be entertained. I adopted the practice of turning out all the lights in the bottom part of the house and coming up here to the study at night—but one night when I was creeping out to mail some letters I ran right into two people who were about to knock on the door. The last week I have given up trying to fight them off, but have sidetracked a lot of people who have just come or announced they were coming, into a giant picnic tomorrow (Sunday). So far as I can see, there will be Gardner Jackson and his wife from Cotuit, bringing Felix Frankfurter and his wife and a young Englishman I used to know and his wife, John Bishop from South Harwich and Margaret Bishop and her sister and her sister's daughter from Martha's Vineyard, the Dos Passoses and odd people from Provincetown to whom I owe invitations. If, however, the weather isn't good enough for a picnic, it won't be quite so easy, because they will all have to come here. But Carlo Tresca has offered to make spaghetti—so that would somewhat simplify the problem. Mary Vorse is here, too, seeming rather old. She seems to think she is going out to Pittsburgh about the steel unions and I'm going to tell her to go and see you.

Thank you for letting me know about the WPA. I've sent my plays on to them. No: I never heard another word from Erskine.

The avocados are good for you: they are fattening.

I am not precisely clear as to just how long the money I have sent you for the hospital will last. Will it last till the week of the 20th? Please let me know about this right away—writing to me at Red Bank. I'll send you some more, then.

Rosalind has gone over to play pingpong at the tennis club with Ann de Silver, who is staying with us while her mother stays with the Dos Passoses and Jeannie Clymer. She loves all the visitors and guests: great excitement for her! When I asked her the other day whether she wanted to go over to the Walkers' with me, she said, "Yes: I like to see how people live."—I forgot to mention that the Walkers (you remember

Charlie Walker) are coming tomorrow, too, and bringing numerous house-guests.

I hope you got out for Labor Day.

Susan Glaspell has just gone away on her way to the Middle West, where she has been asked to select plays for the WPA. I think it will do her good. She has been talking for several years about going back to the West. She has come out of a period of drinking and demoralization at splitting up with Norman somewhat aged but more dignified and sensible. Nilla had just been up to see her and she, too, seems somewhat sobered by the years—though still a bit hyperthyroid or whatever it is. She has been writing her autobiography in some gigantic number of words. Alan Ross MacDougall was visiting there too.

I don't know what I am going to do when I get back—wish I did. I guess a little house in the country is indicated. Margaret de Silver has just offered me her house at Cos Cob rent free, but I don't know that I should like Cos Cob and it is four and a half miles from the station and I don't drive a car.

I'm sorry I haven't written in so long, but have been trying to work and as I say, distracted by guests. Recently I've given up work till I get away. Write to me soon, my dear. Best regards to Connie.

Best love, Bunny

My life, my father's life, the lives of some of the people on the picnic guest list were to take many turns. Katy Dos Passos and Carlo Tresca were to die violent deaths.

But at that time, Provincetown still had the wholesomeness of a fishing village, a working town. On the street corners, the men off the boats gathered in their sea boots. Writing wasn't as yet big business. And the town had not yet become a resort for rich doctors and art dealers.

The Dos Passoses' house was charming, with a fenced garden in front and decks and Dos' vegetable garden in back, and a magnificent view of the harbor. We had rented it rather cheaply the summer of 1936 in return for dog-sitting their uncannily intelligent poodle, ToTo, and some Siamese cats. It had been a barn before Katy bought it prior to her marriage to Dos. She had gradually improved it and called it Smooley Hall, a combination of her name, Smith, and the name of her best friend, Edith Foley, whom Katy had known from childhood and who later married Frank Shay. Frank had had a famous bookstore in Greenwich Village and was the first to publish Edna Millay. He had done some anthologies of famous drinking songs and for a while had become the Provincetown drunk. Phyllis Duganne, who had been in love with Frank at one point herself, said she had written Edith Shay off as a somewhat prissy Wellesley girl until one night at a party when Frank was lying on the floor drunk and someone had complained, Edith had looked down at him and said, "He's brave and he's beautiful," which was typical of the romantic spirit of Smooley Hall as opposed to the harsher light my father's marriage to Mary McCarthy brought in.

Before their marriages, Katy and Edie and occasionally a third friend had a going household at Smooley Hall with Katy's two brothers occasionally passing through accompanied by a variety of other people. They kept a large barrel in one corner of the main room to which they constantly added water, fruit juice, yeast, citrus rinds, molasses and other matter. It would make cozy, gluggy noises and was known as "the boy." People would come up exhausted from New York and Boston and be totally revivified after a few ladles, able to stay up talking and dancing all night. One Boston doctor who visited them started recommending it to his patients.

Dos had met Katy and immediately come up and pitched a tent on the front lawn until she married him. She had real cat eyes. Her father was a famous biblical scholar and it drove my father crazy that she would never talk about him. Until her horrible death in 1946, I was part of what Dos called her "Youth Movement," an assorted group of young people whom Dos found entertaining and who hung around the house from time to time.

One of the summers, the Dosses were in Mexico, as they often were. Occasionally they bounced around with Hemingway, to whom Katy had been engaged, having grown up with him. The main floor of the house overlooked the harbor with a large living room with a bedroom, bath and dressing room off it, occupied by my father. The dining room and kitchen were in the basement. I had the upstairs to myself.

As my father was having a very active social life and sleeping late in the mornings, we led more or less separate lives, which I found delightful. My policy was to go into his room around eight in the morning and say, "I need some money for today." He would groan sleepily and say, "Take what you need," motioning toward his wallet on the bedside table next to his gold watch. I would take perhaps a crisp twenty and be off for the day, the only kid in town with twenty dollars for Popsicles and movies per diem.

# VIII

PROVINCETOWN IN THOSE DAYS had wonderful open buses which were very high. They looked like gargantuan touring cars. They had tops but no sides except in stormy weather, when oilskin curtains were let down. They were owned by the Paige brothers' garage and were operated by a driver and a money taker, who was often Harold Paige, a very handsome and personable seventeen-year-old. Harold was one of the main objects of Jeannie's and my day, and a lot of the twenty and the day was spent riding from the Dosses' house at one end of town to the Waugh house at the other end, hoping for some notice from Harold. Anything would do. A simple "Well, I see you're on again" or "I haven't got change for a twenty yet" would set my heart beating.

The summer had begun auspiciously when my father agreed to come and get me and spring me out of Huckleberry Camp, where I was wholesomely incarcerated with my light blue gym bloomers, sailor blouses and ties, wearing what beads I could manage to win for neatness, courtesy, punctuality, sportsmanship, honor, etc. You won them at the campfire every Saturday night. They were different-colored wooden ones and you wore them on a shoestring around your neck. They were awarded to the strains of "Satan is a liar and a conjurer too." You were on your honor not to eat a single huckleberry at Huckleberry Camp until a certain date, when they were all picked and made into pies for dinner. The pressure of wearing my honor beads when I knew I'd eaten some illegal huckleberries was getting to me and I longed for my father's arrival. The Connecticut countryside was hot and stuffy and somehow cramped, although Norfolk where we went to church was an all-right little village; but the little stone church seemed claustrophobic along with the carefully controlled huckleberries.

We were all at dinner in the middle of the day when the old Stutz touring car slithered in with one of my favorite people, Betty Huling, at the wheel, and with Hattie, the black . . . I hesitate to use the word "maid" because her nobility, resourcefulness, spirit and personality put her so far beyond us on a transcendental plane. Hattie (who preferred not to have her last name bandied about, as she like my father was often the target of bill collectors) and her three grandchildren were in back and my father in his brown suit and hat in the front with Betty. The girls began singing, "How do you do, Mr. Wilson. How do you do. Is there anything we can do for you? We will do it if we can, stand by at your command. How do you do do do?"

Hattie and her grandchildren got out of the backseat of the car to stretch their legs. Hattie had a spot on the back of her dress from sitting in melted ice cream one of the children had splashed. I was embarrassed and hated myself for it. Soon the children were wandering around plucking the sacred huckleberries. There was the well-ordered life on the platform of the open dining hall, the girls in their fresh uniforms drinking their mugs of milk, and below were my father and entourage in the light green Stutz, its top down and the unfettered delights of Provincetown in the offing. Though I had brought Huckleberry Camp on myself by shooting an arrow into the sky with Johnny Maguire in Talcottville and having it lodge in the dining-room table, somehow I had made enough noise so I was being extricated. I got in the front seat between Father and Betty and we left to the strains of, "We're sorry you have to leave us, Mr. Wilson, Mr. Wilson." "Lambie," which is what Betty had named the Stutz, broke down every fifty miles or so on the way to the Cape, and when we would be towed in or manage to limp into a garage, the mechanics would invariably lift the hood and say, "What a beauty! They don't make them that way anymore," and then call in other mechanics and anyone who was lolling around. The periods when we stopped made the moments on the open road, touring along, all the more precious and free.

Betty spent a week with us. She was a great tennis player and introduced me to the Provincetown Tennis Club. There were Ping-Pong tables on the top floor where you could play for twenty-five cents a game. They were holding the championships there that year, so there were a great many very good players around. Jeannie and I became good enough so they would occasionally let us rally with them.

Betty Huling and my father had been comrades-in-arms at the *New Republic*, and she was one of his best female relationships, the only one I knew of with a woman who was interested in a competitive sport—tennis. She was of professional caliber, and it gave her a dimension he could not enter and complicate. She wasn't a beauty except for perfect legs, and she stuttered, but she was one of the most lively people around and regarded my father with an amused dispassion.

The summer meandered its halcyon way. Betty had left after a week, Hattie after two, as planned. The idea had been to get us settled and give the grandchildren a vacation until

July. In the mornings, I put on my long shirt over my tennis dress and took the bus up to Jeannie's. The old Wizard and his household were usually at breakfast, served elegantly by their maids.

Wizard Waugh's studio was huge, with canvases standing around and the one he was working on on an easel, always of the sea, which looked as if it were about to roll off the canvas and onto you. There was a balcony in the studio where Jeannie and I slept if I spent the night. It held his collection of strange pieces of driftwood he had polished, called munes. Outside, in the large paved garden with fountains, were great plaques with inset sandwich glass remnants. The Wizard was never idle, and it was a fascinating house to be part of. It was a great showplace and we always felt important opening the gate of the beautiful garden and walking in while less fortunate passersby merely looked.

In the afternoon there was a big tea tray and Madam, Elizabeth's mother, and Mrs. Waugh were joined by various elderly ladies and gentlemen who lived in the neighborhood or who were connected with St. Mary's of the Harbor, the charming little Episcopal church the Wizard had designed.

It was a totally different setting from that of my father in the Dosses' basement dining room with Hattie and her grandchildren in attendance and a still in the corner. Hattie and my father were bound forever. He had spent days on her behalf at various welfare agencies. I used to sit outside in the gloomy offices and hear him patiently pleading her cause and painstakingly doing the endless paperwork (her daughter had mental problems, which is why the grandchildren were with us).

Two occasions in particular had shown her great presence of mind. Once he had invited a distinguished guest to dinner in his house in the East Fifties. He had no tablecloths; one suddenly appeared on the card table that was used as a dining table with a wide blue stripe across it saying YALE CLUB. The guest was a Yalie. It turned out Hattie was doing a little moonlighting for an indigent Yale man down the street who was benefiting from some of our household goods.

One day the sheriff came to throw my father out of the house for nonpayment of everything. My father kept calling for Hattie, who was upstairs, to make a quick getaway. She kept saying she was coming, but it was quite a while before she appeared. Several days later, she explained she had caught fire turning off a heater and was rolling herself in a rug to smother it. She hadn't wanted to worry him by telling him at the time.

He eventually arranged to share her with Margaret de Silver. Margaret was the rich socialite widow of a liberal lawyer, Harry de Silver. She was beautiful and overweight, with tiny hands and feet and a sweet manner. On several occasions after we had seen her, my father would say wistfully, "She was almost your stepmother."

The day of my thirteenth birthday, I made a new friend in Margaret's daughter, Ann. I didn't realize she was twenty-three. She was tragically misdiagnosed as retarded. It wasn't until I was in my twenties that they discovered she was schizophrenic. Ann came with her mother and Carlo Tresca to talk over picnic preparations for the next day.

Carlo Tresca and Margaret were a very husky duo. Carlo was the flamboyant editor of an Italian newspaper, *The Hammer*, and totally anti-Fascist. He would be assassinated in the early forties. By then, Jeannie and I had an apartment in New York. One night around eleven, we got off the Fifth Avenue bus at Thirteenth Street and there was a body covered with newspapers and a policeman standing guard. We skirted it. The next day when we opened the newspapers, we realized it was Carlo. He had turned and walked toward his assassin. Margaret, who had many connections in the newspaper world, would spend years and vast sums of money trying to discover his murderers. But she had been like a European woman in her relationship with him and kept herself aloof from his professional career. Carlo was mammoth, over six feet, and portly. He always wore a black cape, liked pretty young girls and made superlative spaghetti.

It had been a summer of people. Louise Bogan had come down on the Provincetown boat with her daughter, Maidie. On the way, she had been picked up by Zoltán Horasti, who was the colorful Hungarian rare-book man at the Boston Public Library. He became a lifelong friend of ours, and through the years it seemed to me that every woman I met around Boston of Louise's vintage had been entangled with Zoltán at some point. He never married. I had quoted some popular quatrain in front of Miss Bogan. My father harshly reprimanded me: "You mustn't recite things like that in front of Miss Bogan. She's a lyric poet. It will trouble her."

Betty had driven us to Martha's Vineyard for a few nights to visit Max Eastman and his wife. To my adolescent embarrassment, he and his entourage were cavorting around the beach in the buff. My father and e. e. cummings both had terrible sunburns. cummings wore a beach robe and my father sat in his hat and brown suit, an odd contrast to the naked faction, who encouraged me to be free and take my clothes off. I would rather have died, which cummings saw, and made them stop trying to persuade me. I always loved him for that and a remark he made many years later when I was involved with an indifferent Englishman. "Some people," he said, "have a cold in the nose. Some people have a cold in the head. The English have a cold in the heart."

The next summer in Margaret de Silver's house in Stamford was the last summer my father and I were to spend alone, and it was a painful one, a far cry from the beloved Dos Passos house.

The foreshadowing of pain started when my father came to my graduation at Wykeham Rise school, where I had gone at eleven.

Wykeham Rise was very strict. We wore blue serge uniforms and were inspected every morning to see that our black cotton stockings met our uniform pink cotton underpants. We answered roll call with the Latin *"Adsum."* It was high Episcopalian, which as I pointed out to my father when I tried to get out of it was an odd paradox since he had refused to have me baptized. It had been founded by a remarkable Scotswoman and went on the skids as she got older, closing down the year after I left. I was there five years.

It was the proud boast of Miss Helen Tucker, a pretty, petite English teacher, that she had never lost a girl on a college board.

After the graduation ceremonies, there was a garden party, and I watched with alarm as my father sought out Miss Tucker. The icy hand of terror clutched my heart as I watched them engage in earnest conversation. I sensed she was beseeching him to help her, a lady in distress, who might lose her first girl on the eventual English college boards. If only it had been one of the less attractive teachers. Miss Tucker's academic robe swirled in the breeze around her pretty ankles and size-four pumps. The tassels from her mortarboard tickled her piquant little face uplifted admiringly, confidingly, winningly to my father. His voice carried, and such words as "I see work in grammar" came drifting over the otherwise happy throng. As we got in the taxi to leave, my father said as he slammed the door, "I shall have to tutor you this summer."

Margaret's house, Trees, was a depressing place set in acres of thick boring woods about ten miles outside of Stamford. It was a one-story stone house with two ells, each containing a bath and two bedrooms, off either side of a courtyard. It was surrounded by spooky rocks and a nasty unswimmable little river running below. There were several green screened outbuildings such as they had in old-fashioned Salvation Army camps. Kitty-corner downstream from the miserable river was Libby Holman's house. That terrain cried out for trouble. Miss Holman might have attributed some of her problems to the ghastly landscape, and perhaps did. There was a large all-purpose room between the ells, and underneath that a tin-lined room in which Margaret's lawyer-husband had kept important papers.

The driveway was a mile long. We had no car, of course. Hattie got our meals and the terrible grammar lessons began. My father loved to teach, especially his family, and was a terrible teacher in that respect. Tortuous tirades over nouns in apposition—"The man is a ballet dancer. What's 'ballet dancer'?"—and over the parsing of sentences. I was too upset by his bellicose approach to learn. Some years later when he was teaching at the University of Chicago summer school, he was the soul of patience with a woman who had been writing a thesis on "The Idiots in Dickens." She'd been at it seven years and he discovered she had an idiot relative.

Betty Huling came out. As the copy editor of the *New Republic*, she knew more about grammar than he did and, taking in the ghastly situation, taught me in three hours what he hadn't been able to in three weeks.

I read the complete works of Havelock Ellis and Henry James that summer, which added to the gloom of the place, and thought of Jeannie having Harold Paige to herself in Provincetown. My father was desperately lonely and would spend a lot of time at the upright phone in the living room calling various ladies and proposing to them, especially an old girlfriend, Louise Connor. Several times a week, he'd make forays in a taxi into the outside world. He was so desperate there were shades of what I'd heard of Sandy Kimball's behavior in it. The thought of returning to Red Bank seemed wholesome and exciting to me.

One winter evening, he called me at school to say he was getting married. One weekend Jeannie and I went to Trees to meet his new wife, Mary McCarthy. He had tactfully invited Jeannie's parents too. Had Mary come on the scene during the magical Dos Passos house summers, I might have re-

95

sented her, but after the grim Trees summer I regarded her with relief as a potential buffer. She had her hair in a braid around her head and was wearing a taffeta print dress. She did the best she could with the situation, and there was no foreshadowing of the hysteria, mayhem and destruction brought on by the intricacies of character of both my father and herself. There were some entertaining times, and I learned two practical things from her: how to make the best cucumber sandwiches and Tom Collinses in the world. She never managed to teach me how to dress, which she did very well.

# PART
# II

# IX

MARY MCCARTHY WAS TWENTY-FIVE when she married my father and he was forty-three. It was her second marriage; and she'd done the affair circuit. She had been traumatized by an unbelievably harsh childhood which had left her with symptoms of apprehension. Her scenes had a quality of sameness, unlike my mother's scenes, which were theatrical and reminiscent of some of the plays she'd been in. My father and Mary had a swift intellectual give-and-take, but in the end it didn't compensate for the fact that some of his psychological problems didn't dovetail with her eccentricities. He felt she'd bamboozled him by not telling him some of her problems before they were married.

There were some happy social times, but on the whole it was a tense and tortuous household. For instance, they were two people who should never have eaten a meal together at home. Mary was a very good cook of the gourmet-perfectionist variety, not the girl to get the meal on the table for the threshers at harvest time. My father was always ready to criticize the food and really wouldn't have felt everything was normal if he didn't. He was compulsively late for meals, so the soufflé whatnot had fallen or the meringue had toughened up. This combination made for some ghastly meals preceded by dread on all sides. Mary longed for the constant assurance that everything was perfect, and my father was the last person to give it to her.

She actively disliked music, said she really couldn't differentiate between the sounds, except she had some idea that when people put on their coats, the symphony was about to end. My father loved music, and some of his happiest moments were spent with the phonograph blaring full blast, often playing the same piece again and again while he drifted into a world of sound and scotch.

My grandmother's attitude toward the marriage was one of fearful discouragement. My father had told her of Mary's interest in cooking and gardening in much the way a salesman tries to talk up his product to a reluctant client. She had nothing against Mary per se, but her clinical view of my father's previous failures, his psychological difficulties and the difference in ages made her beg him to wait. When he didn't, she felt she was shouldering another burden. She'd been opposed to the marriage to my mother because she felt she wouldn't have time to be a housewife. My grandmother felt Margaret Canby drank much too much. My grandmother was tired and felt she could no longer deal with the needs of neurotic and brilliant men—rather than wishing to hang on to him, she wished to relocate his emotional needs. She had a great deal of medical knowledge, acquired from her father, her brothers, their doctor friends and years of dealing with her husband's doctors. When Mary came down to Red Bank and made a scene, she slapped her face and brought her out of it.

Mary did like cooking, did like gardening, but in small,

perfect portions. Great bowls of flourishing peonies and roses were not for her. Bud vases were more her style.

My grandmother's distaste for the mismating of circumstances took the form of having a phobic reaction to anything Mary gave her. Mary wanted to be liked by and to accommodate my grandmother and among other things gave her an eminently suitable bed tray. My grandmother threw a tantrum of her own when the pretty thing arrived from Bonwit Teller and demanded it be taken out of the house.

Mary and Father remained at Trees for a while. The peculiar atmosphere of the place was enhanced by the fact that there was an accident while my father was doing one of his card tricks. It involved a person's picking a card from the pack and replacing it, at which point my father, with the aid of an elastic and a thumbtack, would nail it to the wall. The card overshot, pinning itself to the very high cathedral ceiling. No one around had a tall enough ladder to get it down; so it remained.

He was a very good sleight-of-hand magician and was appreciated as a serious scholar by some of the good magicians. I'm convinced he pulled his last great magic trick a few days before he died. It was always amusing to go into magic shops with him; and sometimes in the more distinguished ones there would be famous magicians in the back room, gossiping and showing tricks, or the proprietor might sell him a new trick he'd learned with a coin, some newspaper and four aces, for instance. It was a funny dichotomy in his character, this love of illusion and magic contrasting with his career, which depended on analyzing and taking apart literary works and removing the magic. My mother had come to know Houdini when they were on the same bill together, and she and my father had visited with the Houdinis on several occasions. He, like Houdini, knew what frauds most of the psychics were with their vast filing and communications systems, which gave them information about the people coming to them and enabled the psychics to hoodwink their customers with the seemingly inexplicable knowledge they had of them.

When Mary became pregnant with my half brother, Reuel, named after my Great-uncle Reuel, she started seeing a psychiatrist; and they took the house of a retired sea dog on Shippan Point in Stamford for the summer, which was almost next door to the house of her psychiatrist, Dr. Sandor Rado, one of the strangest people to enter our lives.

That summer he made only fleeting appearances in our social life, but his presence became very evident when they moved back to the Cape. He had been a pupil of Freud's and he was interested in psychosomatic medicine. He was not a man who went and worked among the poor. Charlatan? Or dedicated healer? He had great psychological problems of his own, which he had never succeeded in ironing out.

Sometime after my brother Reuel's birth on Christmas Day, they started moving back to the Cape with thoughts of buying a house in Wellfleet. At approximately the same time, Sandor Rado discovered Provincetown with a whole group of New York doctors. There were skin specialists; there were internists cavorting on the beaches with heavy, expensive striped bath towels and Hammacher-Schlemmer thermoses. The nicest of the group were Dr. Milton Rosenbluth and his wife. He was an internist and one of those geniuses as far as diagnosing went. Some years later, I took Jennie Corbett to him. She'd had a large brown growth on her forehead for years. She'd been to four skin specialists, all with different recommendations—electric needles, X-rays, operations, all with warnings of risk. Rosenbluth took his thumb and forefinger and pinched it off in a second. My grandmother wasn't surprised when we returned from New York and told her about it. She said it's just the sort of thing her brother, Reuel, would have done.

Rado was very short, anything but good-looking, with bright beady dark eyes. He had taken the only really upper-bourgeois house in Provincetown on Commercial Street, a few houses away from the Dos Passoses. He was Hungarian, and his nicest side was the one which dispensed Hungarian hospitality. He had really established for himself the sort of life in which my father would have functioned well. He had a nice and efficient German housekeeper and a sort of all-around unromantic gofer companion named Lottie. His older son was around sometimes and also his younger son by his second wife, a former patient of his from whom he was more or less separated. Mary thought Rado looked like a honey bear and called him her honey bear—not to his face. I may have been the only member of the family to ever meet Emmie Rado, who was perfectly beautiful and very good quality—a tall, dark beauty with a perfect figure. She had come up for the night and took her young son, his tutor, Jim Powers who was a friend of mine, and me out for a bang-up dinner at the Flagship, buying herself, Jim and me a lot of zombies, which were then in vogue.

One aspect of my father and Mary's marriage was that they analyzed people until nothing was left of them except a few nail parings. Rado excelled even them in this respect; after all, in his case it was business as usual. The Dos Passoses were the social elite of Provincetown. They had the most attractive house, and everyone loved going there. Rado would have liked to be among the happy groups invited there; Dos, who was very un-Freudian-minded, was bored by the prospect of him.

Mary and Rado spent hours on the Cape beaches on the subject of the Dosses, whom Rado analyzed to anyone who would listen. As I sat with my mosquito-bitten legs listening to all this, I couldn't help feel that Dos and Katy, who had a very happy marriage and gave other people happiness and laughter through it, were in far better shape than Rado or

Mary. Stories had reached the Dosses of Rado's compulsive chasing of young girls. One very young waitress who had rejected him had to take his breakfast to his room and found him sitting cross-legged and naked in a purple turban as he grabbed for her ankle.

Soon I was telling Katy Dos Passos about Jeannie Clymer's adventures with him. Jeannie and I had gotten on the boat for Boston; as we went up the gangplank, there was Rado. Jeannie, whom he had never met, was at the height of her blond beauty (my father had made her mother furious by saying she looked like Rita Hayworth, whom Gwen, her mother, thought was tough).

Rado literally chased her all over the ship. Jeannie was going on to New York, and when we got to Boston there was no way we could avoid taking a cab to the South Station with him. I was staying in Boston; Jeannie on the New York train, The Owl, had a frightful time. He literally knocked on her compartment door every twenty minutes or so, asking her if she didn't want sleeping pills. She said she never knew what the word "satyr" meant until that night with Rado. I knew what she meant, as his eyes had had a glazed look like an animal in heat or rut. When Dos wrote about the incident in one of his books, he said, "Two little girls, one the daughter of a distinguished friend, had had their little behinds pinched black and blue on the Provincetown boat." That wasn't true; Rado had no interest in me whatsoever as he jumped from camp chair to camp chair grabbing for Jeannie while she leapt from one protective barrier to the next.

Dos and Katy also had a charming house in Truro, where Dos went out to work sometimes in the summer. Katy was very entertaining about people in a very different way from Miss McCarthy. Mary saw people from a socio-psychoanalytic point of view. There was always some romanticism in Katy's outlook. Katy and Dos always called my father Antichrist. Katy was Possum, Dos was Emfish. They were unable to have children after an unfortunate miscarriage of Katy's. Dos traveled a great deal, often doing reportorial assignments, and when he was away, Edie Shay would often come over and stay with Katy. Mary made a great deal of this, implying they were lesbians, which was untrue, and saying Edie was all over the house like a Dalí painting. Actually, Edie and Katy collaborated on several books together, which had respectable sales, one of them becoming a best-seller.

Katy and Edie were not homosexuals any more than are little girls who go to slumber parties for the excitement of it; and neither was Dos—although he did have a theory that every artist has a dash of the homosexual. One of his best friends in Boston was a rich and famous one. One night when the Dosses and Edith Shay were dining with him at the Hotel Vendôme (people were always going up to Boston to see their doctors or publishers and spending the night at the Vendôme or the Bellevue), he kept grabbing the bus boy, saying, "You're a lovely boy, sonny. Let me catch you." When the Dosses got back up to their room, there was a fly buzzing around. Katy kept grabbing for it, saying, "You're a lovely fly, sonny. Let me catch you."

Katy and Edie's books were about the Cape and its history, and when Dos was away was a good time for them to drive around together doing the necessary research and writing. It worked out well for all concerned, giving Dos the freedom his nature needed to go off alone at times.

Because I had been brought up with my grandmother's library, I was much more at ease with Edie and Katy's Somerville and Ross approach to life and literature than I was with the cold, white light of Miss McCarthy.

Dos always pretended not to be interested in gossip; and if anyone made some personal reference or analysis of another person, he stuttered a lot looking over your head and puffing his cigar. Katy had a very acute eye and fed him everything when they were alone. She had her own snobbisms and

Dorothy Parker was one of them. One night when Miss Parker had been there, she said to her in a sweet voice as she was leaving, "Well, Dorothy, it's been absolutely horrible having you." Knowing how Dos hated any sort of direct confrontation unless it was in a verbal political argument, I asked how he'd reacted. Katy said, "I regret to say he rushed to Miss Parker's side full of solicitude."

Dos was the son of a Portuguese immigrant, which was evident in his looks and put his relationship with the Portuguese in Provincetown on a different level than the other later arrivals in the writing set. In those days, there was still a great rate of intermarriage among the Portuguese and a fair number of retarded children in ratio to the population. On Christmas Eve, the natives held open house, the women staying behind the men as Spanish custom dictates, and not mingling with any outlanders who came in. There was constant traffic between Provincetown and the Azores, which kept the local Portuguese in touch with the old customs.

It seemed to me strange that Rado was willing to see Mary socially, although it was always pleasant to go to the beach. She had been a patient of his. I felt he badly longed to get into the hard-core literary set. We were renting a house in Wellfleet the first Rado summer. In addition, my father had rented a studio next to Elizabeth Freeman's, the local real estate agent. To get there, he walked half a mile through the woods on a narrow dirt path. Either Mary or I took his lunch over every day, prepared with perfection and trauma by Mary. Looking back, it was symptomatic of the household that the obvious course of preparing his lunch in advance so that he could take it with him was never taken.

When I came for vacations, Mary always said, "I haven't had a chance to make your bed." It was a roundabout denial of my arrival, and who could blame her? It meant added commotion.

Mary had brought the *Partisan Review* crowd with her to

the marriage. The Shays had been the people to first leave Provincetown for Wellfleet and Frank Shay boosted it by organizing local fairs and with his slogan "Well, well, Wellfleet." The chain of five freshwater ponds a quarter of a mile or so from the ocean was still wild, and Gull Pond was still regarded as the place Thoreau walked around. Wellfleet oysters and scallops were abundant and famous. Ten years later, it was full of remainders of the *Partisan Review* crowd, among others, with their new wives, while ex-wives had cottages nearby. The scallops and oysters were being overharvested; and my father was one of the few people who really worked anymore. Vladimir Nabokov had appeared on the American scene and came to visit. My father was trying to help him and sent a story of his to *The Atlantic*. They kept it forever, which added coals to the fire of my father's real dislike of Edward Weeks, the editor.

If anyone was a match for my father and Mary's ability to dismember people mentally, and love of torturing intellectually and analytically, with endless ramifications and complications, that person was "Volodya" Nabokov. He could take them on with both hands tied behind him. Then he'd slip into things lepidopterous or Russian grammar, worlds of which he was king and where they could not enter. Eventually, my father decided he would attack Nabokov on a point of Russian grammar—with disastrous results. Nina and Paul Chavchavadze begged him on bended knee not to. "You'll be bested." And he was! Nina Chavchavadze came every afternoon and taught my father Russian. There was no car at that point and my father had established his usual relationship with the local taxi driver, Bill Ceerun, a true Wellfleetian. Although my father kept Bill waiting for hours and paid him modestly, Bill took it, waiting in his dignified car with his straw hat, clean shirt and bow tie. Mary said someday he'd explode; but he never did. On some deep level, Bill must have realized that my father was like himself, basically a serious person compared to some of the newer arrivals. Volodya had been an admirer of Nina's when they were young in Russia. When I was working at Houghton Mifflin in the early fifties, Jack Leggett, who was then also working in the New York office, asked at an editorial meeting if we would like to see a book by Nabokov about an older man in love with a young girl. We all said *no. Lolita.*

Mary's book *The Company She Keeps* was ready to come out that summer, and she went into a swivet because she didn't want me to read it. My father said if you published you had to bear with the fact that people were going to read you.

Rado's tinkering around—seeing a still potential patient socially—blew up in everyone's face when his comrade, Lottie, told Mary a lot about just how neurotic Rado was. Things blew over, but there wasn't quite as much socializing on the beach.

I liked Rado more than I disliked him, but it seemed to me there was no one at home a lot of the time. His behavior toward me was impeccable. He rather touchingly arranged for his older son, George, to serve as an escort for me to the Provincetown Art Association Ball. But Rado was really incapable of conversation. He had to hold forth on people as he did about the Dosses. Any form of give-and-take in a political conversation, for instance, was unknown to him. His eyes would dart around the room and his hands would become fists. An opener such as "What do you think will happen with the situation in the Persian Gulf?" would leave him blank.

Looking back, I think Rado just never read the papers and, like his patients, was ensconced in a world of his own in which any form of abstract thought had no part. His eyes were expressionless. Perhaps he'd had to keep them so for so long for his patients that it had become a habit. But I don't think so. Take away the mechanics of analysis from his mind and there was nothing. The attractive Hungarian hospitality was simply a national trait, like most Spaniards' being dark.

There were some jolly evenings at home with Fred Dupee, Philip Rahv, Charlie Walker and his wife Adelaide, among my father's oldest friends, and occasionally the Dosses, with everyone screaming about Trotskyism, Stalinism. Later in life, people were always saying to me, "Didn't you learn a lot?"—a question the Walker boys also got. The answer was, I didn't. We explained we were always out getting the ice. Usually, we stayed out as long as possible, as we were on the whole bored with the refighting of the Russian Revolution and its aftermath.

Mary and my father could be very amusing, but cozy and tranquil were never words you'd apply to their household.

# X

MARY AND MY FATHER eventually moved into the house my grandmother had bought for them in Wellfleet, which had belonged to Aunt Betsy Freeman, Elizabeth Freeman's aunt. It was a large house right on the main road, and had the first bathtub in Wellfleet in it. It was one of two identical houses built by two ships' captains. As Aunt Betsy had been a professional florist, who sent flowers to Boston, the garden, although overgrown, had all sorts of strange flowers, including one night-blooming one. Eventually my father hired some professional gardeners, but they tore everything out, wrecking it. He had tiny windows put in his study so he wouldn't be able to see out and be tempted by the outdoors on beautiful days.

The tortuous household continued, interspersed with some very good parties for Mary and Father and their guests and even for me, sitting on the sidelines. Mary became briefly involved with someone, and during my Bennington winter work period she began a series of abortive leavetakings, sometimes actually going. Other times she'd only get out to the car with her suitcase. She was Anna Karenina without the warmth, and if there was a Vronsky, he was not a handsome officer but a complicated Jewish intellectual. It was hard on my brother, Reuel, who was a darling child, and hard on the people who had to sub for Mary—sometimes me. Some days I'd do everything to make it easy for her to go, some days I wished she'd stay. Luckily, I had Jeannie and the Dosses in Provincetown. Mary went to the Dosses, had a miscarriage, and Rado had to be summoned. Dos and Katy thought she'd planned it and were not happy about it, discussing it cynically afterward. I went and brought her home in our old car. The brakes gave on the way home and it was frightening: part of the whole ambiance of our lives.

The Waughs en masse had given a party in the old Wizard's studio, a wonderful party at Christmastime, with dancing, to which everyone was invited, including lots of young people. It was very exciting, with naval officers who were then stationed at Highland Light. At one point, I stood on the studio balcony watching Father and Mary attempting to dance together. They were hopeless, Mary shuffling around with no sense of the music and my father clumsily steering her in the wrong direction. That's the way they were all the way through, although I think she woke him up at a period in his life when he might have gotten stodgy. And though the bad times were very bad, there were some good times.

The marriage eventually broke up completely when they were living on Henderson Place in New York; and it was completely my own fault that I happened to be there for the denouement, as I had left Bennington in the middle of my junior year against everyone's advice. Dorothy Thompson had come up to Bennington to urge us on to farm, which is what Bennington was doing for the war effort. She held out her hands and said they were "working hands" and spoke movingly of starving people. My father ran into her and her husband during the war in a restaurant in Greece where there were a lot of correspondents, most of whom were ordering meager portions as the faces of hungry children pressed against the glass front. He said Miss Thompson and her husband sat ordering up course after course, complaining occasionally if something wasn't rich enough.

I had won the *Mademoiselle* story prize and was living in New York City in a piecemeal sort of way. First Jeannie and I had had an apartment on University Place. She was a secretary for a downtown firm and I was a copygirl, first at the *Daily News*—until one of the top editors began making me go out and buy mattresses for him—and then at the *New York Post*, which was a lot of fun, as it was a lively place. Victor Riesel, the famous labor reporter, was there; later he had acid thrown in his face by hoodlums. There was also a man named Mr. Gibbon, who seemed able to recite all of Joyce, and a charming gray-haired man, Mr. Mulligan, one of the chief copy editors, who was given to seizures, especially when Elsa Maxwell's copy came in. Her society column was so full of mistakes, bad grammar and loose facts, it was often practically irretrievable.

Then the Lonergan case broke. It was the first time the newspapers used the word "homosexual" on the front page. The *Times* did it first; and the other papers followed suit. A woman named Patricia Lonergan was murdered in her fashionable apartment. Her husband, who was in the Royal Canadian Air Force, was accused of coming down from Canada and hitting her over the head with a candlestick. People at Bennington had known Patricia Lonergan. Her maiden name was Burton. Lonergan had been a boyfriend of her father's. The interesting part which never appeared in the papers, which my Bennington grapevine told me, was that she had been dead set on having Lonergan, knowing full well what the situation was with her father, and had heckled him to marry her until he did, against many protestations on his part. She would say, "What's good enough for Daddy is good enough for me." A girl at Bennington, who had known both Lonergans, said "Patsy" Burton was a bitch—citing the fact she had 500 nylons hoarded during the war as one unpleasant aspect of her character. My friend said many people felt Lonergan was a sweet guy who had been pushed into an impossible situation by a spoiled, willful rich girl. One thing which precipitated the death blow was that Patricia Burton taunted Lonergan about his lack of masculinity. He was convicted of the murder and died after serving his prison sentence. I was writing my father on *New York Post* stationery, "You have no idea just how sordid New York has been lately. The Lonergan case has wafted a whole new flavour into society. People who never heard the word 'homosexual' before are sporting it like a boutonniere. Little boys on the street hold hands and say, 'We're going steady now.' "

Jeannie and I were so light-headed we eventually gave up the apartment for some frivolous reason, say, a summer vacation. The old Wizard had died in Provincetown; his daughter-in-law, Elizabeth, who had been so full of nutty ideas about how Jeannie and I should be brought up, was dying of cancer. She talked Jeannie's grandmother and mother into selling the Provincetown house and buying a huge house on East Seventy-second Street which had belonged to Mrs. Gorham of Black Star. It was a terrible thing to do, uprooting old Mrs. Waugh and Elizabeth's mother from their cozy, delightful Cranford-Provincetown life. But Elizabeth, who had moved herself and her husband, Coulton, to Newburgh, New York, couldn't resist tying up everyone's life almost from the grave and tying it up in the wrong way. She had become paranoid about Provincetown, saying everyone hated them because they were in trade. People may have been irritated by her, but the older Waughs and Jeannie's parents were adored by everyone.

Because of the shortage of nurses due to the war, I also

worked as a Red Cross nurse's aide at Bellevue Hospital. An earlier dealing with the Red Cross had proved less rewarding. I had gone to see Richard Rovere, who was editing *Common Sense*, to see if he had any assignments. He sent me to do a story on the American Red Cross. In the course of my interview with a handsome, opulent-looking PR type, I asked how much they spent on advertising in ratio to charity. The man put me off; and by the time I got back to *Common Sense*, Rovere had obviously been called and was furious. "I don't want to muckrake the Red Cross." I slunk out.

I alternated between Jeannie's, Henderson Place, and Red Bank. As the poor old ladies were miserable and immediately began to fail, and Jeannie's mother worked, they were glad to have extra hands around. Occasionally, I lived at Henderson Place, baby-sitting Reuel. I caught chicken pox from him, and Mary, who had her bags packed to leave, stayed to nurse me through it. I was fond of Mary; in many ways she'd tried to do the best she could by me, but the situation was unpleasant on all sides and soon became more so.

My father's lawyers wanted me to testify at his divorce trial, which I really didn't want to do. It wasn't until I got to the trial that I realized Mary was claiming I'd seen my father kick her in the stomach, which I hadn't. Mary was a big girl and strong physically. On occasion, her childhood trauma made her think she was about to be beaten, when she wasn't. She would wake up screaming "Don't hit me" when my father wasn't in the room. Perhaps her therapy corrected this later.

When *The Little Blue Light* was staged at the Brattle Theatre in Cambridge with the superb English actress Jessica Tandy in the part based on Mary, she played it so well it was like having Mary in the room when she had one of her attacks. Miss Tandy must have gotten some medical coaching. My father was totally ambivalent about her in the part, and he really didn't know why; it's because he was seeing Mary on the stage. He'd say Tandy was no good, then he'd say,

"These truly competent English actors were hard to beat." He was much more comfortable with Arlene Francis who gave a pedestrian performance in a production ANTA (American National Theatre and Academy) put on in New York. Miss Francis was uncomfortable with the play, which she had taken to please her husband, Martin Gabel. My father walked out during the opening night of the Tandy performance, and I found him all by himself at the bar of Seilers, a lonely figure in a white suit saying, "There's a double Manhattan here which will be my friend." They managed to get Adelaide Walker, one of his oldest friends, to appear as a character witness against him, which hurt him deeply. Mary could be very persuasive. For years Adelaide tried to make up with him; and they did eventually, which was generous of my father. I was tired of Mary and my father's quarrels, and felt stupid for getting mixed up in the divorce instead of staying in college. Mary and my father were two supersurvivors who left emotional destruction in their wake.

One thing any woman who had lived with my father longed for, including myself, was order as far as finances went. Because of the neurotic situation with my grandmother doling out the money, he was always at the precipice of financial ruin. He knew if things got bad enough my grandmother wouldn't let him go to jail, and of course it was a period when a five-hundred-dollar advance was considered lavish for a writer. It would have done no good to have given my father a sum of money and said, "Here's your inheritance, that's it," because he would have spent it; and the situation would have reestablished itself. For years we didn't have a telephone in Wellfleet because my father's payment record was so bad the phone company demanded a ten-dollar deposit, which he refused to pay. We were always having to use a neighbor's telephone; they sometimes were not happy to have their meals interrupted by my father's voice booming in controversy with some publisher over the phone. It was unnerving having to face disgruntled tradesmen and not knowing if the lights would be turned off the next day.

Checks were always coming back. My father really didn't know that two and two were four. Mary did. Though they didn't live lavishly, the rented houses, huge bills from the grocers, my father's penchant for taking long trips by taxi, and Mary's psychoanalysis all added up. My father had written *Memoirs of Hecate County* and Mary had written *The Company She Keeps*—neither of them great romantic books, though perhaps important from a view-of-the-times standpoint. One could get awfully bored with reading about their sexual adventures and begin to long for Willa Cather, Thomas Hardy or some of the other understated greats.

During one of my Bennington winter work periods, I helped Miss Janssen in the filing department of the *New Yorker*. That wonderful woman had come to the magazine when the filing system was an old couch everyone dumped things on. She turned it into one of the best filing and information centers anywhere. She had me on her hands at the first of the year when the files had to be changed. She said one day, "A Mr. Broadwater may invite you to tea." He was one of the fact checkers with thick glasses. It crossed my radar then that he was fascinated by my father. Mary Meigs, in her book *Lily Biscoe: A Self-Portrait*, published in Canada in 1981, is ambivalent about him. But he seems to have had better luck with her than my father. Such are the rounds of love. Mary Meigs' book is a plea for her gay lifestyle. He never did ask me to tea.

Mary McCarthy began dating Bowden Broadwater soon after the divorce and eventually married him. Perhaps he brought order and gentleness into her life that enabled her to work. My father would say somewhat wistfully and enviously in later years, "I think she's got her life arranged so she can work." I imagine she and Bowden spent many hours gossiping about my father, many more than he did about them. My brother, Reuel, said he was very bright and nice to him.

My grandmother's attitude about the divorce was one of resignation mixed with nirvana, except she was glad Reuel had been produced. She more or less tried to forget the whole thing, except questions of alimony kept intruding. She'd always had doubts about Mary's touted gardening and when one of her bridge friends pointed out "The Weeds," Mary's story in the New Yorker about her troubles with crabgrass identified with those she had with her hateful husband, my grandmother commented that if you knew what you were doing you could punch a hole in the ground and squirt in weed killer with a syringe and rake the grass away.

She took my father's giving up his lucrative New Yorker reviewing job very well, as she had her husband's rejection of high-priced offers from New York firms. She did say to me once, "I don't know why your father always appears in the back of the magazine."

She had become more frail and couldn't take the emotional onslaught of my father's visits and really didn't want him down. She liked having me down as I had no divorce troubles. We sat on the porch and watched the squirrels and went to the movies and had Cream of Wheat or Wheatena for supper. My father felt some resentment toward me because of this. I'm sure he was still first in her affection; she just couldn't bear to have the turmoil which accompanied his presence.

He was to go to Europe for the New Yorker. I was left in the Henderson Place house in New York to tie up the details and try to rent it, which was difficult to do, as we had a lease on it. I had returned to college via Columbia Extension School. Mr. Clisby, the landlord, was a southerner determined to extract his pound of flesh. After weeks of being heckled by him, I wrote my father on April 21, 1945, "You have $30 in the bank. Roosevelt's death was a terrific thing. Everyone grieved outwardly, even *Time* magazine; but since the day of his death, the stock market has been taking huge leaps upward. It will be very easy to rent the house now. . . ." (But it wasn't, and we lived in it the winter he returned from Europe.) And I described what was to be my last meeting ever with Mary alone. "I met Mary on 57th Street the other day. I have never seen her in such a state. She talked very fast and told me everything that had happened to her in the last few days." That summer on the Cape, at a cocktail party, Dwight Macdonald took it upon himself to reproach me for not seeing Mary, saying she was hurt. It had been a temptation to see her; but the whole tenure with my father had been so convoluted, I saw no way of doing it without getting involved in labyrinths of gossip. My father and I were stuck with one another. Mary did write me a very nice letter when my mother died.

After my father and Elena had been married several years, Mary and Bowden bought a house in Wellfleet. They, of course, came to pick up Reuel sometimes; and came in on several occasions. Mary really did want to have her cake and eat it too: the stimulating conversations with my father with none of the trouble. Elena said she felt like Kay Boyle with all the ex-wife embroilment. In her devious way, instead of any direct confrontation, she called out the Russian Mafia, of which Nina Chavchavadze was lead lady. These ladies were either well-born Russians or married to distinguished Russians. They all saw each other at Russian Easter. One of the Russian ladies said, "You should have been there when Nina spoke to Sofka Winkelhorn," White Russian nobility, on Russian Easter. I gathered in the tone of command used by high royalty to lesser royalty, Nina had made it known Sofka wouldn't be received at court anymore if she encouraged Mary in any way. Nina also took this line with some of the Americans, the Francis Biddles, *par exemple.*

Katherine Biddle said to me, "Mary didn't fool the old judge," meaning Francis. The Russian Mafia could be very strong. Another lady they blackballed was the harpist Daphne Hellman, because they felt she'd behaved badly to her ex-husband, Harry Bull, editor of *Town and Country*, whose secretary Elena had been at one point.

My father and I had quite a stint at Henderson Place. I'd have to go out when he had ladies in. On the other hand, he needed my domestic services—cooking and shopping—and I had a few of my own romantic irons in the fire. Out for his romantic dates with his ladies, in for Arthur Mizener and W. H. Auden. Auden was very cozy in his suede quarter boots, and our cocker spaniel, Bambi, adored him. Bambi had a thing about licking people's feet, especially if they were bare, and Auden's soft boots were the next best thing. The two of them would sit happily for hours adoring one another. Bambi was a dog with a past, having eaten Peggy Guggenheim's memoirs as a puppy.

I felt about Mizener as if an undertaker's assistant had come to call. Perhaps it was because there were so many undertaking homes I had to pass every night coming home on East Eighty-sixth Street. Mizener, who was doing a biography of Fitzgerald, would sit solemnly and reprovingly (I thought) while my father got jollier and jollier, drink after drink, as he remembered the old times. I could see that Mizener was like the kid who hadn't been invited to the party. Things which seemed totally normal to my father—and to me—shocked Mizener. Zelda, flinging her skirts above her head and dancing, was just another dance and good time to us. Not so to Arthur M. Once when my father left the room, he confided to me that Scotty Fitzgerald had propositioned him. I didn't know Scotty well enough to ask her, but a "Come up to my hotel room and we can talk" might have seemed like seduction to Arthur. Or perhaps she got tired of his questions about her parent and wanted to give Mizener a turn. My father said

Arthur's wife had hidden fires burning in her. Perhaps Arthur did too; if so, they were well banked.

Years later, when I was an editor at Houghton Mifflin in Boston, they published Mizener's *The Far Side of Paradise: A Biography of F. Scott Fitzgerald*. I wrote my father, "I have just read Mizener's manuscript on Fitzgerald, unofficially, not in the line of duty; and I am appalled at how clinical it is, like a coroner. His accuracy, if he is so, is of a mathematical variety. He has a prissy cold point of view on things which are natural and gay. It's sterile. I'm really worried you have him as your literary executor."

Scotty had the Princeton Library send up the photographs of her father for *The Far Side of Paradise* on the condition that only I see them, and after looking at them I felt it was lucky Mizener hadn't chosen them then, although she may have opened them later to the public.

Before he went to Europe, my father, in typical fashion, instead of paying Clisby's rent, went to Sloane's where one of his ladies picked out a lot of ghastly imitation antique furniture with some horrible modern purple chairs. The musical *Carousel* was just a hit on Broadway and my father would turn the phonograph on full blast and bellow the words "What's the use of wondering if it's good or bad or if he can pay the rent" as he packed for Europe.

One night the following spring, after we had survived an on-again, off-again winter together, I came in late with a Bennington friend. A thin blond woman I had never seen was coming out. "She's beautiful," my friend said. "Where does he find them?" It was Elena Thornton, to be my father's fourth wife. Their marriage, although it came to the point of divorce many times, would be his most successful.

# PART
# III

# XI

I N THE DAYS when Nina Chavchavadze had come to teach my father Russian, Mary always said, "I feel as if she is your father's friend." Nina would arrive in the afternoon, all business, and she and my father, teacher and student, would solemnly retire. Eventually, they would emerge and have a social hour or two, Nina in jeans with her cigarette holder and her totally American accent. Somehow she and Paul, who were multilingual, had managed American accents. Many of the White Russians, after their sojourn in England, had ended up with English ones or a polyglot intonation. There was some chitchat, often about what a bore Vera Nabokov was. The feeling seemed to be that she was a governess type. Personally, when I eventually met Vera, I found her delightful and very good-looking with her silver hair. But the more successful Volodya became, the more people complained that Vera was dull. Perhaps Mary was right that Nina was my father's crony. Nina said later she had enjoyed Mary well enough but thought she was impossible as a wife for my father. Elena, who had known Nina since girlhood, as their mothers were acquaintances, had been a paying guest at the Chavchavadzes, where she met my father and Mary. Elena thought them an ideal couple.

My father met Elena again when an excerpt from *Hecate County* appeared in *Town and Country*. He began talking about her, saying she'd had him over with some Russians connected with the ballet, and he thought she had prettier hands and feet than Mary McCarthy. The romance slipped into high gear the following summer when Elena went to Wellfleet while Nina had great fun with Dwight Macdonald—notoriously thick about some things—by giving him the impression she and my father were hot and heavy for one another. Dwight had dropped in one day to pick up his son, who was playing with Reuel, and found Nina ensconced on the couch, my father beside her. They were studying Russian, but she hastily shoved the book under her. The last thing anyone wanted, with all the divorce difficulties, was word to leak out about my father and Elena's romance. It was typical of Dwight's lack of perception in personal matters that he should have thought my father and Nina a passionate duo. Nina soon would have told my father off, as she was a stickler for having meals on time. "You're quite impossible," she would have said autocratically, as she often did when someone had displeased her. Royalty, no matter how well adjusted in exile, is still royalty. Dwight Macdonald was a sterling person in many ways, and some of his causes and articles were important, but the lack of human perception which he shared with other members of the *Partisan Review* made them pygmies compared to Dos Passos. They were constipated in their frame of reference.

The following fall, Father and Elena went out to Reno, and Nina came to stay with me on the Cape, as Paul was still away with his Red Cross war job.

I certainly enjoyed being lazy, as I loved a slow-paced country life, horseback riding along the flats at low tide and swimming off the Dosses' dock. The Gulf Stream was enough on course in those days so that you could swim in Provincetown Harbor until mid-November, or at least Dos and I could. Nina and I became great friends, and she told me about Elena. She said Elena's mother was extremely amusing but a bitch who had sometimes made Herr Mumm pay to sleep with her. She had married Elena off to Jimmy Thornton, the son of Sir Henry Thornton, founder of the Canadian Pacific Railroad. Jimmy was rich when they married, but the money had waned and Jimmy had still insisted on living as if it hadn't and belonging to all the right clubs.

The only time I met Jimmy Thornton we inadvertently ended up in a cab together after his son's wedding. I was struck by the fact he was the same physical type as my father, shortish and sandy-haired. Nina said Elena had never really loved Jimmy. She and Elena had shared a best friend, Alwena Riggs, so she knew a lot about Elena indirectly. She assured me Elena was not neurotic but that her reactions to some things were "quite extraordinary." Nina felt she was part of the making of the Elena-Edmund marriage and suffered terrible pangs of guilt when the first glimmerings of disaster appeared shortly after they were married. Eventually, as the sometimes grisly drama played itself out, Elena would say, "Nina is like a rock remaining firm in her friendship to both of us."

My grandmother was happy to have me ensconced in the Wellfleet house with Nina, whom she didn't know but automatically approved of because Nina was not divorced and had a stable marriage. My grandmother much preferred not to have me doing what was known in Red Bank as "banging around New York."

I was soon being seen around town and at the Dosses with a young Greek, Sirius Proestopoulos, known as Topie. He was

Susan Glaspell's step-nephew and the grandchild of Jig Cook, the Grecophile of Provincetown Players fame whose advances my mother had so deftly avoided.

Topie had gone into the Greek army at thirteen or fourteen and was on the Cape with Susan so he could catch up on some of his missed education by being tutored and pass his examinations for Harvard, which he eventually did, going on to law school. He knew a lot about Greek politics, which fascinated Dos, so we were perpetually at the Dosses. After all, Nina's mother had been queen of Greece, which fascinated Topie. Christmas at the Dosses was almost enchanted that year. They gave a huge party in the afternoon with presents for everyone. It was delightful to sit cozy and warm in their great downstairs living room overlooking the cold gray little wavelets to the Long Point lighthouse beyond.

They had a lot of local people in. Dos gave me a little hand-painted coach with horses which he'd crafted himself that said "On the way to Champagne Rosie's" on the side. I felt I'd come a long way from the days when my nurse had watched the Dos Passoses' still dripping its crude white liquor. Katy was at her best. She never wore any makeup—her looks depended on her extraordinary, ever-changing cat's eyes. She did dye her hair a lot; you never knew if she'd be a redhead or an ash blond. My brother, Reuel, fourteen years younger than I, told me years later he had the same feeling about the Dosses': It was his very favorite place to go.

Dos had been to interview Douglas MacArthur. He said, as did General Eisenhower, that MacArthur was a great actor and he had liked him. He kidded me because I had thought Betty Crocker was a real person at General Mills, where he had also been. For ages, I'd heard Grandmother and Father talk about "Emma custard." One night at a restaurant, I asked my father why one never saw it on the menu. "Rosalind," he said in a desperate way, "you've been in Red Bank too much." It turned out that Emma was a cook at my grandparents'. My father used the same tone when I was fourteen and he discovered I didn't know the difference between a sweet and a dry sherry.

Dos' switch to conservatism was beginning to irritate my father and others, but often one felt when being an audience at these arguments that Dos' grasp of American history was so sound and broad and his all-around political knowledge so far and wide that it was convincing. It was a little like Valadya's taking on Father and Mary in tortuous analyzing; Dos left the field, if not triumphant, at least with the enemy confused. It had been one against many.

My father had all sorts of theories about the Dosses: that Dos paid too much attention to Katy's physical ailments and not enough to her psychological ones. He said that Katy only liked animals like Siamese cats and brown French poodles because they looked well with her. They certainly loved their animals—one brown poodle, known as Mr. Gooser, they kept through thick and thin. One day a saleswoman at Bonwit's in Boston had turned around after the dog had lived up to his name and said dispiritedly, "Oh, it's only a dog." They seemed perfect to me, totally happy with one another, completely well adjusted in their life together and with a modus vivendi that accommodated whatever neuroses they had. The Dosses might well have said to my father, "Who, you! on the subject of our psychological difficulties."

Of course, everyone thought Hemingway (Jasper in Dos' *Chosen Country*) was mad, and the Dosses saw quite a lot of him. But he seemed to go on writing, getting better and better.

Antichrist (my father) had an imitation of Hemingway's shooting some poor animal, cradling its head in his lap and then moaning, "It looks at me with so much love," which was considered a sidesplitter at the Dosses. My father dined out on it quite a lot.

And there was the usual less classy social life going on at

the Cape. I wrote my father while he was in Reno waiting for Elena's divorce about a party at Topie's uncle Harl Cook's:

> We attended a rather wild party at the Cooks where all sorts of scandals occurred. Polly Boyden kept turning to me and saying, "I despise Edmund Wilson. He has got to choose between George Orwell and me." Eben Given, sitting nearby, said, "Maybe he has," which threw Polly into an utter rage. Polly and Cappy Captiva made violent love until Dodie Hall threw a pail of water on them. She was rather upset as she and Cappy were getting married the next day, but not so upset she postponed the ceremony. Polly left for California the next day and isn't coming back until spring.

Polly Boyden was a well-known Cape character who kept divorcing and remarrying her husband, a successful Chicago divorce lawyer. She had become a Communist, then reneged; Polly at her best could be charming, gay in the straight sense, and wonderful. Eben Given was a handsome and amusing man (Katy Dos Passos said he was the only person she knew who spoke in complete paragraphs); he was an artist, married to Phyllis Duganne.

In spite of the marriage, he and Phyllis both more or less lived with their mothers for years, he in Provincetown, she in Truro. People began saying again, "Why don't Phyllis and Eben get married."

Nina and I gave a big party for Father and Elena when they came back from Reno sometime after Christmas.

It was impossible for my father ever to talk to one of his children about any arrangements or anything important simply in the course of a conversation. He called you into his study as if you were a pupil called into the headmaster's office. It was part of his communication difficulty as a result of my grandmother's deafness as well as a sort of one-upmanship on the child. He said he had to pay for Elena's divorce and promise to pay for her son's education, was damned near broke again, and quite rightly that I should get a job. I'd been planning to change venue anyway, as the truth of the matter was I preferred the Wellfleet house at that point of my life without him in it.

Elena certainly generated many more pleasant vibes than Mary as mistress of the house. Elena had obviously set out to make him the best possible wife and to make it a comfortable household. She did begin talking about wills right away, asking me if I realized the Wellfleet house had been left to Reuel, saying she was going to leave me some plates I liked. I wasn't very worried about that sort of thing, as my grandmother said she'd taken care of me. I went to Red Bank for a while, then got freelance work doing feature stories for the *Boston Globe*. I had to come back to Wellfleet to get some things and unfortunately was there when Elena hit the first reef of my father's personality.

One summer's day, when my father was in a bachelor phase a year or so before his marriage to Elena, we had gone down to dinner at the home of a distant cousin, Carolyn Wilson Link. She lived in Orleans, fifteen miles south of Wellfleet, in an ordinarily furnished country house. Carolyn was married to a psychiatrist, Henry Link, who wrote a best-seller called *The Return to Religion*. After dinner the Links had driven us home and came in for an after-dinner drink. We sat in the front parlor, which had the Sloane sofa and some other atrocities. My father began to expound on how carefully he'd decorated the room. Henry got up and a professional gleam came into his eye as he said, "Why, Edmund, I never knew you went in for all this interior decorating," eyeing a couple of prints of Roman baths. "Well, well, well," Link continued, "tell me more about it." And my father did, elaborating on how he'd carefully chosen everything, including the rugs, which looked like large dust mops, one of them exactly matching the Sloane sofa.

After his marriage to Elena, my father went up to Boston

for a few days. Nina was still at the house. The two ladies ripped the front parlor apart, painted walls, floor and woodwork, working against time and energized by the wonderful surprise they'd have for him. They even moved the bookcase to another room. I arrived on the New York bus an hour or so before he did, and as Nina and Elena showed me with glee and pride the newly decorated and improved room, a sinking feeling came over me. In a cowardly way, I said I had to pick up some things at the Dosses and would probably be over there for quite a while.

My father came back and was totally enraged by the changes made. It was the first time the ladies had seen him in action. He told Elena she could leave. Nina realized it was one case when saying "You're absolutely impossible" would do no good. The next morning Elena went around saying, "I hurt Jimmy and this is my retribution." My father had wanted a woman who would make a home for him in Wellfleet and eventually Talcottville, but he fought Elena every inch of the way.

# XII

ELENA TOLD ME LATER she had decided early in the game she wouldn't be "kicked out like the others." Inherited beds were a big thing in our family, the kind it takes several carpenters to put up. Although not on the gargantuan scale of Lord Marchmain's Chinese bed in *Brideshead Revisited*, they were still always a lot of trouble. My father had inherited a large four-poster with great carved pineapples on the posts from his Great-aunt Addie. The posts were so tall they had to be cut off to fit in a room of average ceiling height. For years the bed was in Red Bank. One morning he'd woken up with a terrible hangover to see a bat sitting on one of the posts "smiling at me." "What do you think I did?" he asked me once at a cocktail party in the middle of a political discussion as the incident came back to him. "I called Jennie, who came in with an old badminton racket and a broom and shooed it out the window." Everything halted as people wondered who the heck Jennie was, possibly an old mistress.

When my grandmother bought the Wellfleet house for him, the bed went to the Cape, where it remained a theme in his marriage to Elena as he perpetually tried to kick her out of it—and she stubbornly remained in it. Talcottville was full of great beds originally made for ropes slung across the bottom, converted for slats; they were always falling down. It was considered a great show of affection for an elderly relative to leave you her bed. The men never seemed to leave them. I myself was left the cannonball bed in which my Great-great-aunt Huldah Kimball had died of a toothache while waiting to marry the Reverend Brainerd, D.D. There is a biography of Brainerd published by Lippincott in 1870. It neglects to mention that he and Huldah, whom he refers to as his sweet "Northern Flower," sawed the bottom cannonballs off the bed to use as croquet balls.

Elena certainly did the best she could to make it a happy household. She had a friend, Reine de Roussy de Sales, the widow of Raoul de Roussy de Sales, who had written *The Making of Tomorrow*. She eventually spent a summer on the Cape. She had known Elena in her early twenties in Paris and said she thought Elena was shy, without being silly, and that she suffered from the fact the Germans were anything but popular in France at that time. Elena always wrapped her men in pink cotton wool and had told Reine she was going to spend the rest of her life taking care of Edmund Wilson, which she pretty well did. Years later, after she had met Mary McCarthy in Venice, Reine told me, "I marvel at your father's catholicity of taste."

Elena put up with a great deal that first summer, including opening the icebox one morning when she was pregnant and finding it full of toothy dogfish Topie had caught with his bare hands. She was wonderful with Reuel and his friends. "I must have the soul of an old pansy, I like boys that age so much," she said.

As her family made champagne and wine, she understood

drinking and drank very little, practically never a second drink. She was horrified at the kind of heavy drinking which went on at the Cape in which you were considered something of a sissy if you didn't have at least four drinks in the afternoon.

The cocktail hour as a formality was unknown to my father. If people came, we served drinks—usually there wasn't enough ice—and then he went on drinking after they left. He went for days not drinking at all, but a cocktail hour in which the man of the house dispensed the drinks didn't exist; and the gentlemen retiring separately with the brandy after dinner was unknown to us. When I went to Boston to live and men began acting as if it were rather vulgar for a woman to make the drinks, I'd been house barmaid for so long, I couldn't get over it.

Elena loved the beach and the ocean, which were her refuge when my father began to try and destroy her systematically. He did it by resenting her presence, except when it pleased him, and by being unreasonable about domestic matters, trying to pick fights at meals. She was someone who tried to arrange every aspect of the lives of those around her. He was to say until the end, after years and years in which she had proved herself, that "Elena's only fault is that she likes to have people dependent on her."

What he did when he set about destroying a woman was almost incommunicable because it combined the conscious and unconscious to such an extent on his part and constant criticizing from morning until night. I said to her once after they'd been married for fifteen years that it must be an effort not to show any reaction. She said, "I went beyond that point long ago; the trick is not to just become numb, to still have some reaction." Eleven years later, when I was having a bad time with him in Talcottville, she said, "Well, he's having one of his bouts of sadism with you." And it was true, although I'd never put it that way to myself.

She was physically very strong when she married him, and during her pregnancy with my sister he was very considerate of her. Elena did not have a basically happy nature, but by creating a shield of positiveness, "Yes, dearest, you're brilliant, dearest," she survived, because the most dangerous repercussions of my father's destructive forces were the deeply negative emotions they engendered, especially in women.

He had naturally taken Elena down to Red Bank. My grandmother was over eighty by then and the war had changed her life as it had everyone else's. She had to give up going to Talcottville in the war years, except for one trip up when the Munns made her a present of some gasoline, available to them because they were farmers. She and Oscar drove around in an old LaSalle two-seater with a rumble seat; it was very amusing to see him get out in his chauffeur's outfit, walk around and open the door for her with the same formality he had had with the Cadillac limousine. She was living very frugally and found three weeks at an inn in New Hampshire while Jennie went to Asbury Park on the ocean a poor substitute for Talcottville. If Henry VIII had had a mother at court, she would have felt about Catherine Parr the way my grandmother felt about Elena—nothing against her, nothing for her. She had made all her arrangements as far as wills went and had no intention of changing things—no matter what happened—leaving me a small trust and my father a modest one from which he derived the income and which Reuel and I would inherit upon his death.

My grandmother begged Elena to see I didn't go barefoot, which terrified her because the red clay soil from which Red Bank derived its name was a good breeding ground for tetanus. Elena said she went barefoot all the time herself.

Jennie's judgment of Elena was that "nobody could be that nice all the time." When I said, "European women had a different approach to men, perhaps a better one," Jennie said, "Horsefeathers, an American woman went and took the old

King of England off his throne, didn't she?" Grandmother and Jennie felt very close to King George and Queen Elizabeth of England, as they had passed right by Vista Place on the Rumson Road in an open car on their way to Sandy Hook, and my grandmother said, "The king smiled right at me!"

My grandmother did manage it up to Talcottville one more time after 1946, and it's amazing that she did. Oscar had died, and she had a tall black chauffeur, William, a wonderful man, but people around Talcottville had never seen a black before. No one gave him a hard time, but they stared in awe. My father was beginning to think in terms of upstate, and there is a letter from my grandmother on embossed stationery saying "The Stone House, Talcottville, New York." Her handwriting is amazingly strong and large for an old lady.

> Your great-grandfather Miller was a fine man, very homely, a martinet with money. Whenever your grandmother had a child, he arrived, tormenting father (who was the doctor). When your father was born, they did not call him, he slept thru it all—making him so mad he left on the first train, never forgiving father. Love to Rosalind. Remember me to Elena.

(The modern spelling of the word "through" is interesting considering the period in which she was educated. She must have picked it up later.)

But the Red Bank house was still run like clockwork. Jennie felt that Gerta the cook and my grandmother sometimes ganged up on her. But she had one friend—a rat. I went down, and every night Grandmother and Gerta would bait a trap and put it down in the cellar. I discovered that after Gerta went home and my grandmother went upstairs to read, Jennie would go downstairs, remove the trap and leave some lettuce leaves. "Poor old fellah," she said.

I wrote my father on April 24, 1949:

This is going to be a rather morbid little letter. Mrs. Sherwood next door just died and Grandmother is in a terrible state. She has been bursting into tears and begging Jennie and me not to ever let her go to "that cold dark place," meaning the undertaking parlor. I have promised her that if anything happens to her, everything will be done here. I just wanted to tell you in case I should be away or something and you should hear first.

She was wonderful on her birthday, but if one is here with her a few days she really is not all right at all. It is an awful effort for her to get upstairs; and she practically collapses afterward.

One of the interesting aspects of my father's saving my letters is that he'd always been critical of them, getting me in his study, pointing to an offending missive, saying, "They always look like balloons. Can't you fold them properly. You never answer any of my questions. . . ."

# XIII

**E**VERYTHING SEEMED TO BE GOING WELL for the Dosses the year my father and Elena were married. Dos had been in fine fettle, free from his periods of invalidism brought on by the vestiges of rheumatic fever from his youth. Katy had a theory every house should have an invalid in it, someone who couldn't get away when you complained, which would do away with the Rados of this world. Dos had won back his ancestral home in Virginia via a lawsuit against his half brother.

Dos was illegitimate. His father, a wildly successful corporation and criminal lawyer, who had received the largest fee ever paid a lawyer to that date, had lived with Dos' mother fourteen years before they could marry. He could not divorce his first wife, an invalid. Upon the elder Dos Passos' death, Dos' half brother had taken over their father's property in northern Virginia on the grounds that he was the legitimate heir contesting the will. When the judge asked Katy when she had first suspected something sub-rosa was going on, she said, "Something in the way he flicked his coattail going around the corner of the door."

It was late summer, and they were planning one of their trips south; I went over for dinner one night, as they said they were cleaning out the icebox before their trip. As was the custom, I went over at about four to swim, and then they served tea as they always did, with cheesy accompaniments, followed by drinks; supper usually showed up around eight-thirty or nine. Dos' vegetables were magnificent that year. We had a long talk about the fact that a single personal tragedy affects people en masse more than a mass tragedy. Dos said one old lady killed in her wheelchair by a drunk driver was more shattering to the public than a hundred old ladies dead in a nursing-home fire.

Katy kidded me about the fact that a certain segment found me a bad influence on Topie. "The Nemetouchepas [our name for them], were here, Katy said, "and I entered the room just as Mrs. Shay was defending you." Apparently, Edie took umbrage when they referred to me as "that Wilson girl." Mr. Nemetouchepas was Topie's tutor. They thought I was distracting him from his studies. "Why, why, P-P-Possum," Dos stuttered as he always did at any really personal reference. Mr. Nemetouchepas often boasted he had never been to bed with his Mrs., as he wouldn't *do that* to a woman. The Dosses had a mythical undertaker they often referred to, Hugh Mangor (human gore), as I had a mythical poet Oliver St. Paul, a Kansas poet, who occasionally lived in Europe with an American eagle on a leash. They loved this sort of foolery.

A few days later they stopped by our house in Wellfleet for a minute. We waved goodbye. An hour later, Katy was dead.

At Wareham, the sun was in Dos' eyes; he didn't see the cranberry truck parked with its rear end jutting out over the road. As they went under it, the end of the truck ripped the canvas top off their Chevrolet convertible, decapitating Katy completely and taking one of Dos' eyes.

A few years before, Edith Shay had fallen downstairs, cutting her eye. Primary healing had set in, as no one had realized how serious it was. Eventually, they had to take her to the emergency room of Massachusetts General in Boston. There Dr. Abraham Pollen was on duty. He and Dr. King, the reigning eye surgeon in Boston at that time, operated on Edie under a local anesthetic. Edie realized Pollen was controlling things, saying, "Doesn't that piece go there?" etc.

Dos immediately told the police and ambulance to get him to Dr. Pollen, who later told me that Dos was sick to his stomach on the operating table and kept apologizing. Pollen thought, "My God, he's lost his wife, his eye, and he can still be polite." Dos was in Massachusetts General with contusions, various injuries, and his eye operation and couldn't be at Katy's funeral. But some of the ladies, all very well-meaning, went their own sweet way in spite of Dos' instructions.

Katy had been essentially a man's woman. Any need she had for close female companionship was met by her personal and working association with Edie. Their husbands had been proud of the books they did together and grateful for the added income. As for the best-seller *The Private Adventure of Captain Shaw*, Dos loved to say, "Yes, the girls did all right."

Edith Shay was so distraught she was really in no condition to attend to the practical side of things, and it was left to other ladies, some of whom had never been crazy about Katy. Eben Given's sister, the violinist Thelma Given, lived a few doors from the Dosses with her mother. The Givens were what my grandmother referred to as "funeral hounds," rather enjoying and being evident at funerals. Sometimes, in the nicest possible way, they invited people into their burial plot, as for instance Susan Glaspell. One afternoon Eben had driven her out to the Truro cemetery and, pointing to a piece of sod, said, "You can be here, right here, Susan." Anyway, the Givens, who were very sweet people, did enjoy a good funeral. Dos had requested that Katy have a white coffin. Thelma and Phyllis Duganne Given, who really had not liked Katy, told me with some glee later that they found a white coffin would be very expensive—so they took a white shawl Thelma had and slung it over the coffin. "Of course, there was no way it could be an open coffin." Dos, when he emerged from the hospital, did manage to get the tombstone up the way he wanted it, saying, "My sweet, my lost love." And his book *Chosen Country* was really for Katy. One couldn't imagine any member of the *Partisan Review* set writing such a book.

When I went to work for Houghton Mifflin, which had published both Dos and Katy, Katharine Bernard, the book designer, told me how impressed everyone was by Katy's concern for Dos first, to the neglect of anything to do with herself.

One late afternoon some years later, when I dropped in on Edie Shay after Frank's death, I realized things hadn't been going as well with the Dosses as they had seemed.

Had Frank been alive, Edie probably wouldn't have told me what she did. She'd been knocking back a few. Edie said she usually bought only a quarter of a pint of a dreadful bourbon called Imperial, beloved by the Chavchavadzes and herself, so she wouldn't go on drinking, but since I was visiting, she'd bought a quart (I have never been known to touch whiskey). "It's gin that's mother's milk to me, Edie," I said. "Oh, I forgot," she said, pouring herself a mahogany drink and downing it. It reminded me of Katy's story about Scott Fitzgerald. She said she'd always heard awful stories about him when he was drunk but whenever she'd seen him, his face was scrubbed and he was beautifully behaved and utterly charming. Only once had she seen him even take a drink. She and Dos had gone up to his room at a hotel in

Baltimore and sat around with Fitzgerald drinking ginger ale. Suddenly, he got up, poured himself a highball glass of straight whiskey, and drank it in a couple of huge gulps, turning to her and saying, "Did I just drink that drink?"

After the accident, Dos had given the Shays the house next door to his. He and Katy had bought it to protect their privacy. That house is now Norman Mailer's. Edie said how glad she was that she and Frank had sold it, as it would have been unbearably poignant to live there without the Dosses next door. I said, considering what really bad eyesight Dos had, being very nearsighted, always with his eyes pressed almost against the windshield of the car, it was a miracle he could now drive again. A cagey Celtic look came over Edie's face. I said, "A lot of people had said Katy was very ill with cancer, and it was just as well she'd gone quickly." Suddenly Edie burst out and said, "Oh, Rosalind, what rot. She'd had a breast removed down at Johns Hopkins when they went down after their Christmas party. When she came back to Boston, Dr. Murble had told her, 'I don't believe you ever had to have that operation.' " It was a terrible thing to hear, but it certainly settled her fears about the cancer returning, although she was worried Dos would find her less appealing. "Time and again," Edie said, "she came here and walked up and down the room wringing her hands, saying, 'I know we will have a terrible accident on one of these trips. We've had several near misses. Dos will never get off until late afternoon when we're already tired, and his eyesight is bad.' " Edie said Katy felt absolutely doomed. Knowing her, it was certainly the sort of thing she would never have gone to the mat with Dos about. It explained his state of almost suspended animation when I went to see him at Massachusetts General.

It was beyond shock or grief; he could either transcend his own guilt and be suspended like an Indian fakir or drop forever into a morass from which he'd never emerge.

One day he called me over to his house and gave me a

carefully put together little box of jewelry and trinkets of Katy's.

Soon he was giving the Provincetown gossips something to sink their teeth into by doing what is known in the vernacular as "running" with a redheaded divorcée with two little boys, a lady about Provincetown, and a friend of the young lady who eventually incurred Humphrey Bogart's wrath. Like her friend, she was a very pretty, full-blown girl. There were naturally all sorts of stories; Edie had by accident met them at the Vendôme in Boston, not a good place for an affair, as Cape neighbors were always staying up there. She said they'd met in the dining room and although the lady was on the blowsy side, there was something in the turn of her head that reminded her of Katy. Dos was a gourmet and loved to fuss around about food. Someone said there had been an argument in which the woman in question had said, "To hell with you and your damned suckling pig," and walked out.

I wrote my father:

> The rumour is that Dos is going to marry Mrs. Parker and is in Cuba with her at present. I rode down on the bus from Boston with her. She is not so bad and I think very much in love with Dos. Everyone has been saying how wonderful it would be if Dos could marry and have children. Now everyone up here is in a state of terror about it and feels how much better it would be for him not to marry this number. I am becoming more and more impressed with people's sweet solicitude over one's welfare when it involves their own convenience or plans.

The last sentence may have been aimed at my parent.

Dos eventually married an eminently suitable woman who had been an editor for *Reader's Digest* and whose husband had been killed, I believe, in a plane accident. Betty was statuesque, unlike Katy, and very much her own person; but there was something about her delivery of a joke that was reminiscent of Katy. Dos and she had a daughter, Lucy, named after his mother. They came to the Cape upon occasion in the summer to see his old friends, one time staying in my family's house while they were away. When I got off the bus, there were Dos and Betty with some small bottles of champagne, saying, "Here's our Rosie." He had a heart attack on one of these return trips and stopped coming to the Cape. He made his life in Baltimore and Virginia, where he did some serious farming.

Dos' departure from the Cape left a big hole in my father's life. Several times a week, they had visited back and forth in the late afternoons. The Shays and the Givens were dear old friends, but they couldn't fill the gap left by Dos. The person who came the nearest was Charlie Walker, a classicist, whose field was labor relations. "It's after all just a step from Greek tragedy to labor relations," my father commented. But the fact that Adelaide Walker had testified at his divorce from Mary McCarthy that he was a man of bad character took years to heal, because he felt Charlie shouldn't have let her do it. Charlie and he went way back and had been at Fort Dix together, where Charlie "would leap out of his tent like a young Apollo." My father was on visiting terms with the Walkers, but it wasn't until Charlie and my father's last years, when both had failing hearts, that the closeness returned; they were deeply and touchingly close.

Adelaide is a beautiful and highly intelligent woman, generous and kind, but she did overidentify with my father's wives. After my father married Elena, Adelaide was soon calling Charlie "dearest" and imitating Elena. Whenever my father entered the room, she'd greet him with "Here comes the master."

But nothing filled the intellectual void left by Dos in spite of what my father regarded as Dos' reactionism against the beliefs of their youth. He, like Dos, went back to what he considered his roots when he inherited the stone house in 1951 in Lewis County, New York. Dos had gone to Westmoreland County, Virginia. There was no substitute for Dos as an afternoon companion. No one who had such a wide knowledge of literature, politics and Europe. In a sense, it devitalized my father and turned him more to drink, although he never drank as much as some people thought he did. If he had, the work wouldn't have been there.

After I went to Houghton Mifflin, Dos and I would meet occasionally for a drink at the Passion Pit at the Hotel Bellevue, just up Park Street on Beacon Street. The Bellevue lobby, with its pillars, made you feel you were in the Parthenon. The Passion Pit bar was the size of a ballroom. Very, very dark except for the illuminated passion flower over the bar and great comfortable sofas against the walls, with long tables exactly the right height in front of them. The sterling black waiters, whom we had all known for years, seemed to float in their spanking white coats like beautiful clouds or angels on the horizon—so much more curative than most doctors—appearing at your side, intuitively knowing when the next drink was required. Dos said you always knew those waiters could fix whatever was wrong in your life. One time he and I, both without our glasses, waited for each other for an hour in there, discovering each other only by chance when we got up to leave at the same time. Many romances were sealed, many business deals clinched, many hangovers cured in that wondrous bar. The day it closed, as the Bellevue was becoming a residential hotel, many people grieved high and low, my father not the least among them.

Dos always referred to Houghton Mifflin as McHoughton and McMifflin. They naturally thought they were giving him enormous advances. Once I told him what they were paying me, which was too little, on my third drink at the Passion Pit. "I'd stand up to McHoughton and McMifflin," he said. "I'd get more money or see them taken out on a stretcher." I remarked, "They are all so nice and gentlemanly it is hard to do." "Well, make it a tweed stretcher then, but do it." I was surprised; he was always so almost bumblingly amiable. At that time, McHoughton and McMifflin were listed in Dun & Bradstreet as the richest publishers in America.

# XIV

T HE REVOLUTIONARIES IN LITERATURE and politics who had come to Provincetown in the twenties, eventually mellowing into the Old Guard, were dying or leaving. At approximately the same time as Katy, Susan Glaspell died. After her marriage to Norman Matson, a writer some years younger than she, had dissolved, she had led a quiet life in her drearily furnished house except for the advent of Topie. She and the Dosses had for years lived on top of one another, separated only by narrow Commercial Street, so narrow there was no sidewalk on the Dosses' side, their picket fence was right on the street, and her right-of-way to the harbor bordered the Dosses' vegetable garden. She also had a house in Truro.

Susan and her husband George Cram Cook had founded the Provincetown Players in 1915 and she was known as "the mother of the American little theater" by some. She had won the Pulitzer Prize for *Alison's House*, based on the life of Emily Dickinson, in 1931. One of her plays, *Suppressed*

*Desires,* was well known, and her *Road to the Temple,* about her trip to Greece with Jig Cook, had been published. After a long interval, she published *The Morning Is Near Us* in 1939; after that, no big work.

PBS did a program in which she was portrayed by a young actress, encouraging young artists around the Wharf Theater. The actress who can best portray her in her later years is the television star Betty White. Only Miss White has that super-sweet delivery of a damaging sentiment. It always took a while for you to realize that Susan's honeyed tones had suggested you were a good-for-nothing or that she'd like it if you took so-and-so out on a dark night and whomped him one. You always did a triple take on any conversation with her. She remained attractive-looking as she got older—tall and straight, with clear eyes and curly gray hair.

Although Susan's writing had sloughed off in the later years, she wrote two epistles which were masterpieces. Edie Shay told me about the first, personal one; the second one was public. Susan's lawyer had been caught by his wife with his young mistress. His wife said it was definitely splitsville. The troubled lawyer poured his heart out to Susan, who, as she was fond of both parties, decided to play Cyrano de Bergerac and composed a beautiful letter to the lawyer's wife, signed by him. They were reconciled as a result, and the wife kept it in a casket on the table, saying, "It's the most beautiful letter a man ever wrote a woman." Another similar case, only it was a much bigger job, was Reine de Sales' ghostwriting Pauline Potter's letters to Baron Philippe de Rothschild (as in Mouton-Rothschild) before their marriage. For five or six years, when I'd go to Reine's, Pauline would be there. After she left, Reine said they'd spent hours going over a letter for just the right wording and many more hours on the telephone between sessions. Reine's husband had been a longtime friend of Philippe de Rothschild. They'd been schoolmates. Reine said his interests were artistic and literary and not in banking.

So she saw to it that Pauline emphasized these things and that Pauline had probably been the woman who was closest to Glenway Wescott. She was the dress designer for Hattie Carnegie and helped Reine out enormously when she was in financial difficulties, leaving huge orders of food to be sent up to her at frequent intervals.

Susan's second letter was a great one to the Provincetown *Advocate* about a stranded whale in the harbor which was being tortured by grown-ups and children throwing beer cans and other things down its spout. Provincetown was becoming a place for drifters as the solid fishing industry waned and people like the Waughs receded. Susan, in an interview, had told how she and others had come to Provincetown to lead a gentle life and tend each other's fires. There were some not-so-gentle fire tenders coming in.

My mother died in Pittsburgh in 1947. That she went on as long as she did was a miracle. They had taken out portions of her ribs, leaving her hunchbacked, and she spent months lying with sandbags around her. Eventually, they let her out of the hospital, as there was nothing more they could do.

In 1945, I wrote my father:

> I have been to Pittsburgh; it is exactly the same as the last time I was there four years ago. Connie and mother both look as if they would fall apart at any minute. They drink from morn till night and never eat anything. Connie still works in Gimbels's Rug Department; he still carries on those endless disconnected monologues.

One morning my mother simply did not wake up. She died at fifty.

She and Connie had had a little apartment in a residential hotel, two tiny rooms with some pieces from their luxurious duplex which heartbreakingly dominated the rooms—the

great blond Throckmorton-designed bed, a long Tudor dining table with massive chairs, the Djuna Barnes portrait. My
mother still threw her theatrical scenes, interrupted by
coughing. The doctors said the quantities of beer she drank
were what kept her going and, of course, she was a chain-
smoker.

I appreciated her. I was proud to be her daughter. I was in
awe of her courage. But I never loved her. I was twenty-three
when she died, and all the time we had spent together barely
added up to less than six months. I adored her Swedenborg
family and loved her older sister Lois and her husband, a
newspaperman.

Once when Jennie had gone with me when my grandmother sent me up to Redding Ridge, Connecticut, to get me
settled, she met Connie for only a few minutes. He was at the
height of his success then, handsome and affluent. "He's
handsome but weak," Jennie said. "Something will give in
him." After they got the apartment, my mother would berate
him unmercifully for hours in full voice, which would have
carried to the back rows of any Greek amphitheater. He'd just
sit, saying, "Mary, oh Mary darling."

After her funeral, I went with Connie to the apartment; he
was completely sober. He gave me an emerald-and-diamond
bracelet from Tiffany's he'd given her when they were
engaged. All those years when they'd had nothing, they'd
saved it. I tried to refuse it, but he was insulted. He disappeared and no one ever heard from him again. His son tried to
locate him.

My Aunt Lois told me much later that my father had paid
all the funeral expenses and helped out on many occasions
among minor matters he didn't even mention in his diaries. It
was nice of him not to tell me.

Two excerpts from Louis Sheaffer's *O'Neill: Son and Artist*, a biography:

"Mary Blair," said O'Neill, "is cast for Ella in *All God's Chillun Got Wings* because I have always had her in mind. Her performance in the very difficult role of my *Diff'rent* convinced me that she is one of the most talented actresses on our stage. She is playing Ella in *God's Chillun* because she likes the play and the part. As a true artist, she does not recognize any considerations but these as having any bearing."

One evening, during a desultory conversation at O'Neill's home, someone mentioned Mary Blair. "Gene," recalled Madeline Boyd,* "suddenly came to life. His face glowed as he began talking about the Provincetown Players, Jig Cook, Fitzi, and others but mostly about Mary. He praised her talent, her courage—he said he'd always be grateful for her appearing with Paul Robeson when no other actress would— and he wound up calling her 'one of God's Chillun.' "

* Madeline Boyd was a literary agent, wife of the writer Ernest Boyd.

Nelly Wilson with her cherubic son, Edmund, Jr. (Courtesy Hartshorne family)

Susan Wilson, middle, and siblings, circa 1906.

Edmund Wilson, Sr. (*left*), attorney general of New Jersey, and Dr. Reuel Kimball, prominent diagnostician.

Caroline Knox Kimball (Mrs. Reuel Kimball), the woman most sympathetic to Nelly Wilson aside from her sisters. No one ever accused Aunt Carrie of not having class. (Courtesy Hartshorne family)

Edmund Wilson, Jr., with friend. (Courtesy Susan Wilson)

Drawing by EW in his childhood copy of *The Ancient Mariner*.

Poem by EW written in the same book.

EW at Hill School, inscribed to Susan Wilson. (Courtesy of Susan Wilson)

The stone house, Talcottville, in Nelly Wilson's day.

*Above left:* With my mother, Mary Blair, outside Red Bank house.

*Above right:* With Jimmy Canby, O'Neill-Dodge-Wilson house at Peaked Hill Bars, Provincetown, 1931.

With EW, Peaked Hill Bars, early 1930s.

*Above left:* Mary Blair Eakin, Redding Ridge, Connecticut, 1930s.

*Above right:* With my mother, Redding Ridge, early 1930s.

With my mother and Constant Eakin, Redding Ridge, 1930s.

*Top:* O'Neill-Dodge-Wilson house, Peaked Hill Bars, 1931.

*Middle:* EW and Margaret Canby, 1930s, surveying O'Neill house disaster after a hurricane delivered its *coup de grace.*

*Left to right,* Phyllis Duganne Given, Susan Glaspell, Norman Matson, at O'Neill house, early 1930s.

John Dos Passos, Peaked Hill Bars, 1931.

EW, Peaked Hill Bars, early 1930s.

Egg race, Orthodox Easter. *Left to right*, Paul Chavchavadze (*in bushes*), Natalia, Rosalind, Wendy Day (Clarence's daughter), David Chavchavadze, Alexander Romanov.

Prince George (Pickerel) Chavchavadze, Mantua, 1949. (Courtesy David Chavchavadze)

Rosalind (*second from left*), Topie (*third from left*), Natalia (*sixth from left in white dress*) and David Chavchavadze (*turned away*). (Courtesy David Chavchavadze)

David (*first from left*), Nina (*seated fourth from left*) and Paul Chavchavadze (*far right*). (Courtesy David Chavchavadze)

*Les Wilsons*, Wellfleet, 1946. *Left to right*, Wrecky (great dog); Reuel Wilson; Elena, holding Helen; Bambi; Rosalind; Edmund; and Henry Thornton. (Courtesy David Chavchavadze)

Frank Shay (*far left*), who
first published Edna Millay;
Edith Shay (*in hat*), who
wrote best-sellers with Katy
Dos Passos; Rosalind; and
unknown blond woman.
(Courtesy David
Chavchavadze)

At Wellfleet, Fall 1968.

EW and Dorothy Walsh,
philosopher, in living room
of stone house, Talcottville,
late 1960s. (Courtesy Helen
Muchnic)

EW leaving Villa Rosalinda,
late 1960s. (Courtesy Helen
Muchnic)

EW asked Helen Muchnic to pose him "where Mother's garden used to be." (Courtesy Helen Muchnic)

Huldah Loomis, Spring 1973, with a larger lady-slipper than EW ever had, although she lost the Red Plush War.

EW at the desk he worked at until the mid-1960s in the stone house at Talcottville, late 1960s. (Courtesy Helen Muchnic)

# XV

PHYLLIS DUGANNE GIVEN had, in a sense, all the other ladies of the set my father saw outclassed because she was a native of the Cape, having been born in Brewster. Her mother, Maude Emma, was part Indian and lived to be 104 or so. Phyllis also had the handsomest husband. She had been brought up partially by her Aunt Inez Haynes Irwin, one of the first fighters for the women's movement, and her husband, William Henry Irwin, a newspaperman, foreign correspondent, and novelist. Inez hailed from Scituate, Massachusetts, and had been discovered in her teens by Gelett Burgess, the well-known editor and writer, when he visited Scituate and saw her work. Burgess, much to his grief, was coauthor of the famous quatrain beginning "I never saw a purple cow." To his grief, Mrs. Irwin said, because a lot of people knew him for that and not for some of his important writings. A Radcliffe graduate, she was founder with Maud Wood Park of the College Equal Suffrage League. She was on the National Advisory Council of the National Woman's Party and in 1921 wrote *The Story of the Woman's Party.* From 1916 until 1918, she was a foreign correspondent for various magazines in England and France; from 1931 until 1933, she was vice president of the Author's League of America. Aside from all this, she was famous for her children's stories, *Maida's Little Shop* and the Phoebe and Ernest stories. She was in her middle seventies in the first years of my father's marriage to Elena and came to the Cape to visit her niece as winter closed in. Phyllis decided to give a bang-up, polish-all-the-silver dinner party in her honor, featuring my father and Inez's first meeting.

Phyllis' first husband had also married Miriam Hopkins, and there was a similarity between the two women, something about the mouth. She had the ideal flapper figure and great triangular blue eyes. Her husband, Eben, said you could see through her on a clear day, and she could outdrink anyone. Her discipline was such that she could function no matter how much she drank; when she got older and Eben would occasionally remonstrate with her about drinking, she'd say, "Get yourself another general," referring naturally to Lincoln's remark that he wished he knew what brand Grant was drinking so he could give it to the rest of his generals. Her attitude toward my father was to let him have it when she felt like it, although she would never have done as Adelaide Walker did and gone into court as a character witness against him. She did not identify with my father's wives.

My father told her she was a "small, bossy woman like my mother," and so it went, sometimes very hot and heavy, with Eben saying to his wife, "Avaust there." She and her mother were superb housekeepers and cooks. Eben Given, his sister Thelma and their mother were awash with spiritualism and mysticism, totally the opposite of Maude Emma and Phyllis. After old Mrs. Given's death, when strange lights were seen in the Provincetown house, said to be the dead lady's doing, Phyllis said she'd like to see the electric light bill.

Eben and my father had many arguments over spiritualism. Eben saying the psychic who didn't do it for money always had clear dark brown eyes of a certain kind. My father would try to explain that he knew how all the tricks were done and that psychics had whole files on the people who consulted them. Eben said my father rejected the whole concept because he had psychic powers himself and it scared him. And there was something to be said on both sides. Things did crowd in visually into my father's mind, and he says in his piece on Edna Millay that he had a psychic bond with her. After all, a Cornell team discovered only a few years ago the voice box which enables elephants to communicate with herds hundreds of miles away.

I came down from Boston to find my father in an anticipatory frame of mind. He had been to Hyannis to buy a new shirt, a bright blue tie, and some expensive after-shave lotion for the party. Since Dos' exodus, after work he usually got dressed, shaved, drank scotch and played the phonograph in his study. In later years, he saw something of Waldo Frank, who would come over and take walks with him. But Waldo's house was set apart from most people's in a little hollow and because he didn't drink, he wasn't seen around at a lot of the parties. Phyllis Given's attitude toward him was "him and his virgin Spain." Waldo claimed that one day when he and my father were walking in the woods and became lost, Waldo guided them out. My father turned to him and said, "Waldo, as a woodsman you're wonderful." Waldo, who once told me he was as great as Dante, said he always felt the woodsman remark was what my father really thought of him—a good woodsman, not a writer. At times, Waldo had a lot in common with A. A. Milne's donkey, Eeyore, in *Winnie the Pooh*.

The day of Phyllis' party, my father was absolutely jovial,

had brushed up on Mrs. Irwin's works (although he knew all about her), was whistling, and exuding a strong, sweet after-shave smell. Off we went, arriving at Phyllis' on the dot. The Givens' house, with its large living room and antique furniture, was shined and polished to the hilt. The room was always dominated by a mammoth deep blue velvet couch, a couch you could move into knowing they'd never take you alive once you sank into its comforting depths. It had been the casting couch of Jed Harris—the notoriously lecherous producer—and had eventually ended up at the Givens'.

Dominating the couch that night was Inez Haynes Irwin, a powerful and attractive presence. Dressed in black, her hair parted in the middle, showing the definite features of her face, she exuded graciousness and intelligence. She was a large woman, but her feet were tiny and elegant in black satin sandals with rhinestones, the same kind my grandmother and countless ladies of quality felt were fitting for evening wear after you reached a certain age. My father made a beeline for her and sat by her side, his considerable weight lowering him into the soft down of the sofa until he was almost at her feet. From 6 P.M. until two in the morning they talked, forgetting everyone else. He was fifty-two and she was seventy-six, but I honestly believe that for eight hours they were in love.

When we went in to dinner, their meal was taken to them on the sofa. The Yale crowd was there and there were some very pretty young women, Helen Carter and her good friend Miss X of the Humphrey Bogart–panda debacle. Miss X was used to being the center of attention at events where men were present. She played the guitar, her long dark curly hair swishing around her plump white shoulders. My father snuffed her out. "Quiet, you are interfering with what Mrs. Irwin is telling me." The room was lit by the fireplace and candles in Mexican-silver candle holders on the walls, and Mrs. Irwin and my father seemed the same age in the light—like a girl with her suitor. They discussed juvenile literature book by book, England, Paris, the wars, the suffrage movement, literary figures they both had known. Mrs. Irwin had already become a famous woman by 1927. A chapter had appeared about her in a Dutton book called *Girls Who Did* by Helen Ferris and Virginia Moore.

As the rest of us made our piddling conversation, the Yalies and I tested out who had heard of Oliver St. Paul and who had not. Mrs. Carter and Miss X had. But we were minor characters in the presence of greatness and two legendary people having one great shock of recognition. We weren't even a chorus. Elena became rather miffed and was taken home early. It was usually my father who left at ten. He had drunk practically nothing.

The next morning, instead of complaining about his breakfast and being disagreeable, he was exhilarated, like a young man who has met a fascinating woman at a ball. As Edie Shay said, "It had been a party at which all men were handsome, all ladies fair."

For several months after Phyllis' bash, every mail would bring a book, inscribed to my father in Mrs. Irwin's hand, slender old volumes, reproductions, *The Scholemaster*, written between 1563 and 1568, first edition, 1570, edited by Edward Arber, A. Constable and Company, 1815. One book was *Ralph Roister Doister*, the first comedy in the English language.

Even later, when Phyllis would become angry with my father, she'd say, "I think of how nice he was to my Aunt Inez," and calm down.

I'd say, "He wasn't being nice." But Phyllis preferred to think he was because, although she was a remarkable and competent woman in many ways and her *Saturday Evening Post* stories brought in a good income, my father could never talk to her on the same level as he had to her Aunt Inez. Never mind; she could still laugh up her sleeve when the other ladies talked pridefully of how they were liked by "the local people."

They might do very well in New York and Chicago, but Phyllis was socially top dog locally. The born-and-bred Cape Codders were snobs about what they referred to as "the summer complaint," and most outsiders coming in longed to be thought of as natives.

# XVI

NOT ONLY HAD THE DIFFICULT SIDE of my father's character begun to assert itself in his marriage to Elena, but she had had his financial carelessness thrust upon her many times. Wilkins Micawber seemed like Bernard Baruch compared to my father. And the financial tie-up between my grandmother and my father had to have dawned on Elena early in the game. A bounced check was run-of-the-mill to him. She found herself in the same penurious situation as she had been with her first husband.

The situation in Red Bank became very ticklish as my grandmother's last years approached. She simply did not want my father there, though it was important that someone go down. She still ran her household and attended to all her business affairs, but it was desirable to have tradesmen and neighbors know that someone was coming down and taking an interest in things. But it was impossible for her son to be the one to visit without upsetting her and often making her physically sick.

Her questions—"Edmund, why are you so disagreeable to me? What makes you so disagreeable? Do you know what makes you so disagreeable?"—were real questions to which she longed to have the answers. At that point, she was really scraping and saving too. It cost her far less to live for a week with three servants than it did my father in Wellfleet. Elena didn't drive; she was a good cyclist and for a while we went everywhere on bicycles, but then Bill Peck and his large Chrysler entered our lives, and he taxied us everywhere. The taxis, the liquor bills, the hotel bills when they went to Boston for four months when their daughter Helen was born, all added up.

My father did have two great economies: First, if he stayed at a hotel, he always ordered rolls, butter and milk with his room-service meals, which in those days were gratis. He would put them on the mantelpiece or bureau of the hotel room where the rolls and butter and milk would slowly deteriorate over a period of days. If you went up to see him in his room, he'd ask if you wouldn't like a snack. The second economy was that he always saved used wrapping paper and ribbon Christmas after Christmas after Christmas.

My grandmother quite rightly felt that my half sister Helen, who had been partially named after her, had a very solid mother to stand between her and the world, for Elena was a very maternal woman.

My grandmother was fading out; her son either didn't see it or didn't want to see it. Of course, he did have to speak to her through her ear trumpet, a three-foot job with a hose in the middle, a horn mouthpiece on one end, and a tubular piece she inserted in her ear on the other. He would bellow. "Not so loud, Edmund, not so loud. You're blowing my head apart," she'd plead. She loved hearing about Reuel, who had been down to visit them for a week at one point, but Father's speeches were so often about money or what was wrong with what she'd had for dinner. It reached a point where my position was very difficult because she wanted me to come down but not him. She wanted Jennie and me to tell him not to come down anymore because she couldn't stand it. On several occasions when she knew he was coming, she'd had minor heart attacks. Jennie and I certainly couldn't tell him not to come. Anyway, it was important for people to know her son came and went. I finally got up my nerve and wrote him saying, "It would be a shame if you or I ever did anything to dangerously upset her." But he really had no idea what it was he did that troubled her.

All his life he'd turned to her, depended on her, and because of the, to him, insulting terms of his father's will, had been under her thumb for his economic needs. It had been a place he could come to always, where he had no worries. My own friends used to love to come to Red Bank as a surcease from their hectic lives in the city. They regarded it as a great luxury hotel. But I hadn't brought anyone down in the last five years. Of course, quite often when he came to Red Bank he had been whooping it up on binges in the city. And if he were living in the city for a few months in the winter, saying "Oh, I must go down and see how Mother is" was a fine way out if something came up he didn't want to do.

But in the very last years of my grandmother's life, she was adamant about not wanting him down, to the point where Jennie's miming during the phone calls did no good. She couldn't mime him home anymore. My grandmother would say, "Tell him I don't want him. He makes me sick." Of course, he could hear her and she knew he could hear her. It went so far, she said, "Tell him if he comes I won't send the car for him." And that was very far indeed. From her point of view, she had had to say one too many times, "If you're going to come down here, Edmund, why can't you be amiable? Try to be amiable."

I had seen an angry God once, in the Boston museum— Chinese, I believe. He looked just like my father when he switched to his difficult self. For he was like a person possessed in the old-fashioned sense. Elizabeth Waugh, whom he had admired so long ago in Provincetown, had thought my father looked like Caligula. Liquor may have brought it out sometimes, but it was fundamental and had nothing really to do with drinking. He may have had hangovers at my grandmother's when he came down late from a party in New York, but he didn't drink in Red Bank, except for Canada Dry ginger ale, a great Red Bank standby. Bottles were kept on ice and tall ginger-ale glasses always awaited his pleasure.

The worst part was that he wanted to comfort his mother, whom he finally realized was failing. But some rage in him took over. Perhaps his forebear Cotton Mather had seeped through the generations because the often amusing, warm, sensitive person would disappear and a tight-lipped, vengeful and mean expression would change his face. "Edmund, you distress me so I wish you wouldn't come down anymore. Leave me alone. Leave me alone," my grandmother would repeat.

He was fascinated by monsters, loved movie ones, referring to them affectionately: "There's the old monster." He doted on a record I gave him a few years before he died called "The Monster Rally." These creatures appealed to his terrible, lonely, isolated, evil side. David Chavchavadze always called him "Monstro."

Aunt Addie had died and could no longer be sent for to recall him to his better self. On several occasions, Jennie, who seldom angered but when she did it was all the way, berated him, saying, "You will kill your mother if you keep this up. She can't stand it any longer." When Jennie became angry, she became repetitious and all the wrath of Ireland tumbled out.

But, of course, my father and I were still eating our hot cereal from our childhood bowls in Red Bank. Mine had a picture of "the house that Jack built" at the bottom, his of "the cow jumping over the moon."

But my grandmother, through no fault of mine indirectly because I was happy-go-lucky and loved a casual life and a good time, was to gather her forces for one last great row over my right to use the Wellfleet house.

I had been commuting between Red Bank and New York, doing some piecemeal work for George Davis, who was then editor of *Mademoiselle*. At one time, he, Auden, Carson McCullers and Gypsy Rose Lee shared a house together. Elena came down with pneumonia on the Cape and my father asked me to come up and help out—no great chore— which I did. After things straightened out, he kicked me out very disagreeably and I took a room at Mrs. Pickard's in Wellfleet for twelve dollars a week. I certainly was no longer trying to play the situation about the Wellfleet house; because of my grandmother's health, I longed to conceal it. Elena got my father to agree not to tell my grandmother that I wasn't living with them. (If I was at Red Bank and took a train somewhere, she and Jennie worried until I called her.) It was in late spring and Father and Elena were going away in August.

Whenever Jennie called Wellfleet, Elena said I was out for the moment and that held them in Red Bank until Father and Elena went to Europe. Naturally, I wrote Red Bank not mentioning Mrs. Pickard's. Hers was a fine family of Finnish extraction. The rooms were spotless, with beautiful quilts made by Mrs. P. I was to have a whale of a summer, my last careless Cape summer before I went to work for Houghton Mifflin in the fall.

The pleasant men came in groups; some tree surgeons working on the road were staying at the Pickards'. People would yell "Happy Arbor Day" as they dropped me off at night. I met Henry De Gafoy and his brothers (they were artists), who had a house on a pond, then there were some attractive physicists on the same pond, and Edwin O'Connor and Charlie Nelson, writers on another pond. Reine de Sales had come to the Cape that summer. Her son was Elena's son's best friend. She and another woman had rented a house in Wellfleet, a stone's throw from where I was staying. Dom Perignon flowed at Reine's, and they had in their orbit an actor, George Roy Hill, who had been in the Marines and a friend of Reine's friend's nephew who was killed. He was at the Wharf Theater. Occasionally, my father would pass by in Bill Peck's car, meeting me with one of these groups, turning his head away angrily. We weren't speaking. Elena came to see me occasionally. None of these men were serious beaux. Mrs. Pickard kept saying, "You keep sifting and sifting with flour and there is nothing left but some grains."

Ed O'Connor later became wildly successful with his book *The Last Hurrah*, based on James Curley, the governor who had governed Massachusetts from jail, and George Roy Hill became an important director, directing *The Sting*, among others, bouncing around with Newman and Redford. Ed and George were comrades of mine, no hint of romance, and went under the heading of men who first asked how my father was, then how I was. Charlie and Ed, being Catholics, gave Sunday morning brunches after mass and fought off a group of nudist divorcées across the pond. One Sunday morning, as we were munching our eggs Rockefeller, a naked woman in a large hat rowed across the pond to borrow a cup of sugar.

George naturally brought his colleagues from the Provincetown Players to Reine's. And she loved having the men floating around my life at her parties. It was a particularly hot summer and often George, Reine and I would take blankets and sleep out on the cool beach at Highland Light, tying little bottles of champagne on a rope to cool in the ocean. One night, they slipped their moorings and George and I dove for them desperately. The Provincetown Players put on a play by

Conrad Aiken called *Mr. Arcularis,* and George and I spent quite a lot of time at the Aikens' in Brewster. They served giant goblets of gin colored with orange juice. And I read George's reviews out loud: "Whenever George Roy Hill walks on the stage . . ." All very flattering. "Read that again, Rosalind," George would say.

Before going away, my father arranged for Peggy Bacon to stay in the house and take care of the dogs. It was then that my grandmother found out I was staying in a room in Wellfleet. Queen Victoria and her "We are not amused" routine paled next to my grandmother when she entered the ring. Everyone was left hanging on the ropes. A letter she wrote me at school when I was lightly contemplating going to Swarthmore will give some example of the tenor of her disapproval. "Any idea you have of going to Swarthmore you give up! I absolutely refuse to pay your expenses at that place. I know all about it; it is a nasty little quaker college. It is also coed." The combination of God and peace as personified by the Quakers was not sympathetic to my grandmother.

Miss Bacon, with her little drawings of cats, her Victorian way of dressing, had never been a favorite of mine. She had been staying at the home of Edmund Duffy, the cartoonist, in Truro, but they had another guest coming or something, although she was to return there. She certainly wasn't taking care of the dogs. They came down to the Shays. Edie called Peggy and asked if she was enjoying the dogs. Peggy said, "Yes. They are right here with me." Edie looked down at them, lying at her feet.

Upon discovering I wasn't in the house, my grandmother had Jennie trace me down through Jeannie's mother in New York, who called Edie Shay. When Red Bank got hold of me at Mrs. Pickard's, I said the phone was in the Pickards' kitchen, and I couldn't bother them by standing there talking. Jennie told all this to my grandmother sitting by the phone; I could hear my grandmother say, "Tell her to go up to the house and call me. I'm supporting that house." By the time I got up to the house, Jennie had called Peggy Bacon and said, "Mrs. Wilson had been very surprised to find you instead of Rosalind there taking care of the dogs."

I had been corresponding with my grandmother about a large beach picnic I planned to give to pay back the brunches after mass, the Aikens' orange blossoms and Reine's champagne, and my grandmother sent me a hundred dollars for it. She had always felt troubled and totally unnecessarily so about the fact that she was removed from an active social life by choice and deafness; when I was younger, she had had Esther Hartshorne give parties for me. Now she told me that unless I gave the party in the house I was to send back the hundred dollars. She wanted Jennie to speak to Miss Bacon. Jennie told Miss B. that Mrs. Wilson saw no reason her granddaughter should be "banging around a beach" when the house was there. I found out my grandmother had wired my father, "ROSALIND TO ENTERTAIN IN HOUSE OR WON'T PAY TAXES OR ANY BILLS." Ever after, my grandmother pretended she didn't remember Miss Bacon's name and referred to her as "that woman who has something to do with pork."

The upshot was, I remained at Mrs. Pickard's but gave the party at the house. A hundred dollars went a long way in those days. We moved in a small piano of the Walkers', had champagne punch made according to Elena's fantastic recipe, and stuffed bass. It was a shame George Roy Hill became a famous director, because he was such a great singer of light songs, putting Alfred Drake and Howard Keel to shame. His rendition of the Irish classic "Phil the Fluter's Ball" would make severe arthritics leap up and into a jig. He played and played and sang that night. I had, of course, invited Miss Bacon, who declined. She returned tight-lipped the next day to an immaculate house, which we had left after cleaning our hearts out. I wickedly rubbed salt in her wound by telephoning Red Bank and telling all about the party. Jennie sang a few stanzas of "Phil the Fluter's Ball" over the phone herself. I, for one, was happy at the Pickards' and would have been with a beach picnic. It was one of life's little dividends that my grandmother had chosen to put Peggy Bacon to rout.

When Dawn Powell, author, wit and family buddy, surfaced later that summer, she said Peggy droned on to anyone who would listen about the party I'd given with a lot of actors. "You would have thought they were going to steal the silver," Dawn said. I begged Dawn to remind Peggy my mother was an actress and that Miss Bacon had partaken many times of her hospitality and consorted with actors there. Dawn did.

When my father returned, he was even angrier than when he went away: at his marriage, at the world, at me. I was happy to be out of it. His eyes had begun wandering to other women, one of them a cousin of Nina's, Natalia Galitzin Heseltine. The Galitzins were the family in Russia considered more noble than the Romanovs. Natalia's mother had literally walked out of Russia with nothing but her pearls. Natalia was a brilliant conversationalist, with great dark eyes. As one gentleman said to me, "In the evenings when those great eyes shine, she looks like all the heroines out of Tolstoy rolled into one." Natalia had no interest in my father; in fact, she rather disliked him. Even if she had, Nina would have squashed it. Natalia worked for the U.N. and was a divorcée with a daughter. Her other vacation place was in Ottawa with the Alexanders. General Alexander was then governor general.

Again, we had all been caught in time by the war and the fact that many men were still in college at a late age. Natalia referred to the Chavchavadze weekends as "Operation What-the-Human-Frame-Can-Stand," and said it was "good to get back to my British colleagues having tea and translating minor Serbian laws on Mondays."

She said that although she had rather disliked my father, there was one night at a beach picnic when she saw him in a different light. We were all sitting around the fire near the ocean singing with guitars. David Chavchavadze was singing a Russian song and suddenly my father, who was sitting halfway up a sand dune wearing the brown felt hat he always wore, chimed in with his resonant voice. "He was so completely himself then, no one else," Natalia said.

# XVII

PAUL CHAVCHAVADZE was having a book published by Houghton Mifflin, and I met the managing editor, Dorothy de Santillana, at the Cs'. When she was young, she had entered into a very unhappy marriage with the poet Robert Hillyer; she later married an historian of science at MIT, Giorgio de Santillana. She had gotten me in to see Paul Brooks, the editor in chief, who hired me. So I moved into a large old kitchen running the length of a house, with a garden, a great sandstone sink, pantries, and a toilet—but no bath or shower—at 4 Louisburg Square. The rent was forty dollars a month. At the suggestion of Austin Olney, the only young male editor of that period, who managed to last and rise to the top of the firm in the most decent way, I bought a children's wading pool, which I would fill every morning with pails and then bail out. It eventually sprang a leak and, as I couldn't afford to replace it on a Houghton Mifflin salary, I had to blow it up every morning and take my bath very quickly. It was hard on mornings after late parties. I'd had a small room for a while but had to give it up after one evening when Ed O'Connor and I sat chastely in the horrible stuffed chairs after a meal at the Automat and the alcoholic landlady came in and said, "Here, here, we won't allow that sort of thing with the doors closed," then leapt into Ed's lap.

Ed was very much on the make in those days, but for success, not women. He had taken up legerdemain as a means of ingratiating himself with my father. I had mixed feelings about him, for I'd heard through the grapevine that *Time* had suggested he do a story on my father, and he had replied in a memo that "Wilson was nothing but a hopeless drunk." After that, my father published *Classics and Commercials; The Shores of Light; Five Plays; Scrolls from the Dead Sea; Red, Black, Blond and Olive; A Piece of My Mind; The American Earthquake; Apologies to the Iroquois; Night Thoughts* (my favorite); *Patriotic Gore; The Cold War and the Income Tax; The Bit Between My Teeth; The Duke of Palermo and Other Plays; O Canada;* and *Upstate.* Not bad for an old drunk!

Ed used my father's name all the time, saying to editors, "I must call Edmund Wilson and ask him" or "As I was saying to Edmund Wilson" or "Edmund Wilson says I should write this novel." It's known as hoisting yourself on someone else's petard. But Ed was extremely amusing and knew a lot about James Curley and Boston politics. He was a great dinner guest when I finally could entertain, having moved up to the attic of 4 Louisburg Square after a couple of raises. I wrote a memo saying I knew Ed would write a successful book about Mayor Curley. Lovell Thompson, the general manager, said he didn't want a book about a crooked Irish politician. I was rather relieved, as Ed had a habit of coming into my office to visit even when we didn't publish him.

The only time my landlords, the St. John Smiths, ever complained about too much noise in my apartment was the night Ed and George Roy Hill (doing "Chekhov at the Brat-

168

tle") got in a fight over the word "internecine." They were both large men with commanding voices. Ed dined out a lot on stories about his landlady. He'd come back from weekends to find a circle of chairs around the television set, and when he went to the hospital nearly dying of bleeding ulcers, and people would call, his landlady would give the most gory description. "I've seen the Brighton abattoir," etc. After he was successful, Ed bought a palatial home on Marlborough Street overlooking his old room at No. 11.

After my tumultuous family life, Houghton Mifflin, where everyone was pleasant and softspoken, seemed an oasis of calm. Ferris Greenslet, who had been editor in chief for years and a great fly-fisherman, was still a director. Although retired, he would come in and give me fishing rods. They could still remember a reader who sat with a cat in her lap in front of the fire. One day when I felt faint, Miss Salmon, the personnel manager, came up and looked around accusingly at the people in charge as if one of the girls in the Lowell mills had slumped over her sewing machine. There were, of course, no women on the board of directors. My father had been published by them years before, but his connection, Bob Linscott, had been ousted in some coup and had gone to Random House. Still, he came in to cash checks occasionally and saw my employment as a way of getting some of his old buddies published, such as the Haitian novelist Philippe (Phito) Thoby-Marcelin.

My father had written a virulent review of a book by Anya Seton for the *New Yorker*. She was our best-seller, of course. He came in to see me about a check just as Paul Brooks was ushering Miss Seton to the open-cage elevator. Upon seeing my father, he shoved Miss Seton into the elevator quickly, saying desperately, "Up, Mrs. Williams. Up! Up!" to the elevator operator. Anya kept saying, "Oh, it's Mr. Wilson. Let me meet him." (The "at him" was implied.) My father and I stood below while the elevator stopped for a moment mid-

floor with Anya saying "Down" and Paul Brooks saying "Up."
Luckily for all of us, Mrs. Williams obeyed Paul. He had
presence of mind. The story was that once as a young editor
when he was dealing with Olive Higgins Prouty, the author of
*Stella Dallas*, she'd lost her underpants, a pool of pink silk
around her feet. Paul said, "Mrs. Prouty, I believe you've lost
your underpants." She thought he had such presence of mind
that he would rapidly rise in the company, which he did.

Although Houghton Mifflin paid badly, there were com-
pensations. It was a pleasant working day because the hours
were loose and everyone behaved with courtesy. They were an
exceptionally congenial group of workers and it was a first-
rate firm. They really did first readings and got some of their
best and most successful books that way, and they never would
have entered into the situation Doubleday got into with my
father and *Hecate County*. I had liked Donald Elder enormously, who was editor in chief when *Hecate County* was
contracted for. He was a fine editor. I met him at a lot of
parties of the Irish writers Padraic and Mary Colum, and we
had a running joke about an electronic book which sighed
when you were supposed to and cried and laughed. Apparently, the people at the top at Doubleday really didn't know
that *Hecate County* contained material that would cause
trouble. Because at Houghton Mifflin books had to be passed
on by the president and the board of directors, all would know
ahead of time what they might be up against and could stand
behind it.

At one editorial meeting, I realized the separation between
me and my colleagues. A memoir of Bartók, written by my
friend Agatha Fassett, was being discussed. Everyone kept
saying how perfectly horrible Bartók sounded, so rude. It
hadn't seemed that way to me, as it was merely a description
of a day at home with my father.

Norbert Wiener, who worked with Giorgio de Santillana,
had just had *The Human Use of Human Beings* published by

Houghton Mifflin. His thesis was that machines were coming down with human diseases. About forty-three years later, the newspapers began using phrases like "computer virus." Houghton Mifflin had just given the largest advance in the history of publishing to Churchill for his memoirs. The president, Henry Laughlin, had a wonderful story about going down to Chequers, getting drunk with Churchill while they both cried over the proofs. I was sharing an office with the great history book editor, Craig Wylie, who was reading the Churchill as it came in, and it was all very lively. He referred to Churchill as "our sailor boy."

Until my half sister, Helen, took her last years of school at a day school near Cambridge and my family spent the winters there, my family was either on the Cape, in New York or in Princeton. I often made the time-consuming trip to Red Bank for weekends as my grandmother was fading. But my father and I were apart enough so that I would write him gossipy letters from Boston. An excerpt:

> I had dinner last night with the Irish Vice-Consul, among others. We first caught each other's eye when a typical Cambridge lady started running on about that wonderful moment of clarity which tea gives you as opposed to whiskey. In any case he says that Padraic's name is still one with which to conjure in Ireland and that he thinks he will have a great fuss made over him there. The next night I went to a much less pleasant event featuring W. S. Merwin and his English wife. He was more anglophile than she although he comes from Pennsylvania and is full of how there is no American literature and fake English nature talk. However, he had seen John Berryman. He said he was very happily married again with a son. And he had seen Nabokov who sits in front of a washing machine (the kind with a window) watching his sneakers go round. He says, "It's like a window on the world."
>
> Boston was very quiet until a few weeks ago, when it was shaken by Philip Hamburger's profile of Marquand. I have

gotten rather friendly with a crazy family who are related to all the Cabots, Sedgewicks, etc. And their inside stories are all something you wouldn't believe. Ye Gads, if it isn't incest, it's perversion, if it isn't perversion it's a mad member in the attic. I just listen openmouthed.

I was particularly impressed by the attitude about one young man at Houghton Mifflin, who murdered his mother by dragging her around the room by a scarf around her neck. "Poor old X," they said. "He was having one of his black days. We must all rally and have him to dinner." I hadn't had him to dinner before he murdered his parent and saw no reason to do so after.

My father had written a Christmas poem for Elena because she said no one had ever written a poem for her. He got a young man in the production department at Houghton Mifflin to print it up on his own hand press. A couple of years later, he noted that the famous Boston rare-book dealer, George Goodspeed, was listing it in his catalogue and was quite rightly irritated, as he'd paid for the printing. Goodspeed was a few doors from Houghton Mifflin. Goodspeed agreed to give him a certain number of Audubon prints to assuage his anger. Occasionally, my father, if he was in town, took me to lunch at Locke-Ober's, the great Boston restaurant. He had first taken me there when I was sixteen and explained what brandy with a bead in it was. I have a menu of Locke's from that year: Filet mignon was $2; large live lobster was $2.50; large Cotuit oysters, 40 cents; best champagne, $7 a bottle; pony of best brandy, 45 cents.

Anyway, we trundled around to Locke's one day and had quite a few Gibsons (by that time, I'd learned not only the difference between sweet and dry sherry but between sweet and dry martinis too) and then went into Goodspeed's, where I was to choose my Audubon allotment. I chose some mice, some gray squirrels, and some rats eating someone else's eggs.

Goodspeed and my father kept saying, "Are you sure you want the rats?"—an unspeakably brutal scene to have hanging on one's walls. "Yes, yes." The rats turned out to be very valuable. Later when I felt I was being treated rather unfairly by Houghton Mifflin, I wrote to my father, "Please send me gray squirrels so I can outgames Paul Brooks." Paul had Audubon wallpaper in his office. My father, who had become devoted to the squirrels, wrote back, "Why don't you try the rats on Brooks."

# PART
# IV

# XVIII

**M**Y GRANDMOTHER'S LIFE and vitality were slowly ebbing away. Jennie said it was better if I was there when my father came, so sometimes when I came down from Houghton Mifflin for weekends, my father would be there as well. Nurses had been brought in, which naturally was bound to irritate Jennie, although she had had plenty of experience with them during my grandfather's time. They didn't have to work very hard, as my grandmother could still bathe herself. She kept to her room. One nurse was full of stories about her husband's beating her, and although my grandmother couldn't hear, she sensed the woman's aura and asked me to fire her. It was unpleasant of her to bring her sordid problems into a sickroom even though the patient was deaf.

It was strange to go into the house and not find my grandmother, who always dressed, though informally, for dinner, sitting in her rocker by the window in the living room. On the half-moon table against the wall next to her chair were some small brass figures of characters from *Pickwick Papers*, Sam Weller and others, a picture of Talcottville and her beautiful garden, with flowers: rows and rows of bachelor buttons, also known as ragged sailors or cornflowers. They were prominent in her Red Bank garden too. Like her, they were dainty but sturdy. There was also a tile of the stone house.

I would get in late from Boston and go up to see her lying small and neat in her wide bed with old-fashioned cotton blankets drawn tightly across her, and hospital corners—like a raft going out to sea. One such night when I came, she said she wanted some old-fashioned coffee, which was the kind always served in Red Bank, boiled with the grounds and an egg to clear it. I went down and made it, knowing she wouldn't drink it; it was the smell she longed for, which permeated the house. I came up with it, lifted her head to smell it, and she died.

The next day, Father and Elena came down, but Elena went back that night. He didn't really want her there, just as he didn't want her to go with him to Sandy's funeral years later. Father and I sat by Grandmother's coffin in the living room that night. I had asked that a pin made of her parents' hair and her wedding ring be left on her. My father fought that night to have me take the wedding ring off and again the next day when the undertaker was there. But the undertaker was on my side. I finally said she'd left *me* her jewelry, and that was that.

A few neighbors came in to see her, and we drove out to Fairlawn Cemetery, passing the Molly Pitcher Hotel and Aunt Addie's old house.

My father inherited the Red Bank house and its contents, except for the furniture in my room and Jennie's, and Talcottville with its contents, constituting between them a very fine antique collection.

Jennie was bereft. But she had a house in Red Bank and planned to live there eventually with her niece, Helen Cluisy, whom she loved and who was a very gentle, caring girl. My grandmother's will was probated within two weeks, as is the custom, in Monmouth County where she lived. It never occurred to either my father or myself to have any dispute over it. It certainly never would have occurred to us to try and get her to change her will during her last illness, although her mind was perfectly sound.

The Talcottville house was my father's at last. It would change his life.

One of my father's characteristics in handling the ladies around him was to repeat to them unpleasant things others had said about them, something most people try to conceal. It was usually for some purpose of his own. Jennie was a case in point. I had gone to Europe, which made him feel insecure. He wrote me that Jennie said I'd gone highbrow. If she said it, it was said as a joke. I felt impelled to write:

> I have just written Jennie a letter. If you remember, when I was in Europe she constantly complained I was not writing her, when I was all the time. If I repeated all the remarks she has made to me such as, "They care nothing about me," you would be just as discouraged as I was at your quote about my being highbrow.

Playing the women around him against one another was a very integral part of his character.

Shortly after my grandmother's death, Jennie fell and had to go to Riverview Hospital. I went down to see her and stayed in the house by myself, where I spent the two loneliest nights of my life. In the mornings, I half expected my grandmother to come in and sing in her toneless voice, "Lazy Mary, will you get up, will you get up," as she always had.

What my childhood and adolescence and girlhood would have been without her constancy, I don't know. I would probably have ended up in a juvenile booby hatch for I would have been prey to the theories and whims of every lady my father fancied.

The contents of the Red Bank house were divided up between Wellfleet and Talcottville. There were a great many pictures around the house—me at various ages, my grandfather on the steps of the stone house and in other poses, my great-uncles, and my father's cousin Susan Wilson in her naval uniform. She and my father had been brought up like brother and sister. She was the one relative who remained close during his lifetime. My grandmother had only one picture of my father, in a silver frame on her dresser. Was it because she, like Jennie, felt something had happened to change him after Princeton? If so, was it the incarceration of his doppelgänger Sandy? Jennie felt the change occurred before the war, or was it that a mammoth ego controlled by his parents had simply been unleashed to roam untethered? Or did she simply prefer to see him as a slim young man, her boy, before life had knocked him about?

People who had known my grandparents together didn't think they were a mismatched couple. My grandparents didn't think they were. Jennie was a good witness to the marriage; but there were many others—my great-aunts, Susan Wilson, her father (my grandmother's brother), and the charming southern family into which he married, the Minors. As I have said, my grandmother said, "I married the best man who ever lived." He told people, "I would have sunk many times without the rock which is my wife."

The nearest she'd ever come to Mary McCarthy's encounter with the man in the Brooks Brothers shirt had been before her marriage when her sister Laura and she had been looking in Tiffany's window. A man had grabbed her hand and said, "If I take you in and put a ring on your finger, will you come with me?" But she wasn't some sexless, removed woman. (Even though she and her sisters had put cotton in the potties in their room so their brother's friends, home from Princeton, wouldn't hear the tinkle.) She came from a medical family and had a very earthy approach to the bodily functions.

Once, when I was sixteen, I told her I was embarrassed because my father flirted with Jeannie. "Don't be silly," she said. "Of course, they all do it. My father did it. They want to catch the caboose as they get older." She had been a very pretty, stylishly dressed woman. Men liked her and she understood the attraction my grandfather held for the friends of her young nieces. She was secure enough, so it didn't worry her.

My grandmother had an extensive knowledge of antiques which her son didn't. When he cleaned out the stone house after his mother's death, he gave away some of the best ones, such as the old harmonium, while coveting ones that belonged to other people which he thought were "the Baker" antiques.

# XIX

TO SAY THAT ELENA DISLIKED TALCOTTVILLE would have been a great understatement. When she hated, she hated; and she said quite rightly that my father didn't like her there. Nothing there was any good for her. The eggs were bad. She claimed it wasn't dairy country. When Nina came up for a few days (she had been brought up in dairy country in Russia), she had to say, "Elena's wrong there," although she was trying to be a peacemaker. Elena had to admit the house was an architectural gem compared to Wellfleet. She regretted it was stone and wouldn't burn. She had never experienced American rural life. A few visits to Binghamton to see her first mother-in-law were nothing like Talcottville. I tried to cheer her up by saying the Bourbons had settled farther north; not even the fact that there was a Russian monastery at Jordanville—just beyond Herkimer—helped.

Once, around milking time, I was driving and stopped for some cows crossing the road to their barn. "Go on," she said.

"They won't hurt you." I explained that one stopped as a courtesy to the cows and the farmer. She complained to the widow of one of my grandparents' friends that once she'd crossed a field to reach a swimming hole and had been surrounded by cows. "Well," said the woman, a Mrs. Burnham, looking at her sharply, "cows know when you're not one of their own." The only person she liked was one of the Loomis girls—Florence—who had taught German in Switzerland and had arterial sclerosis. "I only like one old lady there and she's going potty."

She counted the number of people who had died in the house. Actually, more had been married there. Huldah Loomis did an imitation of her saying in rolling Teutonic tones, "It is a gloomy house."

But the fact of the matter is, Talcottville saved a marriage which had floundered many times. It saved it on one level because anyone living with my father was on constant floor duty, and her refusal to go there gave her a few months' rest. But for twenty-one years, the battle raged every spring; and they weren't silent about it. Elena, in tears, would call me up every day before I went to work saying he was going, going, going. He said she was surprised every year that he was going and injured herself in some way. She said he could have made her like it, which wasn't true. He didn't want to. He didn't want her in "Mother's house"; and some wild, lonely part of him rebelled against the perfect household she had made. There were never any dusty corners in Elena's house. But you can't clean out the dusty corners in people's souls.

On several occasions, after an evening of Europeans at Wellfleet, he had turned to me and said, "Don't forget, Rosalind, all these people are exiles," which was true. They were wonderful exiles, but had they been able, they too would have retreated to their roots as he did.

There were people who used the annual battle for their own purposes by renting the Wellfleet house from under

Elena cheaply. My father would make the arrangements in front of her. Eventually, she paid her own expenses when she was there in the summer, which silenced his complaint that he was keeping up two households. Once she was all ready to go up on the Fourth of July with a poached salmon in her arms, as he wanted to give a party, when he called and said he didn't want her. Her son said, "Oh, go, he'll snap out of it." He did; but it was the sort of situation which was nerve-wracking. He said they'd both had different dreams. They certainly had different literary frames of reference.

One day in Talcottville, I was standing to the side watching the two of them on the porch. My father had just come out the door and was at his most portly and squirish. He was pointing to the three-quarters of an acre in front of him across the road, saying, "That's mine, *mienne!*" "Sir Roger de Coverley," I said. He gave me a sort of irritated cognizant look and Elena said, "You must have known him before we were married." Of course, I had never heard of *Elizabeth and Her German Garden* by Countess Mary Annette Beauchamp Russell (married to Bertrand Russell's brother) until Phyllis Duganne had explained it to me. It accounted for a lot of Elena's attitude.

It was a popular book about a woman with a German mentality whose husband, whom she referred to as the Man of Wrath, was away a lot. It tells of her involvement with her garden ad nauseam and her day-to-day life alone in the German countryside.

It shed light on Elena's psyche: *When my dearest one [Edmund] is far away.* Yay, even in Talcottville.

One problem Elena had when she was in Talcottville was that it was impossible for her to dress badly. She couldn't help looking as if she'd just stepped out of Chanel or Dior with her clotheshorse figure and the rhinestone earrings she always wore. She simply couldn't look sloppy and countrified. My father wasn't a tweedy type either. A raggedy bathrobe was the order of the day until early afternoon. And he often could be seen walking across Route 12D to Mrs. Maguire's in it. In Wellfleet, he was often seen on moonlit nights bicycling down Route 6 in his pajamas to bring our dog, Wrecky, home from "that bitch who wasn't good enough for him." Wrecky liked to go down and sit with his love and his pups. He couldn't booby-trap Wrecky's homecoming.

Mrs. Maguire and another lady in Talcottville spent quite a lot of time at their windows with binoculars watching what went on at the stone house; and there were some really pro party-line listeners. The stone house was always on a party line with five other people. One of my father's economies was not paying the hundred dollars a year extra a private line would have cost. People whose vocation and recreation is party-line eavesdropping get up in the morning and have their meals at the table where the phone is, taking the phone off the hook while getting the meals so it will register busy and they won't miss anything. Then they return to the table, placing their hand on the phone, which gives off a slight vibration when anyone is on it. As my father transacted all his business, personal and otherwise, on the phone, he gave several idle people much pleasure. Of course, the phone calls with the *New Yorker* about punctuation must have been dull. But the interesting conversations were so full of anger, sentiment, and fascinating private facts it was probably worth waiting out the *New Yorker* calls.

My grandmother gave candy to kids as they passed the house, taking the younger ones on her lap. And people knew she knew what was what as far as workmanship and gardening and antiques went. Her relationship with the hamlet was good, my father's with the younger set was not, which was partly their fault. If they'd ever come in and asked him about books or anything for that matter, he would have been pleased, but their minds were on demolition—of their cars and each other. There were always demolition derbies at the local fairs which encouraged this pastime and the Talcottville stretch of road was perfect for drag racing, even more so after the new road went in. The new road is dangerous with its overwide shoulders; although it's a two-lane road, a lot of people use it as if it were a four-lane highway.

# XX

THE ONLY ONE of my father's female first cousins (on his father's side) to come up to Talcottville to see my grandmother over the years was Susan Wilson because her job involved visits to the state school for the retarded in Rome, New York, twenty-five miles or so down the Gorge Road from Talcottville. Unlike Dorothy Stilwell, who was very pretty, with a witty, bright chatter, Susan was a different kettle of fish, and provided a steadfast relationship through my father's whole life—one which was never severed nor did it falter. Whereas Dorothy had been vivacious and easygoing, Susan was the opposite.

My grandmother complained that when she took her to Princeton football games with the boys, she spent the whole time primping instead of vamping the young men. Susan was a beauty with perfect classic features and grew enormously as a person during the course of her life. My grandfather's brother, John, had married a lovely southern woman from Charlottesville, Virginia. She came from a delightful family—the Minors. They had had three children, and Susan was my father's age. She used to come up and spend long periods of time with my grandparents. When John Wilson died, the womenfolk in the family were helpless, having been brought up in the southern tradition. I can remember their coming, Mrs. John Minor Wilson in heavy widow's weeds, after her husband's death. They were unlike my grandmother, totally untutored in the ways of business. Susan's two siblings died at an early age, her sister of diabetes and her brother, Minor, a lawyer, was shot by the jealous husband of a client in a divorce case. Susan, who'd been brought up in the most helpless way, showed great character and went to New York, where she got herself a job as an occupational therapist in the Brooklyn State Hospital, becoming an expert in the field. She often came down to Red Bank for weekends, although sometimes Jennie had to mime her in acting out her life among the mental patients, her lonely life in her rooms at the hospital. Sometimes Jennie got down on her knees while trying to get some member of the family in the door. The only thing my grandmother had against Susan's coming down was that she picked at her food. Once when I went up to visit her at the hospital, it was depressing—two postage-stamp-sized rooms with a narrow bed with hospital corners, a narrower box bed, and you could hear the screams of the patients, and everything was thrice locked. She was totally southern, and the thing which kept her going was the house she planned and did build in Charlottesville upon her retirement. I loved hearing her sing "A Froggie Would A-wooing Go," a southern song of which she knew the myriad verses. She often spent the holidays with us or with my father. Mary McCarthy would spend hours talking about how Anglo-Saxon and prissy she was.

I'd once spent a harrowing evening at Red Bank with Susan and Dorothy Stilwell, who had just gotten her settlement from Cecil and was talking about the wiles she'd use to snag a new husband. "Really, Dorothy," Susan would say, "that sort of talk belongs in the stables." Then Dorothy would relate how she'd had me out on Long Island when I was fourteen and the tax commissioner for New York State had tried to kiss me until Dorothy whomped him one with her evening bag. A doctor had to be called. The Stilwell girls had looked me over, saying, "Maybe something can be done with her hair eventually," but on the whole, they decided I wasn't millionaire bait. Adeline Stilwell had had a house with pools, slot machines, yachts, the works. Her mother, Aunt Addie, was a prop. She had her sitting on the sofa and turned to her, saying dramatically, "Mother, have I ever lied to you?" "Yes, all the time," Aunt Addie said. Someone had poured me champagne in a water glass. Adeline spied it and said, "No one in my house drinks champagne out of a water glass" as she poured me a large hollow-stemmed glass of the bubbly which led to my getting involved with the tax man.

Susan joined the Waves during the Mary McCarthy period and sent a picture of herself in uniform. My father patriotically displayed it in a prominent place; as a result, Mary would go on for hours negatively about Susan's miserable qualities. Poor Susan did a lot of crying in uniform until my grandmother wired her, "SAILORS DON'T CRY."

Susan was much more like my father than anyone else, only she had to be practical; but it went against her vague nature. She took up Anglo-Saxon and really learned it, but she missed trains as he did and was actually an intellectual whose education had been neglected. She was the only relative, except his children and his mother, with whom he corresponded throughout his life and never turned on completely as he did Helen Augur. But then Susan never had time to be ensconced as temporary chatelaine in the stone house.

She had a charming southern accent. Her routine for getting out into the world in the morning was to get completely dressed with her white button gloves on, then say,

"The daily miracle has occurred. I am dressed." Then she would take one single jigger of bourbon. One. Only. In the evening she would ask for bourbon, pointing to the three-quarter mark on a highball glass, then say, "Just slosh a little branch water over it." Dos had gone down to see her and disappeared for two weeks. The only answer anyone got when calling any of the Minors or Susan was a maid's saying, "They've gone to a party."

When my father tried to be disagreeable to her, she said, "Edmund, it's no use trying to be disagreeable to me because when people are disagreeable to me I just pretend I'm a feather bed," which must have come from dealing with a great many mental patients. Once he said, "When I pass on . . ."; she reproved him: "Edmund, in our family we don't pass on, we croak."

After my father's death, when she came up to Talcottville to see me, she brought a little box with a semiprecious stone in the top my father had sent her from Gump's in San Francisco when he was on his honeymoon with Elena. "Isn't that just like him to send one woman a box when he's on his honeymoon with another." It showed her almost romantic view of their relationship. Elena had enormous respect for her and said she was the only person she'd be kicked out of the famous pineapple four-poster for when the house was crowded. As Susan grew older, the prissiness disappeared. She remained a beauty till the end but a much more open and jovial one. When my father's trained nurse, Mrs. Stabb, came in to give some shots to Susan, who was visiting after Father's death, Mrs. Stabb said she had a turn, Susan's manner and expression were so like his.

# XXI

ELENA WAS FULL OF DEVIOUS PLANS to keep my father from spending too much time in Talcottville. But they never worked because if he stayed in Wellfleet later in the summer, he made up for it by staying in Talcottville later in the fall, a time he loved there. One of Elena's plans was to have Jennie come for a prolonged stay. In later years, she would say my sister, Helen, needed him "else she'd turn out like Rosalind." I think "the ne'er-do-well" was implied.

Jennie came for two months and there were two very memorable evenings, one with a man I was semiengaged to, Frank Rounds, and one with the French poet and diplomat, Alexis Léger, alias St.-John Perse, famous for his sea poems.

Houghton Mifflin was publishing a book, *A Window on Red Square* by Frank Wendell Rounds, and Craig Wylie was editing it. Frank would spend hours on end in the office, and Craig decided to do some matchmaking. Frank had just come back from Russia, and was at loose ends. It most certainly didn't work out in the end. I was too wild for Frank and after the night I spent in his house with him and his mother, I woke up the next morning and left before breakfast. I felt trapped. I think we both looked back on our unsuccessful semiliaison as if we'd avoided being in a railway crash and had no regrets whatsoever about it.

When Frank came down to Wellfleet one weekend, Jennie, who had had a few drinks, hated him and told him he was a no-good jerk, which came as a surprise, as everyone had been pushing the romance because he was sterling and so settled. Elena had kept saying, "Marry him before he gets to know you, because if he gets to know you he'll never marry you." When I went back to Houghton Mifflin Monday morning, I reported this in a distressed way to Dale Warren, one of the older editors, who was famous because he'd discovered Raymond Chandler and because he was the person Dorothy Thompson chose to escort Boston lobsters up whenever she gave a party in Vermont. He was often seen boarding the train talking to crates of crustaceans. I told Dale my father kept trying to ease Jennie out of the room; but after several whiskeys she'd have none of it and just kept telling Frank, "Going to Princeton doesn't make everything all right if you're rotten to the core anyway." "Never mind," said Dale, "the nurse in *Romeo and Juliet* got drunk." Frank's contribution to Wilson lore was, "I don't think anyone knows Elena well, not even your father."

In the course of the Frank saga, Elena decided they should come to Boston, staying with me instead of at a hotel as an economy measure because if I decided to get married it would be expensive. It seemed insane to me, as there were four long, long flights of stairs going up to my apartment at Louisburg Square. But I didn't want to seem inhospitable. Naturally, the stairs were too much for my father, so he came down with a terrible case of gout and couldn't be moved. He took over the apartment: two small rooms with casement windows, and I had to spend my nights at the Vendôme. Weeks earlier I'd planned a little dinner party with Curtis Bennet, a professor of Greek at Tufts, and Margeret Ryan, the commercial artist who lived below me. My father announced I shouldn't give my dinner because he'd invited Isaiah Berlin to dinner. I said, "I yielded to no one in my appreciation of Berlin," whom I'd met once in Wellfleet and thought the most brilliant person I'd ever heard, but my dinner party had been planned ahead. I felt I had to hang on to some little corner of my life.

The upshot was that there were two separate dinners—one in the bedroom and one in the living room, Elena getting one while I got the other. Finally, Berlin wandered in to say hello and eventually wafted my guests back with him in his great wake to where my father held sway, thinking my guests delightful.

My father thought the Greek professor was one of the brightest people he'd ever met and was taken by the fact that for an office party, the commercial artist had drawn some faces on potato chips. Her boss's wife then asked her to do the same thing for a party involving hundreds of people. Totally harassed by the stupid assignment, my neighbor put a sign above her desk saying COMMERCIAL ARTIST AT STUD.

When my father felt the first pangs of gout, we had a hard time getting a doctor and did what everyone, including Dos, had done—immediately called Abraham Pollen. Pollen was an eye doctor, but we always got our medical references from him. Pollen said, "If I can't get anyone, I'll come myself." "I wouldn't put it past him," my father said hopefully. He had a mystique about Pollen, who had had physical troubles himself, and said he was "the perfect example of the mind's ability to triumph over the physical."

A very different evening from Jennie's evening with Frank Rounds was her meeting with Alexis Léger. Every fall he came and paid a prolonged visit to the Francis Biddles in Wellfleet. (Biddle and my father had two very different approaches to getting breakfast when left alone. Francis had also always had people taking care of him but whereas my father would drop an egg into the frying pan with no butter, Biddle would toss half a pound of bacon in with half a pound of butter and have to call the Wellfleet Fire Department.)

Everyone looked forward to this *little season* treat. Francis' wife was a very good poet, who wrote under the name Katherine Chapin and was a beautiful woman. It was said that while her half sister, Marguerite Caetani, had *Botteghe Oscure* (a multilanguage magazine published in Italy), Katherine had Léger. In Washington he had often been an integral part of the Biddle household. I adored both Biddles. During the Alger Hiss case, the Biddles, Elena and I thought Hiss innocent while my father thought him guilty. There were some heated fights over it. Biddle kept saying what my father did not understand was that Hiss was a totally inept lawyer. My father said Biddle didn't understand that it was perfectly possible for someone like Hiss, married to the sort of wife he had, to be a Communist in that period.

One fine autumn night, Léger and the Biddles came to dinner. Léger, with his dyed hair and Hitler mustache, was full of charm and politesse. He had been born on the islet of Saint-Léger-les-Feuilles. His full name was Marie-René-Alexis Saint-Léger Léger. In 1939 he was French Secretary General of Foreign Affairs, resisting appeasement policies. In 1940 he declined an ambassadorship and left France on a British freighter, and Vichy deprived him of his citizenship. He was reinstated in 1944 and eventually ended up in Washington as consultant for French literature at the Library of Congress and in 1960 won the Nobel prize for literature. Jennie was still very handsome and distinguished-looking and had often been courted by elderly gentlemen while walking my grandmother's Scottie. She sat on Léger's right at dinner. She knew a distinguished, Grade A gentleman when she saw one. And he devoted himself to her during dinner, asking where she had spent her summers. She said she had often stayed in Asbury Park on the Atlantic Ocean. "Ah," he said and began discoursing on the sea with a few quotes from his poetry thrown in. "*La mer*, mother, woman, great bosom pure white froth from which we suckle."* Jennie was spellbound. The more Léger likened the sea to a woman, the more voluble and sensual he became, first speaking in French, then translating for Jennie: "The rolling bosoms of the waves, wavelet nipples erect, at sunset the great vagina of the ocean." After he left, Jennie said what a wonderful gentleman he was, then, "Jesus, Mary and Joseph, no wonder he's single, he's in love with the Atlantic Ocean."

Ed O'Connor, who had bored my father at first, had firmly gotten his foot in the door by taking up magic. One day, when he was lolling in shorts with his legs over a chair, Jennie said, "That man has the most beautiful limbs I ever saw." Shorts had been a rarity with Ed until then, but after that his limbs were always in evidence.

My father was very good to Jennie. How could anyone not want to be. She combined being shrewd with being good, a characteristic of a lot of saints. She hadn't married, I think, because she was tied to her mother and supporting her and then to my grandmother, and had had a glimmering of men beyond the remnants of the old class system in which she functioned. Whenever my grandmother took her as a young woman to resorts, she was surrounded by suitors. One she favored—a young college boy working as a waiter—but he wasn't going to take on her mother.

---

* Not direct quotes from Léger's poetry, but an impressionistic reproduction of the conversation.

# XXII

HEN MY FATHER INHERITED Talcottville, he tried to take on the role his father had played of taking distant family members on picnics. "I feel I owe the people here something," he said like the good knight de Coverley. The three Loomis girls—Huldah, Gertrude and Florence—were prime targets for picnics, as they had adored the ones his father gave. Florence, as mentioned before, had taught German in a school in Switzerland; Gertrude had taught home economics in New York and was to become sclerotic; and Huldah had been a nurse, traveling all over the world with a well-to-do patient with diplomatic connections who had left her some money. The patient, like Lord Byron, had eventually been sent home in a cask of sherry. Huldah had caught the amorous eye of one gentleman patient at the Hotel Royalton and every time she'd ask him what he wanted for breakfast, he'd say, "A roll in bed with a little honey." When Barry Callaghan came down from Canada in 1973 and interviewed people, he opened his session with Huldah with, "Well, Miss Loomis, after seeing your picture in *Up-state*, I would have come a-courtin'." He was then thirty-five, and she was eighty-five. She looked him right straight in the eye and said, "Well, why didn't you?" "Time in the head of that little old lady," was Barry's comment.

The Loomises were descended from the aristocratic Tal-cotts, and their attitude toward my father with his Baker blood was slightly snobbish. Their house and farm were a few miles north up the road, but the way they always said, "We were all set for dinner and decided we'd send down for Edmund," had nothing to do with that. My father thought Huldah was too property-minded; but she couldn't hold a candle to him. And they each thought the other was hoarding things in their attics and would wheedle around trying to find out what.

My father had three wars going: one with Elena in Well-fleet (if he'd fix a wall in Talcottville, she'd fix one in Well-fleet); and two with the Loomises—the expensive Red Plush War, and the more modest Who Has the Largest Lady-Slipper Blossoms War. The Red Plush War also drove Elena wild. The opening salvo was discharged by my father's having a Victorian slipper chair upholstered in red plush, an expensive thing to do. The Loomis girls came for drinks and admired it, went home, and retaliated with a slipper chair. My father went up there for supper, saw it, called up the upholsterer the next day, and had a small two-seater sofa and footstool done in red plush, inviting the Loomises for lunch the day it arrived. They went home and had a small sofa done in red plush. Of course, he was a footstool ahead, but their sofa was more valuable. At this point, although he was very broke, he brought out the big guns and had a mammoth sofa done in red plush; the upholsterer threw in two pillows. He left the field victorious because the Loomis girls had no sofa that large. He invited them to sit on it, and they said it was handsome, but too much red plush could look like a bordello and that sort of sofa wasn't meant to have pillows. On the other front, while he had more lady-slippers than they did, theirs definitely had larger blossoms.

I loved the Loomis girls, and in the fall we would hit every church turkey supper for miles around. They named the house of theirs where I stayed to watch over things when the new road was under construction and which I eventually bought from them at a token price, Villa Rosalinda.

Talcottville was really too far from Boston to go comfortably for weekends, but there would be bottles and bottles of champagne as a bribe for me to come. In my father's early years in Talcottville, he was very lonely; but he began to make a life for himself there.

In the spring, I usually took him up, and once we stopped in Saratoga Springs at Yaddo, the writers' colony, where our dear friend Dawn Powell was finishing a book. Naturally, a little party was given. Also staying at Yaddo was an attractive young woman, Patti Hill, an ex-model who had written a book. My father was taken with her until Dawn nudged her book toward him, and then like an animal in the forest who hears the crack of a twig, his eyes, which had been blurry after a lot of drink, cleared up as he nudged the book right back at Dawn.

Dawn was always eager to help younger women in her field and as Matthew Josephson said in his article in the *Southern Review* in 1973—"Dawn Powell, A Woman d'Esprit"—she was attractive to both men and women. Her relationship with women being that of an older sister. She was the only one of my father's friends who ever came to Talcottville for more than a few nights who really enjoyed it and who understood the pleasures of sitting on the front porch, watching the hamlet go by, and of driving around (known in that part of the country as "ramming around," which has no sexual connotation).

One day in Talcottville, I took Dawn and my father to town, where they bought some vodka, then we went for a drive. When I had a flat tire, they both disappeared in a cornfield with the vodka, supposedly seeking help. Dawn was tiny and my father rather short, and it was August, when the corn was at its highest. I soon hailed a passing farmer who fixed the tire. I waited two hours for them, and then, furious, went and took a swim, returning home to find them on the front porch. They'd stopped in the middle of the cornfield to kill the vodka, then staggered out into another county where a sheriff's patrol picked them up. To Dawn, Talcottville was just a continuation of her Ohio childhood.

She was the first person my father and Dos called up when they went to New York, supplanting even girlfriends. I had first become really aware of her at Henderson Place when she had appeared—plump, pink and pretty—and taken my parents' mind off the fact that a member of the Yale wrestling team had permanently bent an antique poker in our rented house on the back of his neck. I literally had romantic irons in the fire then.

When I was young and innocent and polishing up the handles very carefully at Houghton Mifflin, the management sent me down to the New York office for the summer. I couldn't believe anyone would pay me to read books. Of course, it was a bit inconvenient sitting at a desk instead of lying in dishabille on the sofa reading them.

The New York office, unlike the home office in Boston, did not have enough reading to keep me busy. I was usually finished by eleven and aside from the daily visit of a benzie-ridden man from Hoboken who rode over on the ferry every morning with two or three pages of religious exaltation for me, I had no work. It was the summer all the men I knew were in Europe, so I couldn't set aside the normal amount of office time to look out the window and worry why no one had called.

Such were the July doldrums on Fourth Avenue. Margaret de Silver had lent me her apartment on Twelfth Street. One night a voice called asking for Margaret. I explained the situation, and the voice said, "This is Dr. Powell." It was Dawn.

I knew she certainly must have a publisher and also that she was always surrounded by young people from the literary racetrack, so I invited her to a business lunch thinking she might know of some likely writer to justify my existence to Boston. We had lunch and from that moment my summer took a lively course. Dawn wanted someone to do a collection of her short stories, which Scribner's had refused to do. The stories were first-class. The Boston office agreed, and whoever published the stories, subsequently printed under the title *Sunday, Monday and Always*, would get her novel. We took her on; the whole thing was arranged in a friendly way between my boss and John Hall Wheelock at Scribner's, the latter saying he felt like Shylock rather than Wheelock in asking for the amount it took to bail Dawn out. Dawn and I had many lunches and drank many diamond gin fizzes— half vodka, half champagne. She remarked at one of our lunches that I was the only editor she knew who ate her own lunch and the author's as well. She always retained a girlish quality, as if she'd just gotten off the train from the country. She told me her husband said I reminded him of herself when she was young because of the belligerent way I walked. She was so small she often worked in the children's room of the public library. She said she wished the girls at Elizabeth Arden would stop bouncing her on their knees, saying, "Here is itsy-bitsy Miss Powell." The only jewelry she wore were some family garnets which slipped off her bosom one night on our way to a party at the Lloyd Frankenbergs and were lost forever.

After our initial dealings, she sent me some cartoons of us in which I am GOMP, Grand Old Man of Publishing, and she is Dean of the Hairy Wordfellows. I always addressed her as Pow Wow.

We began a prolific business correspondence when I returned to Boston. Houghton Mifflin published three books of hers: *Sunday, Monday and Always, The Wicked Pavilion* and *A Cage for Lovers.* Then I left Houghton Mifflin, and she went to Random House. She always had trouble finishing her books, so we put her up at the Boston Ritz for a few days on those occasions. Houghton Mifflin had a rather jolly group of young people in those days, and we kept telling her she should finish the book she was writing, *A Cage for Lovers,* as a happy love story, which she did; she eventually felt it was perhaps a mistake not to have an undefined ending.

She was meticulously observant of people without appearing to be, and one day after we had had lunch at the Louis Quatorze in New York, conversing all the time, she repeated verbatim to me the dialogue of the two ladies at the table next to ours.

Our friendship never included personal confidences, perhaps because it had begun on a more or less business basis and because she was also a friend of my family's. But I realized that perhaps she knew more about me than I thought when an acquaintance of mine looked at me very shrewdly and said, "I wonder where she ever got the idea for the character of the girl in *Cage for Lovers.*" It suddenly occurred to me that the character did have a lot in common with me—psychologically—although I daresay a great many other young women readers felt the same way.

Her correspondence was notoriously amusing. I once asked her to write a recommendation for me. Here is her reply, with a few deletions. Written in 1960, it is on notepaper embossed HOTEL TAFT, NEW HAVEN, J. O. VOIT, GENERAL MANAGER. In her handwriting, it says "from stock stolen during rehearsals, 1941," then, typewritten:

Dear Pub: I took my good time about filling in the form, as I got so carried away with the subject, and the character began to sort of take charge, as we novelists know they often do. It was with genuine regret I stuck the twin masterpiece (carbons were required) into the chute where I daresay it will inflame all the other mail with its passion.

I began with your boyhood in Ireland—(No, I'm thinking of spooky old Frank O'Connor. - - - - I put in a little color about my own literary progress for the next few years with excerpts from my clippings and my sincere debt to my old Lake Erie English teacher, Miss Bray.

[Deletion here.]

I broke down and cried for awhile here and added that morally you were an absolute scream. I enclosed pictures of myself on a bear rug, Max Perkins on a bear rug, a snapshot of me being hooded for a gazelle hunt at Lake Erie College commencement and a copy of The Villager, complaining about the women's prison being torn down.

It has been an ennobling experience.

Yrs. Pow.


I wrote my father, "Have just had letter from Dawn in which she refers to her Margaret (de Silver) as Princess Margaret and speaks of seeing you who, in spite of the gout, had that sunny Wilson smile which lights up Broadway and says, 'Joe and I are the only kids on the block with frozen bank accounts for Xmas, no tinkle of obels for Dr. Powell.'"

She was the only one of my father's friends who enjoyed coming up to Talcottville. Usually his friends came once and even then were anxious to return to the Hamptons, the Cape or Fire Island. But Dawn's Ohio background made her understand the joys of sitting on the front porch in the middle of the American countryside. Most of the literati were nonplussed by being plunked down there.

She certainly was the wittiest person I have ever known, with a rapid-fire running commentary. Phyllis Duganne once said that Dawn was as witty as Dorothy Parker, but she was difficult to quote, which is true. At the same time, she recalled once when she and Dawn had drunk something like fifteen Pernods apiece in the old Lafayette Café, piling up the saucers to keep score as various frightened escorts looked on. But they had both been able to get up and walk out—going on to a party.

A short time before her death, she was invited to lecture at her alma mater, Lake Erie College. The dean told her the girls were crazy about her. I asked what she had said in her speech. She said, "I told them if they wanted a literary career to first settle the man question and pretend they didn't have a brain in their heads; and everything would fall into place from there."

On her last visit to Talcottville, she was dying of cancer and brought with her a puzzle we couldn't solve but which her brain-damaged son had solved right away. She told Matthew Josephson she loved her son better than anyone in the world. It's where all her husband's and her earnings had gone: to schools and hospitals for her son. We had an awfully good time with her upstate. It was all very easygoing and languorous and amusing. She had had a lover for years while living with her husband, and everyone thought she and her husband lived together because of their son and that she didn't love him. I thought the opposite, that her husband had started straying first and continued to do so while remaining loyal to her. In the end, my father, who, in one of his *New Yorker* articles, had placed her in a class with Evelyn Waugh, agreed with me.

One day Dawn and I got lost on some of the really less traveled roads around Talcottville and asked the way of a very pretty young farm wife with no teeth in the real backcountry. Dawn went up to do the asking and we were invited to sit on the porch and have some lemonade. The woman told us all about her life and asked Dawn where her farm was, the sort of thing which never would have happened with Elena. I think because she knew she was dying (she had refused the operation which would prolong things, saying it was "a medical trick and my husband had had it"), she really enjoyed the return to country life, a far cry from her habitual watering holes in New York.

The Loomis girls treated her like a fourth sister, inviting her to lunch on her own and asking if she didn't find all that red plush very prickly to sit on in the heat. She said she thought the presidential rockers on the porch preferable, and they thought her very, very wise.

# XXIII

WHILE ELENA'S LIFE became more and more focused on the Cape, her husband's became more and more focused on Talcottville, partly because of his work: the Indians and Canada. Bill Fenton, the Iroquois expert, had become a good friend and an important reference for him with his vast knowledge of the New York State Indians. One of the most poignant trips was when my father and I drove to interview an old isolated Indian, an Oneida. We asked how we should address him by mail and he said, "Oneida Indian and his township."

The Haitian novelist Philippe Thoby-Marcelin had married a Sicilian girl from Canastota, New York, whom he had met while they both had culture-related jobs in Washington. They had bought a place on a beautiful hill in Cazenovia, New York. Their hilltop house looked over valleys and rolling hills which "Phito" said reminded him of the Haitian hills, totally different than the Talcottville countryside. The Marcelins' presence, not so very far away by upper New York State standards, was a big drawing card as far as my father was concerned.

We had first known Marcelin in his very rummy days when he and a bottle of rum, the Haitian national drink, were always cuddled up together. He and his brothers came from an aristocratic Franco-Haitian family, and he had been plunged into Washington's racial class consciousness because he was dark. His brother, Pierre, was tall and blue-eyed like Elena. Phito had a reputation as a poet in France.

My father thought very highly of Eva Marcelin, Phito's wife. At one point when they had gone to France, he had given them an introduction to Elena's friend, Nelly de Vogüé, whose claim to literary fame was that she'd had a brief affair with Saint-Exupéry. Elena always mentioned this about her, and perhaps there was some girlish rivalry about who had the biggest man of letters on her charm bracelet. My father had a theory that one's wife always had a blond friend the husband didn't like. And Nelly was it. Elena had gone to France, and Nelly had given her one of her mink coats, which didn't help Elena's Talcottville image when she came up wearing it once in the fall. The coat irritated my father, and he accused Nelly and Elena of being lesbians, which wasn't kosher.

In spite of that, he insisted the Marcelins see Nelly, which they did. I had met her once briefly in Paris, a tall blond, handsome woman, and a name to conjure with in Paris. The Marcelins trundled around, and she immediately assumed they wanted some sort of a favor, which they didn't. The last thing they wanted was to meet rich industrialists. Then Nelly told them how unspeakably sad it was that Elena had gone to live with a crude man with an impossible country place. Why had she ever succumbed to all that was inelegant and "unrefined"? The Marcelins went back to their hotel room, reeling from all this, begging Madame de Vogüé to please not introduce them to anyone, they were happy in their simple way. Phito, who had been brought up as a French aristocrat, was an enormously elegant person, even at his rummiest. He always refused to speak English, which was irritating of him.

After John Kennedy became president, Elena found it all very exciting going to the beach near where the Arthur Schlesingers had a house and hearing all of what she thought was the White House (summer and otherwise) gossip. She said she didn't want her daughter growing up in Talcottville, and it was true the seashore was healthier for her.

My father liked settling into a routine at Talcottville; he would get up in the morning, put on his bathrobe and hat, and after breakfast sit out on the front porch waiting for Mr. Iseneker, the mailman, as one waits for a lover. While everyone else had their mail put in their box, Iseneker brought his mail to him on the front porch. It made things impossible when I stayed with him because he always assumed all mail was for him. He didn't mean to read my mail, he just ripped everything open very fast, putting it in piles. One of the people I had an unromantic but amusing correspondence with was the composer Ben Weber. After several of his letters remained unanswered, he called me up and said, "You can't tear up a phone call." That's what he thought as my father's voice gruffed in on the downstairs extension, "Who's that? Who? I don't know you." Slam.

In the early Talcottville years, my father worked upstairs on the third floor in Jennie's old room at a plain white table-desk. In later years when the stairs became too much, he worked at the card table in the long living room downstairs, where Jennie's bed was moved during his last illness.

He and Mabel Hutchins, who cooked, cleaned and shopped for him when he was alone, would get on a schedule. And he functioned very well. Everyone told Mabel when she went that she'd never last. But she did in spite of the fact that one day when she came in and slipped with his tray, falling and spraining her ankle, his remark wasn't one of sympathy but "You've broken Mother's butter dish."

One of the great recreations in the Talcottville part of the world is driving around. Distances which would seem great in Massachusetts seem small there. One thinks nothing of going to Watertown to shop, 90 miles round trip, while a trip to Boston from the Cape, 106 miles, is regarded as quite long. There are many fascinating places to go: the St. Lawrence Seaway, the wine country, Canada in the fall for the beautiful, luscious Ontario peaches, the Russian monastery—there are endless drives. It's what my grandmother did when she came up with guests. It's what everyone does. It's what my father did. As he had no chauffeur, he squirreled away congenial people to drive him to delightful places. When Barry Callaghan looked at the Loomises' diaries, he said, "My God, the whole countryside was driving Edmund around." And the Loomis girls certainly did their share of it. Many of their entries read: "Took Edmund to Speculator to see leaves"; "Took Edmund to see beavers"; "Set off with Edmund for Adirondacks."

Elena walked a constant tightrope, knowing that my father might sell the Wellfleet house and move permanently to Talcottville. She kept trying to make the Wellfleet house pleasanter and pleasanter. But the proportions of the stone house were so beautiful, people felt at home with the universe in it. And he had buddies: the Crostens (Loran was professor of music at Stanford, and they discussed opera), and Glyn Morris and his wife Gladys.

Glyn had spent his life going into small rural communities setting up educational systems, and Gladys was a very good cook. Father loved to go over to the Morrises for supper. He and Glyn would have long theological discussions. Glyn had some of the little educational movies shown at the school. We found *The Life of the Chipmunk* very soothing. Gladys looked like an innocuous missionary's wife of some sort and was anything but. They both were Welsh, and Gladys could remember when, as a child in Wales, the English threw pennies and her grandfather would put his foot on them before she could pick them up, saying, "Don't you touch them." On Memorial Day, Gladys and Glyn would take some of the most impossible dirt roads over Tug Hill and place lilacs on the graves of the abandoned tiny Welsh grave-yards. For the Welsh were among the nationalities driven off Tug Hill, the wild plateau running between Talcottville and Lake Ontario. Dishonest land speculators, the Constable family, had sold the Tug Hill land to wave after wave of innocents, who died on the unfarmable soil. One night when Glyn and my father had been rambling on about God for hours, Gladys said to me in the kitchen, "God, to heck with it. He sacrificed his only son, didn't he?"

At any rate, Talcottville was no passing fancy for my father. And Elena's attempts at compromise—"Let's sell both Well-fleet and Talcottville and go to some middle place"—were futile.

# XXIV

ELENA'S FATHER'S YOUNGER BROTHER, Walter Mumm, came onto the scene sporadically in Wellfleet. He was very likable, and my father was fond of him; but it added sometimes to the overall European confusion. He was a towering wreck full of bullet holes where women had shot him, which he showed to Reuel and his friends. He had friendly brown, totally uncomprehending eyes and remnants of being handsome in a tall movie star way. Elena had fond memories of his taking herself and her sister out for good times to the best beauty shops and restaurants when they were young and treating them like grown-ups. He had worked in a liquor store in New York but was fading out. He had once said to Elena, "Let's have an affair." She had said, "Why, Walter, that would be incest." He said, "Just a tiny, tiny little affair."

He was a heavy drinker, always talking about "martinilets" and using diminutives for liquor just as my father said "a teeny-weeny little drink." He was very good-natured and gallant, but stubborn to the nth degree and was getting slightly sclerotic, eventually, sadly, becoming completely so. The undercurrent of Elena's German affairs, in which the whole family were always fighting over the patrimony, ran through it all. My father said to me he didn't want to know about her German affairs. I'm sure she didn't want to know about his tax affairs. Natalia Heseltine said she'd met some people in Europe who, when they were children, used to go to the Mumms' for dinner when Elena's father was reigning, and he was very chauvinistic and the atmosphere at meals was unbelievably heavy and gloomy. So perhaps she was continuing something in her own life with the meals my father cast an evil spell over.

When Walter was around, the German part of Elena predominated and they spoke in German a lot.

One night at dinner, my father turned to Walter and asked him what the best American champagne was. The veins stood out on Walter's forehead and he came dangerously near a stroke. "Edvmoond, Edvmoond, how many times moost I tell you. There iss no American champagne. There iss only American sparkling wine."

My father had spent some money putting in a heating system in Talcottville and Elena retaliated by having an intellectual turned carpenter add another study on to his study in Wellfleet. Like everything that particular carpenter did, it was cramped, with scroungy proportions, and in any sort of heat made my father long more for Talcottville.

One summer I taxied Elena and Father to Talcottville separately. First him, and he mentioned on the way up that he had left Leon Edel "in charge" of his literary remains. I said that was wonderful because he combined scholarship with some relation to life because of his journalistic experience. That was all we said on the subject. Forever when the subject of Mark Twain came up, he'd say how crazy it was for literary men to let their wives deal with their work posthumously.

A few weeks later, I drove Elena and my sister, Helen, up.

It was like driving Prince Igor—she felt as if she were going into hostile country. A week or so later, she called me and said she'd seen a ghost. I felt again as if I were back in school with Miss Tucker teaching Addison and Steele, Sir Roger de Coverley, *Coverley Hall, the Coverley Ghost.* Elena had come down early in the morning and seen a piece of material flitting about. My father never locked the door at night. Abijah Carpenter's sister Ann, who had had the battle with my grandmother about Abijah's buggy-riding with Jennie, wore long filmy dresses and would have thought nothing of wandering in in the morning and would have loved it once she realized she'd given Elena a shock. Ann Carpenter had no love for the Wilsons. When no one was in the stone house, anyone could get in with a skeleton key available at any hardware store. She'd probably spent a lot of time there. After Ann died, her house was occupied by an old lady who did the gossip column for the local paper and regularly reported that "Mr. Wilson was on from Fleetwell."

Anyway, the ghost and a young woman named Mary Pcolar did nothing to enhance Elena's feelings about her husband's ancestral home.

The first time I had become aware of Mrs. Pcolar was when I had come up for the weekend during my father's first years as squire of Talcottville. He and I were sitting on the front porch when a young woman drove past slowly. He hailed her, yelling, "Come meet my daughter," but she coyly drove away. "That's one of my contacts—and God knows I need them— Mary Pcolar; she's doing some typing for me and left her typewriter here." Then he turned to me and said, "My relationship with these girls is always absolutely proper." I believed it then, and I believe it now.

Mary typed for him, a great convenience, and she drove him around and he enjoyed the connection with her simple family. She was important to his comfort, and as the years went on he was true to character, very naughty, in using her against Elena. Elena referred to her as "the Madame Bovary of Boonville" with some reason: She, like Madame Bovary, knew pharmacists, and longed for a life beyond that offered by West Leyden and its environs. In the last years, Elena said she wouldn't have minded if Mary had "been better quality" and "It's a subject your father and I don't discuss," which was a very good idea.

In the spring when all the wild flowers on their hill were out, Mary would always drive my father over to the Marcelins for a lengthy lunch. It was intensely beautiful then.

There was so much gossip and speculation about Mary and my father, a lot of it much ado about nothing, that I sought out Eva Thoby-Marcelin, the woman I knew who had seen the most of them together. I said that the first time I met Mary for any length of time was in 1966. She was coming to drive my father to Sodom, New York, which he had long been curious about. Mary arrived looking fresh and competent in a pretty print dress she had made herself. I liked her. Barry Callaghan had called saying he was stopping on his way from Wellfleet to Canada. I spent the day entertaining him and his family. When Mary and my father returned, her husband, who had been working at the mill in Rome, came over, a sweetie, and we all had dinner at the Hulbert House together. The next time I met Mary, my father shoved us together when she drove us to Utica. He sat at one table with the man he was doing business with at the Fort Schuyler Club and Mary and I at another. Her eyes never left the table with my father, so I had thought she was rather rude. My father would have loved to tell Elena I had become great friends with Mary. Eva said, "Your first impression was right." Then she used the very words my father had used to me about Mary earlier: "You thought she was rude because she didn't know how to act." On that particular trip back from Utica, Mary told us the instructions she was taught for dealing with people who were being fitted for trusses at the drugstore. I found it very interesting. It was the sort of thing Elena deplored, saying that it was the part of him that liked the funny papers.

Eva said, "Once Mary was going to take her children to Washington. Your father sent her to the Schlesingers and my husband also got involved in showing her around. He was exhausted and famished because she wanted to see and know about everything and was oblivious to the comfort of others." That thirst for knowledge must have been wonderful to my father.

Mary's life started going downhill even before his death in 1972. She was in a terrible automobile accident, which left her scarred. After Father's death, her husband left her. I asked Eva, "Why?"

"Your father."

"But he was dead."

"That's just it," said Eva. "Knowing Edmund Wilson blew her mind. He opened up the world for her. She was a creation of his, and when he died, the part he created went to the grave with him."

He wrote her letters some people might misconstrue; but I've written people I wasn't in love with, letters about meeting me at trains, which I suppose might be misunderstood. His pleasure at returning to Lewis County was all mixed in with the pleasure of having her meet him. She told Barry Callaghan when he interviewed her she'd always dreamed of a younger man of the world like my father. (Nice going, Barry.) Barry thought she had innocence but that she was consumed by *her* grief, *her* relationship with Edmund Wilson. Eva told me that Mary was intelligent and assertive.

Like Emma Bovary's, Mary's life ended badly. She got in some financial trouble, and she and her second husband died in Florida of monoxide poisoning when a trailer heater went awry.

Mary—"Marushka"—had taught him some Hungarian, but as he outran his teacher, he started learning from our

214

friend Agatha Fassett in Boston, among others. Agatha was a Hungarian aristocrat married to a New Englander, a recording engineer, who did all of Jack Sweeney's recordings of the poets for the Library of Congress, and recorded the Boston Symphony as well as various opera singers and others who came through Boston. Often my father and Agatha, being exuberant over Hungarian grammar, as well as stories Agatha had about the Gabors vis-à-vis their past in Hungary, could be heard in Steve's supposedly soundproof part of the house, say, interrupting Ginsberg and Orlovsky. Steve would come up and say, "Agatha, Agatha, please curb your wonderful Hungarian hospitality." Agatha would get calls from Talcottville—my father saying, "Marushka's here and she says such and such." "That's peasant Hungarian," Agatha would say. And they'd go on for hours. You can be sure he was showing Marushka he had other contacts besides her. Agatha knew all about Hungarian literature and could recite all of the aristocratic poet Endre Ady by heart. However, she was a little vague about American history and one glass of wine could send her reeling. At a party of mine on the Cape, she had mistaken the Chavchavadzes' Uncle Horse (General Radzianko, head of the Russian cavalry) for General Robert E. Lee after some wine and in her pretty way asked him about Grant. Horse did look a lot like Lee. As Horse's nephew, David, remarked, "They both commanded losing armies in civil wars."

David also wrote to me explaining how my father and he ended up calling each other "Monstro":

It all started with a line in his play "The Little Blue Light," which sounded to me like something from the pen of one H. P. Lovecraft, who wrote weird books about star-spawned horrors and the like. I mentioned this to your father, who looked at me with respect for having heard of the man. (The only reason I had heard of him was because some of his

paperbacks were scattered about an army transport I was on
and I read them for lack of anything better to do. But I didn't
tell him that.) It turned out that Lovecraft was one of his
many unexpected hobbies, and he showed me a biography of
the chap in which he would address his friends as "Monstro."
This is how this form of address originated, and your father
used to call me that too.

The last time I had any actual discourse with Mary was in
1966 when my father received the National Medal for Literature. Roger Straus had come up for the night. The next
morning, my father arranged for Mary and me to go in one
car to the Fort Schuyler Club while he and Roger went in
another. She was to take us to the Boston plane afterward. He
was still hoping to be able to tell Elena that "Rosalind and
Mary got on famously." Mary took pictures all through lunch
(people tore them up as they were passed around), which
included Bill Fenton and his wife and the New York types
presenting the prize as well as a representative of Oxford
University Press.

My father, Mary and I ended up at the airport bar plane-
waiting. She ordered a pink lady. My father left for a minute,
and Mary said, "Your father's a foxy old man." He returned,
Mary left, and he said, "Funny how foxy the faces of these
Hungarians can become." Well, I thought, "They're on some
sort of a telepathic wavelength." In Article 5 of his will, he
mentions both Danny Walker, the Walkers' youngest son, and
Mary Pcolar. "I give to Mrs. George Pcolar of West Leyden,
Lewis County, New York, my small Hungarian dictionaries
and my copy of Sándor Petöfi's *Poems* and my book of Hungarian paintings in the Budapest National Gallery, and I give to
Daniel Walker of 204 Prospect Street, New Haven, Connecticut, my library of magic and magical apparatus." He thought
of Mary and Danny in the same way: two people with whom
he had shared an interest and for whom he had affection.

# PART

V

# XXV

THE IRS WAS AFTER my father for nonpayment of taxes. His troubles weren't helped by the fact his lawyers in New York City said they'd lost all the papers connected with his problems which showed he'd been trying to do something about the situation. It was a bad time for him. And Elena stuck with him through it all.

In 1958 when he was in the most tortuous phase of his tax problems, I was about to inherit some money and our finances were to become intertwined forever. I tried to help out a little. He wanted to give me Talcottville and in a letter that sounded just like my grandmother's letter to me about Swarthmore, I rejected it: "The idea of giving me Talcottville is unsound although your lawyer may think it's a good legal gimmick: (a) from a psychological point of view, as I assume you are going to spend the summers there; (b) it will make me responsible for all the upkeep; and (c) it will add a large taxable sum to my total income. . . . I will be glad to drive you around in October for a week. Please let me know what week, and please drop the Talcottville idea."

I was being totally pigheaded—I had had so many threats of "If you don't do so and so, I won't leave you Talcottville"—but I wasn't really inheriting so much money that I'd be on easy street. I had to hang around where the jobs were in case I needed one. But it was unspeakably dumb of me. Still, all the years of "I'm afraid if I leave you Talcottville you'll make a ski lodge out of it" had been irritating. The threats had been so endless.

I left Houghton Mifflin in 1958, returning four years later for a year. The summer of 1963 was a wild one in many ways. For the only time in my life, I was drinking three martinis for lunch every day—just the martinis. One of my colleagues, close to the top of the firm, was having a strange passage in her life and with my usual weakness I began to simulate her feelings. Craig Wylie had become managing editor. He was a wonderful man and a great editor, indispensable to the firm because he could not only deal with the big American history books but with fiction as well. His father was the man who ran off with Elinor Wylie, and his mother had brought Craig up in such a way that he had a real split concerning creative people like Miss Wylie as opposed to the other people. He would often go about the office saying, "That woman, that goddamn woman," referring to one of us. I never knew if he really meant Elinor Wylie or his mother. He unfortunately instituted schoolmaster procedures, which were really something he'd imposed on his own character; but he certainly deserved an executive position if that's what he wanted. He became editor in chief but soon after died of cancer of the liver. I shall always remember him standing by himself one day by 2 Park Street with his hat over his heart as a parade with the flag passed by.

I was also going to the Cape and partying quite a lot.

I realized that Nina, Adelaide Walker and Elena were all in a swivet about a social situation which had developed.

There were two ladies in Wellfleet whom the three hostesses had seen a lot of over the years and whom everyone liked enormously. They were Mary Meigs and Barbara Deming. My family always referred to them as "the Meigses." They were lesbians. And the most extraordinary thing was that my father and Paul Chavchavadze, both of whom had been around the block a few times, wouldn't believe it for a long while. Extraordinary, because when I first met the girls at a picnic given by Bessie Breuer, Henry Varnum Poor's wife, Bessie had made no bones about the fact that they were and neither had they, it seemed to me. "They're just like two nuns living together," my father and Paul would say. My family saw a great deal of them, and Barbara had loaned my father money to bail him out of his tax troubles. Mary was an artist, Barbara a peace activist who went to jail on several occasions. They were extremely well heeled. Mary and Barbara eventually went very public about their lesbianism, Mary in her book published in Canada, partially subsidized by the Canadian taxpayer, and Barbara on a PBS program about homosexuals. Life on the Cape was so diversified that I hadn't seen them much except en passant but the other ladies had, and in the winter Barbara and Mary had dinner with my family almost every night. They were very popular socially with the Chavchavadzes and the Walkers too.

When my father was writing O Canada, a young Canadian writer, Marie Claire Blais, had been called to his attention. She naturally wrote in French and had been brought up in the archaic atmosphere of the Catholic Church in Canada. She had come to be in Cambridge, Massachusetts, and came to the Cape. Elena said to my father, "Don't introduce that girl to Barbara and Mary—she has lesbian tendencies and there will be trouble." There was. Before she moved in with her benefactors, one of the Russian contingent had been ferrying her back and forth from Cambridge, as he lived in Boston. "Pray for me, pray for me," she would command everyone. Finally he said, "You've absolutely got to stop telling everyone they must pray for you. Either they do or they don't because they feel like it. Pray I don't throw you out of the car."

When Marie Claire entered the Meigs household, she had a boyfriend; after a while he disappeared.

Marie Claire couldn't have fallen into a cushier berth. And suddenly the Cape hostesses had a flying wedge of three ladies to deal with. One day while Mary and Marie were walking, Marie Claire's eye was scraped by a branch. Mary Meigs says in her book how callow everyone was about it. I was running all over Boston trying to get her in to see Pollen, finally getting his wife at home. Mary Meigs felt responsible for the accident and wallowed in her guilt. And it was a good excuse for keeping Marie Claire around forever.

The person who in the end was the most distressed by the swift developments in the Meigs household was my father, as Mary and Barbara broke up and Mary Meigs and Marie Claire moved to Canada. He was distressed because he was in love with Mary Meigs.

My own point of view on all this was fairly dispassionate, as I'd never seen much of the Meigses. One night I'd sat with my father and Marie Claire while everyone else was out, and he grilled her about Canada. She was very intelligent about it, very different than when she was with Mary and Barbara. Then, she was always being bitchy to Barbara.

I had gone into his study one afternoon to say goodbye before going back to Boston. He talked about the situation, regretting he had brought "the little Canuck" into the Garden of Eden, and at the same time he was rather enjoying watching the setup. He said of Marie Claire, "All my life I've been attracted to women of talent. But I think I'll skip this one."

I thought his attraction to Mary Meigs was based on a time warp. He'd told me she reminded him of girls of his youth. Actually she was just the sort of woman my grandmother would have been glad to have him marry except for the one little barrier of her lesbianism.

She was very rich. She was presentable, pretty and well dressed. She could draw a little, paint a little, write a little, perhaps play the piano a little, but not well enough to have the inconveniences women of real talent often have. She was well educated, with a very American frame of reference, and my father longed for that sometimes. And there was the challenge of her lesbianism. She and Barbara had created a comfortable household with all the little luxuries, sending to the best places for delicacies; and during the Cape Cod winters it was an oasis. He'd exhausted his exploration of Adelaide Walker and Phyllis and a harsh exile Frenchwoman, a year-round resident, long ago. Elena said, "It's the only person since we've been married he's been seriously interested in. I don't make a fuss because she's a lesbian. I do say, 'Let's see who will do what with whom.' "

Marie Claire and Mary went to live outside of Montreal. Marie Claire was not faithful; they eventually split romantically. Whatever happened, Mary Meigs and Barbara Deming had been an important part of my family's life at one period, and there was genuine affection all around. I never saw the Cape hostesses that upset again about any situation. It just showed how popular Barbara and Mary had been.

# XXVI

THAT SUMMER OF 1963 was really the beginning of the first glimmerings of the breakup of what had become the older generation on the Cape. My father had his first warnings of heart trouble and Paul Chavchavadze his. In Paul's case, he fell on the floor. They had their son's old nurse staying with them taking care of their grandchildren, and she said of Nina, "She stands there so bravely while her prince is on the floor." While everyone else was instituting emergency measures, she ruminated on Nina and Paul's wedding, "And there were three queens there." Finally, someone persuaded her to stop her historic monologue and put a pillow under Paul's head.

My martini-izing at lunch and lifestyle caught up with me, and I had a breakdown just as my father was off to Europe. Elena had gone already. He called me from the airport, and I told him off for no reason. He realized something was wrong. After ten days, I got out of the hospital, and he took me back to Wellfleet.

While I was in the hospital, he brought me a copy of *Vogue* magazine. I opened it to an article by Leonard Woolf saying, "Added to my worries about Virginia during her breakdown were my worries about 'her doctor, sir,' whoever he was," which made me distrust the boring resident. They had my father searching my apartment thinking I must have been on something. But I wasn't. A lot of it had been the martinis; I had never been able to do any steady drinking and neither could he. That's what confused people about him. He drank vast quantities at times, but then there were times when he didn't.

In the hospital, I started smoking like a chimney for the only time in my life and had called him in Wellfleet asking him to wire me cigarette money. "Can't you borrow it from Dr. S.?" he asked. It was the first time it ever occurred to me one could hit up one's nut doctor for a fiver.

Whatever our troubles had been, he saw me through that breakdown completely. One of the doctors asked me how he seemed to me.

"The same as ever," I said.

"Subdued," the doctor said.

He was extraordinarily cheerful about postponing his European trip and being on the Cape, buying me birthday champagne and being as pleasant as possible. One of the causes of his cheerfulness became apparent—Mary Meigs was there alone. Mlle. Blais had gone to Canada and Barbara was off somewhere out of state. He walked over there a lot. And she had us for dinner. I was fascinated because she immediately tried to put me in a male role; instead of my parent, she asked me to carve the roast, etc., which I've never been able to do. It was rather eerie.

The worst aspect of my breakdown was the feeling that the real world was unreal. My father said he had had the same feeling, which is why he was so sympathetic with me during my breakdown. After a few weeks, he went to Europe and I went into a psychosomatic ward of the hospital where my doctor was, as I had gagging nervous spasms and was depressed. I went to work from there, doing good work, going back to the hospital at night where people would come and visit me. In fact, I was in a three-bed room where only two were occupied and several visitors found the atmosphere of the hospital so congenial I had a hard time preventing them from crawling into the third bed to retire from the cares of the world.

There was a congenial and varied group at the hospital—a lively, amusing bartender and others. The common room where we watched television and had our milk and crackers had a nursery atmosphere; people would come in to see me fresh from the Parker House bar and find it all very cozy, not leaving until the night nurse threw them out. Kennedy was assassinated and we, and a lot of other people with their minds on themselves, were blasted out of our doldrums. One of the doctors came in and said, "Well, the fairy tale is over." I didn't feel that way. I'd never been that sold on the Kennedys. If you had lived in Boston and weren't one of their loyal following, you were rather likely to believe them a continuation of the old Boston political machine. On one of his birthdays, Elena asked my father what he wanted. "For you not to wear your Kennedy button," he said. Elena was infatuated with them. My half sister Helen's nurse, a Polish woman, had worked for the older Kennedys and said everything was "politics, politics, politics." Any connection would fill Elena with satisfaction. The Chavchavadze grandchildren had come down on the presidential plane, as their mother, who came from Washington, had a connection. Nina had gone to the White House at Kennedy's request and met him. "You're real," he'd said quite rightly.

A really first-class nervous breakdown is expensive. Luckily, Dawn Powell sold the only story I'd written since I'd won the *Mademoiselle* prize to the *Ladies' Home Journal*. It was so generous of her. Broke as she always was, she'd paid to have it typed up. "I'd give up your own mittenwork on the keys," she wrote, and sold it to the editor over lunch, after his third martini, I guess. I wrote another one in the hospital, which they bought, and it helped pay the hospital, which was more expensive than the Ritz.

In January of 1964, my year at Houghton Mifflin was up and I left. The firm went public and some people were flabbergasted to see the salaries the directors had been making as they told people at Christmastime that business was bad and handed out three-dollar raises. It had been a happy experience when I first worked there, a first-rate private firm with its own press, but the pay had always been abysmal (except, as it turned out, for the hierarchy).

In the early spring, I met my family in Rome for three weeks. It was a wonderful time for all of us. My father was paid royalties in Italy and we lived in luxury at the Hotel de la Ville. Natalia came from her home in Geneva and drove Elena, Helen, who was at school in Switzerland, and myself to Assisi as a treat. When we weren't sightseeing, I'd lie in bed, true to Red Bank tradition, reading James Bond, which my father had scoured Rome for, and eating Italian chocolates. Elena was in a good mood in Europe, and she and I saw a lot of her girlhood friend Olga Fersen, whom I knew from a previous visit to Rome. My father described their household in *Europe Without Baedecker* in the chapter "The House on the Hill." Olga was a descendant of Count Fersen, who helped Marie Antoinette over the border, and they were the only Fersen in the Rome phone book. Elena and Olga talked about the balls they'd been to in their youth in Rome as we sat over our Camparis in the sun at the cafés. Olga was still a beauty—tall, blond, blue-eyed, less vivid than Elena but more patrician-looking—and they must have created a sensation together. Elena, for obvious reasons, was much more at home in Europe; her German side came out only once though, in Assisi when she beat her umbrella against a closed church for twenty minutes. We went down into the catacombs and when we were coming up a long flight of stairs and my father wavered, the priest told him, "Pope John was just here. You are walking in the steps of a very good man." Father was so heartened by this thought he almost vaulted up the rest of the way.

We had dinner at the Italian critic's Mario Praz, whom I knew before from Rome and Wellfleet. The Italians thought he had the evil eye because he was wall-eyed. His apartment was all Empire. People said his wife left him when he made their child sleep in an Empire crib. It was rather depressing having the faces of Napoleon's generals looking up at you through your dinner remains.

When he came to Wellfleet, he was sitting in the kitchen the first morning there, very homesick. As I gave him his American coffee, he looked up at the sky and said, "Your sky is so low." Then the village idiot, who delivered our special-delivery letters, came in. He threw his arms around Praz saying, "You've come. You've come from a long, long way." And I never saw him act that way with anyone before or after.

Praz had a grant to come to America and study neoclassic architecture and was astounded to find some of the houses had blown-up plastic pillars. America to him was low sky, plastic pillars, and being hugged to death by the village idiot, and he never understood how my father could read James Bond, though Praz tried after we told him about Agent 007.

# XXVII

O NE OF THE WHOLE FAMILY'S greatest pleasures were the stopovers on the way to and from Talcottville chez Helen Muchnic and Dorothy Walsh. My father had become friends with Helen, prominent in the field of Russian literature, when he lectured at Smith. He was then married to Mary McCarthy. Helen saw him through it all. Dorothy's field was philosophy, and Father took her very seriously, considering her, he sometimes said, "as perhaps the most brilliant woman I ever knew." He said if she had been a man she would have had much more recognition. Dorothy and Helen were both enormously popular with their students. They had bought a delightful, rambling and superbly comfortable house in Cummington, Massachusetts, which, oh joy of joys for my father, was exactly halfway between Wellfleet and Talcottville. Dorothy and Helen were a constant factor in the annual Talcottville-Wellfleet transition. Over the years, Dorothy and Helen hosted Wilsons in various stages of exhilaration, depression, rage and domestic troubles: Elena's crying that she and my father were divorcing; I that I was fed up with their annual Talcottville feud; my father's complaining about all of us.

But they always rolled out the red carpet, with lavish food and drink, and did everything but carry my father in like a pasha in a sedan chair. They would invite various notables around Cummington including our cousin Tom Mendenhall, who for a while was president of Smith. There were some great after-party breakfasts. Both the ladies were stimulating to my father intellectually and more than worthy opponents when they took him on. They were both extremely amusing and attractive people.

While Mendenhall was president, Newton Arvin, who was teaching at Smith, got in some sort of a homosexual scandal with sailors. Tom stood by him. "I'm glad Tom has behaved correctly in this," my father said. Helen said, "The mother of one of the girls had written, 'Mr. Arvin mustn't be fired. Where could our girls be safer.' "

Tom and his renowned mother, Dorothy Mendenhall, were somehow connected with earlier controversies about the inheritance of the stone house. After my father's death, I drove the enormous bust and pedestal of Tom's mother at age sixteen over to him, as it was unnerving me as I passed it at night in the upper hall. It took two men to get it out of the house. When I got it to Cummington, tiny Dorothy Walsh bent her knees and tossed it into Tom's car while we huskier types stood by. She was used to building stone fences on their place. Later I got a note from Tom thanking me for bringing the monstrosity over, ending, "And of course my wife is greatful [sic] to you for making it possible to have the stony stare of her mother-in-law on her always. We have three other busts of the same subject."

Whenever he left Dorothy and Helen's, my father was on an intellectual high. One time he had a slug of their fine Russian vodka before leaving and said as he looked out on the sunlit Berkshires, "Those ladies always exhilarate me, and of course the vodka accentuates and emphasizes everything, the trees seem etched more clearly. How wonderful to be a writer and not have to go to an office." It was the sort of intellectual companionship he often missed and longed for.

The Muchnic-Walsh ménage had several of the Goodspeed Audubons from my father hanging on the walls. They added to the home-away-from-home atmosphere.

After I had left the remnants of my breakdown in Rome, Father and I went up to Talcottville for a while, naturally stopping in Cummington, where they made us sumptuously comfortable as usual. The thought of the stone house—which could be cold in early spring—seemed harsh to me, and I hated leaving the warm comfort of Helen and Dorothy's. The next night we spent at the Loomises, also very comfortable, although not intellectually up to Cummington. By that time, my father was raring to get into the stone house and a more rugged atmosphere. Something elemental in that house called to him. We got on rather well for a while. I was on a nonfiction kick, devouring biographies. My grandmother had said to me when I first went to Houghton Mifflin, "Rosalind, it's such nice clean work." Little did she know that the manuscripts when I did first readings were often the fictionalized confessions of gentlemen's sex lives from A to Z.

Father would work and I would read. We'd go out to "God's own restaurant," the Hulbert House, at night and fight over the Lytton Strachey biography which came in two volumes of bound galleys from the publisher. He reread and I read all the English memoirists: Lady Ottoline Morrell on Bertrand Russell—"bad breath"; Russell on Ottoline—"not a good lay"; and, of course, Strachey's mother's belief that if he'd only go to a seaside resort and take cold showers he'd like girls.

One day a man came around with a map and said the state in its infinite wisdom was planning to widen Route 12D in front of the stone house because there was so much traffic and so many accidents. Most of the traffic consisted of boys on motorcycles going by again and again and again. And the accidents had nothing to do with the width of the road. Anyway, it was the beginning of one of the worst jobs of road construction the State of New York had ever pulled. One of the head road men told me everyone knew it was a silly, unnecessary piece of road, but "the governor [Rockefeller] has been just like a kid with the road bond." It sounded like one of the Russian tsars at his most frivolous: "Let's build a paper village here and a dike there, even though there's no water to keep out."

I moved to Talcottville permanently in the spring of 1969 and was around for the grisly and insane construction. The winter before, I had had a small house in Wellfleet and it was not without interest.

I hadn't actually lived in Wellfleet for any length of time in years and things had certainly changed since my middle twenties. Naturally, the people still vigorous in the late forties were fading away. Waldo Frank had died the year before; my father said he caught the local undertaker looking at him amorously.

One of the symbolic changes was that there had been an old ramshackle oyster house in Wellfleet, Captain Higgins, a crumbling building at the end of a small wharf. Captain Higgins did a small business selling oysters and many older men—his friends—went, played whist, and chewed the rag with a gleam in their eye as they devoured the oysters. Higgins died, men no one had seen in years although you knew where they were, could be found sitting on the public bench in town flushed out like quail. Higgins' was now a place selling clam chowder without a clam in it at a dollar a bowl. I heard a customer ask a pretty little waitress, "Where's Captain Higgins?" "In the kitchen," she said.

The winter was marked by two important occurrences: the advent of Svetlana Stalin, alias Allelueva (her mother's name)—she said that God told her to come to the good old USA and that Paul Chavchavadze had contracted to translate her book.

I had become aware of Allelueva's impact on the American Russian sector when John Alden, who had succeeded Zoltán Horasti as rare-book man at the Boston Public Library, invited me to go to the New England Historical Society to hear George Kennan speak about her advent. Formal dress was required, so I called up Mlle. Richard, a French dressmaker, and asked her to whip up something suitable which I'd pick up the day of the event, as I was going to be away beforehand. She made something you might wear to a dinner at the Académie Française in the days of Anatole France, with a vast expanse of white material on my chest in case someone wanted to drape the Légion d'Honneur across it. It was a white filmy job with a red bolero. As John and I took our seats, I noted Edward Weeks, my father's bête noir, was seated directly in back of me, his foot in a large cast and cane propped up on the back of my chair. The chairs were the kind with a space between the seat and the upper back, beloved by undertakers and caterers. Weeks and I hailed each other cordially, as he'd always been delightful to me and I was a friend of his daughters. Two things became apparent to me during the course of the speech: one, Weeks' cast had a heel on it; two, George Kennan was rather in love with his subject. "This is an amazing woman," he said again and again, elaborating on why.

When it was over and I got up to leave, it turned out my dress was all caught up in Weeks' cast and cane, and we were irrevocably hitched together. It took almost half an hour for passing well-wishers to extricate us, with much physical pain to Weeks. During my father's last year, I told him this story, thinking it would amuse him. "That's just the sort of thing Weeks would do. He shouldn't have done it to you," he said.

I pointed out again it was all an accident. "What you don't

understand is that Weeks is a perfectly dreadful man," my father boomed. A month or so later he said, "One must never remain mad at anyone."

"What about Weeks?" I asked.

"What you don't understand is that Weeks is a perfectly terrible man," was his response. There was one old Bostonian who always used to say the same thing. I still don't know why really. In my father's case, Weeks' keeping Nabokov's manuscript too long at *The Atlantic* shouldn't have engendered that much hatred. Some people did throw up at Weeks' broadcasts beginning, "From my book-lined study on Boston's Beacon Hill." Mrs. Weeks' half sister had been married to Sir Henry Thornton and was Elena's stepmother; Elena loved the Weeks-connection ladies. And it was very embarrassing for her when my father wouldn't give an inch.

The White Russian line on Svetlana Allelueva was that her mother came from a good family, and that you couldn't have been on the outskirts of some of her father's purges without being touched by it. Nina was not at home with the prospect of Svetlana's visit, although she never said so. As Eben Given said, who came from circus people in the West and always wore a broad-brimmed hat, "Her pappy had his boys draw on Nina's pappy." Ms. Stalin stayed at the Chavchavadzes and apparently there were some extraordinary conversations between herself and Nina about "my Russia" and "your Russia." She was an attractive-looking blonde with frightened hands. Her brief stay created quite a wave, and people the Chavchavadzes hadn't heard from in years were calling and asking to be invited over.

Svetlana's visit was not a subject Nina ever liked to discuss after it was over; that and the subject of Anastasia were taboo. One night when I was alone with them, I asked about Anastasia, as Nina had just had to go to New York to see a false one. Nina turned to Paul and said, "Even Rosalind asks about it." I felt badly, but she said several things of interest. One, they were never sure the woman who had stayed with her sister Mrs. Leeds on Long Island was not Anastasia and, two, to me the most fascinating fact, Anastasia had been a very unpleasant child, pulling the wings off butterflies, *par exemple*, a far cry from Ingrid Bergman's attractive portrayal.

And then on the eighteenth of February the Truro murders broke, giving the winter folk enough excitement to last forever and bringing reporters from every national newspaper. I still had enough connections around Truro and Provincetown to get all the dirt.

My father was fascinated by the whole thing. How could you not be? Elena was snobbish about it, behaving the way she did about Mary Pcolar's talking about trusses. The one open argument Elena and I ever had. She said we were morbid and bourgeois to be interested in those murders. And it showed a love of cheap sensationalism. I said it was odd she took this stance, as she had done plenty of talking about Stalin's purges apropos Svetlana's visit. I ended by saying, "Of course, no one ever put Stalin under observation at Bridgewater [the state asylum where they'd sent the Truro murder suspect], but it might have been a good idea."

The discovery of the Truro murders started when a body, horribly mutilated, was found in a plastic bag in the most removed of the Truro cemeteries off the Old County Road which ran parallel to the then new Route 6, the mighty through road. The Old County Road was the road which a person with any knowledge of these parts was likely to take if he or she had been socializing and drinking over in Truro because the police concentrate on the main drag. Or often people took it because it was pretty. The first body was found a short distance from where Waldo Frank had been buried a year ago. The posse of men sent out from the North Truro air force base were reportedly sickened by what they found—one man was unable to eat for days. There was all the excitement and speculation such an event could belch up in the dead of winter: phone calls, conjecture as to whether the dead girl was a local girl, etc. The victim turned out to be a girl from Eastham, a pretty girl, who had always somehow been in hot water of one sort or another.

More and more bodies were discovered. It became like the carnage of some war. Gossip could no longer encompass the facts. The facts were so horrible they needed playing down rather than up. The bodies were those of girls under thirty, reportedly disemboweled, dismembered and chewed. Perhaps tortured while alive. The alleged suspect, a Portuguese boy in his early twenties with an overwhelming interest in taxidermy who had been reading law books in the Provincetown library that winter, and who was described by an extremely realistic and tough real estate agent as one of "the gentlest and kindest presences" she had ever met. He had almost talked her into giving him her studio rent-free that fall.

He had been married to a Portuguese girl, some said retarded, whom he had often burned with cigarettes—his signature when he slept with women? Neighbors in North Truro where the couple were living reported hearing the screams. A doctor and priest had been summoned one night when the girl had either been given or had taken rat poison. An attempt was made to report that to the police.

When the suspect was taken into custody, he was sent for the required observation period to Bridgewater State Hospital, where he was declared "legally sane." He was actually out of jail, where he should have been serving time for nonsupport of his wife, on the recommendation of a member of the Provincetown police force. The suspect had been a stool-pigeon, helping the police uncover a dope ring.

The published number of bodies by this time was four. It was believed the suspect had a heroin supply in the cemetery. At least, a tin box containing heroin was found there.

The victims had been lured to the cemetery, it was

thought, by the promise of dope. Two of them were school-teachers from Providence. Several tradesmen said to me they would be interested to see what Mafia-type lawyer was sent down for the defense. Where was the money coming from for heroin? There is a great difference in the price of a chocolate sundae at Newcomb's soda fountain, as things stood in my girlhood, and heroin. Some thought the murders might be ritual murders like the moors murders in England.

As the suspect was carted off to Bridgewater, many flower people made the Churchill V sign and screamed, "We're with you." The prisoner turned to the police and said, "Keep digging." Was he torturing the police who had had and would have the grisly job of finding an arm here, a leg there, from the numerous bodies? Was there another burial ground of boys who had mysteriously disappeared?

Two young girls, fifteen, one the daughter of an acquaintance of mine, left a piggy bank on Tony Costa's bed at the rooming house with a note saying, "We love you, Tony. This is to help you start your garage." Tony Costa was the name of this apparently appealing young man who knew the terrain of the Truro cemetery so well and used it so efficiently.

The police went through the cesspools of the houses in Provincetown where he had lived and reportedly found photographs and an earring of one of the girls. Some said there was an abortion mill in Provincetown, which seems unlikely. The suspect's mother called his landlady and asked for his hair dryer back. Feeling ran high among some of the Portuguese, who are a feuding and a formal people in the Spanish sense. One relative of the suspect flew at another woman in Bryant's grocery store, screaming, "It's lies. All lies. It was always the fault of his landlords. *They* got him on dope." In the case of the particular landlord whom the two women had been discussing, it was certainly not true.

Wag of tongue had other bodies discovered, bringing the count to nine in all, hushed up because of the tourist trade or for other reasons. The amazing thing about word-of-mouth concerning these murders is that you had the feeling that people were trying to play them down rather than up. And no matter how varied the source, the essential facts remained the same.

Some local people felt Tony Costa might have been led astray by the "brilliant intellectuals" in Provincetown. Well, who? "Well, ah, such as Norman Mailer." I have never met Mr. Mailer myself, but there were many dear ladies who watched from their windows and called each other up as he left or entered his house, much as generals watch troop movements during war. But Mailer wasn't a flower child, and apparently one of the flower-child ideas running parallel with peace through gentle contemplation as you slowly tear the petals of a flower is "purification through torment." Running parallel much as the Old County Road ran parallel to the new and dangerous Route 6 on the Cape. If you love someone you must purify them by tormenting them. I mentioned this to one reporter, very au courant with the hippie scene, who said, "Listen, doll, if I want to be purified *that* way, I'll do the tormenting myself."

Victims so often lack imagination and those poor little murdered girls whose remains were found in those shallow graves surrounding that particular Truro cemetery must have lacked it. Perhaps heroin held out the promise of imagination.

As I said, I knew the geographical terrain well from my girlhood and no place in the environs was better suited to a murderer's purpose. On the beach or on the dunes along the ocean beach, he might have run into beach buggies or park rangers; on the bay beach, an occasional set of lovers or "outdoor nut" who enjoyed a brisk walk on the more sheltered bay side in winter; and the other cemeteries were on a more prominent road, somehow collected on one hill with the town hall and several other churches.

The very excess of mutilation in the bodies in the murders began to give people an almost Grand Guignol feeling. Sick jokes started going around. The first murder had been uncovered when the police chief in Truro made a routine check on an abandoned Volkswagen on the dirt road to the cemetery. Where were the owners? People thought it might have been some sort of a romantic elopement which one of the girls had not wanted to tell her family about. Then the Volkswagen was found in a used-car lot in New Hampshire. The suspect claimed the two schoolteachers from Providence had sold it to him and produced a bill of sale, false as it turned out. The joke goes the suspect tried to trade the Volkswagen for a Mercedes. The car dealer said, "That will cost you a lot." The dealer named an exorbitant price. The suspect gasped. The dealer said, "I told you it would cost you an arm and a leg." The suspect said, "In that case I have the price."

How awful to be so empty that you fall for the promise of dope in the company of a strange young man, only met that afternoon, and go to a lonely cemetery. Much about Tony Costa was perhaps hearsay, but he had shot a girl up there with a bow and arrow, not fatally but severely. Such was his charisma, she took no action against him. His reputation in Provincetown was not savory, yet a respectable rooming-house owner gave him a room. The girls were staying there and met him. They met him again at the F'C'S'L'E, the hippiest joint in town, and off they went to the Truro cemetery.

Many sightseers came to the murder site. Some with shovels, to "help" they said, hoping to find an arm, a leg, an entrail the police had overlooked. Many people took children up there. One, the child of the Methodist minister in Wellfleet, who was taken up by a family not his own, cried all night.

One afternoon my father called and asked me to take him over to the Givens. Eben had called him and said Dr. Heibert was on television holding up some bones and describing the state of the bodies in a tremulous voice. He had been the doctor in Provincetown since the twenties, and there were many fantastic stories about him. We had an orgy of gossip about the murders.

Heibert, in his eighties, had done the autopsies, and the Commonwealth of Massachusetts had clamped down on him because he'd said too much to the press. The suspect knew and corresponded with at least one girl in New York, named Gail, who died mysteriously. A note was found in the rooming-house waste basket, saying, "I still think lovingly of Gail."

One early spring day, I took my father over to the Givens again. We went on the back road really absentmindedly and had a hard time getting through. So many sightseers had come down to "help" dig—children with buckets and shovels, their parents with spades—that it took seventy-five state policemen to cordon off the area. That day he gave his choicest puppets to the Givens' son, Eben, Reuel's best child-hood friend, who had often helped him with his puppet shows. I knew then he was looking toward the end of his life.

# XXVIII

I SPENT THE WINTER OF 1969–70 in the stone house, the first person to do so for seventy years. In the spring, I moved into Villa Rosalinda. I had never lived so far away from a big city before, and I was completely happy and loved it. If I'd lived in the Elizabethan Age, I would have been totally content to be a person of minor nobility who went up to court for a brief sojourn once a year. As my visits had been only short ones, a certain amount of Elena's view had rubbed off on me. I had always liked it, but her view that it didn't exist and neither did its inhabitants was catching. I realized when I came up for good that the people my father saw up here were very real and very important to him. Elena, for instance, always referred to Glyn Morris, one of the most important, as "What's-his-name, that teacher."

It was super evident that the road was going to go through. The Loomises and my parent kept adjuring me to keep constant vigil on the stone house steps, the graveyard and Loomis hitching post in front of Villa Rosalinda. The actual monstrous carnage hadn't begun, but the ominous young men from Rome kept coming around with their maps, supposedly to consult us but knowing exactly what they planned to do. I sent one of them up to the Loomises suggesting they give him a drink and try to win his confidence. He was supposed to come back and see me right away. When he didn't show up for three hours, I went up and found they'd gotten him completely sozzled. "What have you done to this nice young man?" I said, simulating shock. But it did no good. He sobered up the next day and was back solemnly holding up one of his maps asking whether there were any old wells around and the whole routine. I said Talcottville was riddled with them.

I had begun feeling like Barbara Frietchie defending her country's flag. "Shoot if you must this old gray head, but spare Wilson steps, Loomis hitching post," she said.

My father and I led separate existences when he came up. I had my own activities and we had dinner once a week or so. One such night we were finishing up at the Turin Highlands Club when the waitress appeared with two crème de menthes which had been sent over by lawyer More. Al More introduced himself to us; they'd been sitting in back of us. Then More wrote my father a long letter about how the stone house should be preserved forever the way houses in Williamsburg were as it was a thing of rare beauty and historic significance. Eventually, when the road case came up, More said the house was of no significance whatsoever. Several years later, there was a long interview with him in the paper about how the state always paid fairly for land. What had he been up to? He certainly foisted himself on us. Did he want to find out whether my father was going to sue the state? Was he a spy for the state? Or did he hope my father would hire him as his lawyer? Or had he made a deal with the state? What was the point of the whole belabored operation? The state was very anxious to get hold of old deeds, maybe that was his purpose—to get information.

Certainly, from start to finish there was something strange about the whole boondoggle. Glyn Morris thought the road was so out of the way the state might be after my father for what he'd said about Robert Moses. That seemed paranoiac to me, although some other people had the same idea. I had taken my father up to see Jack Johnson, editor of the *Watertown Daily Times*, a man and a paper he thought highly of, and Johnson advised him to go see Governor Rockefeller, but he never did. He was running down. In Wellfleet, he'd been able to stop the new road cutting him off because there was a law saying you couldn't go through farmland and he owned some watercress. The *Watertown Daily Times* was very pro-Moses. When the book *The Power Broker*, a well-documented account of just what unlicensed powers Moses had had, came out, I thought it should be required reading in the schools. The *Watertown Daily Times* commented on what a heck of a guy Moses had been, a wonderful, kindly old man. It was a little like Al More's saying the state always paid fairly for land. Come on boys, go tell it to the Marines!

Elena came up in the summer of 1970 for a few days, and it was one of the worst cases of phobic reaction I have ever seen. If I mentioned anything pleasant about Talcottville, she immediately negated it. I took her to one of the really great swimming spots on the river. She said she was too old for that kind of swimming and reminisced on how they used to swim in the Rhine, going in at one town and floating downstream to another—something that's great fun to do on the Black River. Some instinct of self-preservation made her not want to be part of Talcottville in any way. My father really didn't want to go back to Wellfleet. She kept saying, "I won't leave without him," holding out the night at Helen and Dorothy's like a carrot. She told Glyn Morris, "Talcottville is not good for Edmund." She told me he saw only bootlickers in Talcottville, and so it went.

I didn't think Phito Thoby-Marcelin, Malcolm Sharp,

Walter Edmonds, Bill Fenton, Loran Crosten or Glyn Morris were sitting around saying "How so, Socrates?" to my father, and I thought them infinitely preferable to some of the scavengers of other people's taste who were crawling out of the woodwork in Wellfleet and who were poor substitutes for John Dos Passos. Although I was totally sympathetic to her difficulties with the situation, Elena did like admiring dependents around her really more than my father, who in the last analysis wanted people who could tell him off intellectually, not for an evening perhaps; but when it came down to the nitty-gritty, he scorned people who didn't. Glyn Morris, who saw a great deal of him from 1957 until the day before his death in 1972, said he noticed he always asked for a pack of cards to do a trick when he was being upstaged and then put the tricks away after he was in control again. Natalia said he had once held forth to her and some other people on the fact that Reuel and I were always fooled by his tricks while his daughter Helen saw through them.

One of the prominent things in the long room as I went through the house after his death was an enormous card in a holder with a couple of silk handkerchiefs lying next to a puppet of himself someone had given him which gave me the creeps. They were up on the bookcase as you came in to the right with other remnants of his magic. It was amazing that someone so clumsy manually in some things should have the skill to be a really first-class sleight-of-hand artist.

I always tried not to spend the Fourth of July with him because there was a disgusting piece of early pink and white cloth with Revolutionary scenes on it which was dragged out. The square of material had been put in the bottom of the cribs of all the Kimball babies and was full of unpleasant yellowish spots. My father took it with him to Talcottville and lovingly laid it out on a chair arm the morning of the great day. Some people hoisted the American flag; he displayed the cloth. The idea was, people would come to drink and toast the glorious. One Fourth in Talcottville, he and I sat alone with the decaying fabric for a long while and eventually the Loomises surfaced. Thank heavens we all got out of the house for dinner.

It was always exhilarating when one had the girls in tow to see the reaction of the often young waitresses when they asked the frail old ladies in an and-what-will-you-have-dear tone of voice, and Huldah and Gertrude said, "Two double daiquiris straight up, easy on the lemon juice." The sisters were thin as pipe cleaners and looked as if there was no displacement capacity to hold the huge meals they downed. Gertrude had become very sclerotic and would often put the restaurant silver in her handbag, although she was as pretty and sweet as ever. Sometimes she'd place her hands on her head and say, "This old head of mine serves me ill." It was tragic. She was the only person who thought I had naturally rosy cheeks when I was tarted up with Miss Elizabeth Arden's rouge. At Christmas they kept an eggnog standing by for the twelve days of Christmas. Anyone going in would come away clobbered. The mother of one boy who went up there to shovel snow said, "Of course, the amount of nutmeg they use is a hallucinogenic. I don't mind the Four Roses that's in it." The Loomis girls had been told by a teacher, "Never tell a lie falteringly," advice they adhered to all their lives.

There was always some sisterly jealousy, as Huldah was queen bee. After her sisters died, Huldah went up one Memorial Day to see her sisters' graves, where her footstone was already in place. The woman who worked for her had placed flowers on her sisters' footstones. "Where are the flowers on my footstone?" Huldah crabbed. "There ain't nobody at home there yet," the woman said.

The Loomises kept a picture of their graveyard. To them, dying was just going to another corner of the farm. My father wasn't sure what dying was, but his mind was turning more and more to it when he came up to Talcottville in 1971.

# XXIX

I N 1971 I WAS CAUGHT between the devil and the deep blue sea as far as Father and Elena were concerned. She kept telling me that if he came to Talcottville it would kill him and to discourage him; he was planning to come up no matter what. The road was going through, with one of the most sloppy, careless and dangerous construction jobs any company was ever a villainous party to. One day as I was driving the few paces from Villa Rosalinda to the stone house, a young man in a bulldozer brought me the closest to death I'd ever come, leaning out and crying, "I understand the man in that house is dying, and my wife wants to know about the antiques." Luckily for him, it's practically impossible to attack a man in a bulldozer. The beautiful elms which had lined the road, protecting it from the snow sweeping across so that the truckers preferred it in the winter to the new Route 12 below, were being burned on the hillsides. I wrote him: "As to the road, they have by-passed the cement steps, but it is going through with a vengeance, and Talcottville is almost unlivable. The noise begins at seven in the morning. It's so torn up and full of machines, it takes forty minutes or so to get in or out of town if you can see through the dust. The great supports for the bridge have been sunk. And nothing is going to stop it."

When Father came up, he had to be lowered off the airplane into a wheelchair. Bob Stabb, a master mason to whom he was devoted as a person and because a man who owns a stone house also needs a master mason, had come, dismantling Jennie's old Red Bank bed and bringing it downstairs piece by piece, reassembling it at the western end of the long room on the north side of the house. Next to the bed was a two-tiered table, behind it a bookcase and not so very far away, the chair and the footstool where he always read. By the chair, a birdcage table, and just a smidgeon yonder a large upholstered chair and card table where he worked.

When he first came up, he was in a very depressed frame of mind because he said Elena said he shouldn't even try and sell *Upstate*, he'd make a fool of himself. She'd got him believing what she thought: No one wants to read about a lot of old country people. I said that sort of thinking would cut out a lot of English and American literature. He girded himself for a New York trip. I had an ear infection. When he got to New York, he wrote me, in effect, "I have sold *Upstate* for twenty-five thousand dollars to the *New Yorker* and regard it as the highlight of my journalistic career. Here's a hundred dollars for your ear." I wrote and thanked him, saying it sounded like some sort of matador–bull ring deal.

The next I heard, Elena called me and said he'd been out in New York. He was staying at the Princeton Club. He'd gone to sit on the bed, missed it, and landed on the floor, cracking his back. Elena called her ex-stepmother, Martha James, who went around and arranged for a walker for him. Somehow he got himself back to Talcottville. Dr. Smith came and thought he might have a broken back (which it turned out he had), but he wouldn't go to the hospital to be X-rayed. "I just couldn't face Wellfleet again," he said as he lay in his narrow white bed. My sympathies were with him—the part of the Wellfleet house which had been rebuilt as his study was close in the summer for anyone with heart trouble, whereas the air came through the grand dimensions of the long room at Talcottville where his Uncle Tom Baker had lived, to whom my grandmother had so often likened him. I still have a little *Book of Promises, The Universalist's Daily Pocket Companion, Collection of Scripture Promises by S. Bullfinch Emmons* (a name to be proud of). It's inscribed "July 4, 1857, Adam Frink, 77 years old this day, To His Very Dear Friend, Thomas Baker, Tommy when you see this after I am gone, know that I loved you most dearly."

My father always said the *New Yorker* cut *Upstate* so it made no sense. It was almost a best-seller. When asked about it, he said, "It's selling beyond expectations, almost a thousand copies a week, which gives me one thousand dollars a week." He had no idea of the huge advances writers were beginning to get. Roger Straus was the only publisher who had lasted in the field with him and he liked him, leaving Roger a painting of himself in his will. Roger could always make him laugh. But occasionally he'd put down the phone and say, "Roger is wailing again. He's doing this wailing. And when he wails, he wails."

On one hand, he would talk about the fact he might sell the house; on the other, he called Dr. Smith's office on some pretense, really to talk to Smith's expert nurse, Katrina Seiter. He said he understood her mother had died recently and had any of the Baker antiques become available, not a word of regret over Mrs. Seiter's demise. He'd talk to people who came in and wanted to buy the house, but it was really part of his loneliness and wanting to see people. If he'd really wanted to sell the house, the only thing he had to do was do it.

There was road-digging in front of the house but nothing to what it was to become, with great trenches like something out of World War I. He had to enter and exit through the kitchen instead of the beautiful, majestic front door.

He said he thought a lot about how "Mother must have felt at the end." Helen Muchnic and Dorothy Walsh had been up to see him a few years before, taking pictures of him. They were colored pictures, and his face is very florid in them, terrifyingly so, a bright salmon pink color. He had them pose him for two of the pictures: one sitting at his white table-desk in Jennie's old room where he once worked and at which he is obviously no longer working; and one where he asked Helen to take him "where Mother's garden used to be." As Ms. Muchnic says, "It's nostalgic." There is also a charming one of him sitting laughing with Dorothy Walsh on the loveseat in the living room with an iceless glass of scotch before him under an oval painting of an Adirondack lake, its gilt frame visible (it was stolen in a burglary in April 1973), and one they took of him leaving what later became Villa Rosalinda but where the Sharps were then staying.

He had absolutely refused a pacemaker. He went about his Talcottville schedule, playing solitaire, doing some work, going out to dinner and to the movies with one of his drivers, and in the last years he had salted away a groupie with a large, comfortable heated car for his list of chauffeurs. Like an old concierge, I had seen them come and seen them go, and she was the only truly silly one.

When I had first come up for good, I'd been contacted by a group in Lowville, who had soon lost interest in me socially when they found I wasn't a swinger eager for fun and games. They didn't hold it against me, they just found the thought of me dull. My father's latest companion was an offshoot of that.

One of the group had tried to persuade me as to the "harmless" joys of marijuana. Shortly after, I had gone down to a house party in Washington at Dr. and Mrs. Geoffrey

Tooth's. Xenia Tooth is a cousin of Natalia's and the Chavchavadzes and Geoffrey is an English psychiatrist. He had helped to set up the drug rehabilitation system in England and upon his retirement was brought over here by our surgeon general to act in an advisory capacity. I asked Dr. Tooth which he considered the most dangerous drug. He said, "Marijuana," because they knew the least about it as there were so many kinds.

Ms. Groupie's eyes were as glazed as Rado's had been so many, many moons ago when he sighted Jeannie Clymer on the Provincetown boat. She was better-looking than Rado. She was in heat over fame. Like the moose who used to rush down to the tracks when the Canadian Pacific Railroad trains had a certain whistle that simulated the male moose's call, she was unreachable in her onslaught, her little hand-tooled boots quivering with excitement as she sat cross-legged or bumped around, her miniskirt bobbing up and down. What a great, distinguished plum had come into her life to make up for boredom, rejection. The classicist Edith Hamilton said you should be able to sit in a railroad station and entertain yourself in your own mind almost indefinitely. This little lady couldn't have stood by the Loomises' hitching post and gone any place in her mind for even a minute. Eventually, she showed up in Wellfleet with a man of the cloth in tow. Oh, the thrill of it all!

Elena tried to explain that my father had been on a heart diet for some years, which his housekeeper was following in Talcottville, and that my sister Helen was a follower of Adelle Davis. Reuel lived in London, Ontario, and was well aware of the vitamin E heart clinic there. (A few years later, they sent Phito Thoby-Marcelin back from there unable to help him.) Elena met with the same glassy-eyed response from the single-minded Ms. Groupie. He knew he was dying, and he was meeting death with great courage. Far better to be ramming around the countryside with an eager lady than to sit at home waiting for death. In that way, she served her purpose. The only time we ever discussed her was when he asked me once if she'd ever told me about her life and how she was left while her husband went off on business trips. I said: "No." I had them to dinner once when he was away with some other people. After dinner, I'd come in from the kitchen with a ginger ale and Ms. Groupie had leapt across the room tasting it to make sure it was ginger ale. "How can I communicate with someone who doesn't realize if I'd felt like gin I would have brought the bottle and put it to my lips!"

"She drinks like a fish," he said. "I cajole her along with saying 'I can still get the prettiest ones.' "

He was also doing what we all do sometimes when faced with big disasters—keeping his mind on trivia. He watched Ms. Groupie's life like a soap opera, only there were no commercials. At one point, I came in late one afternoon, shortly before he died. He'd introduced her to Glyn Morris and was doing a little matchmaking. I told him I thought Glyn had other plans. "That's a gloomy thought," he said.

The truth of the matter was outside of its architectural beauty—the stone house was much better suited to his physically deteriorating condition than Wellfleet. In Wellfleet, in order to leave his reading chair and go to the bathroom, he had to navigate four steep stairs up and down. In Talcottville, the bathroom was flush with the floor and adjoining his beloved long room.

My father was having a lot of dental work done by Dr. Edgar Miller. Elena said the dentist in Boston didn't want to do it because he felt my father's health was too precarious. I don't know if this was part of her anti-Talcottville crusade or true. He liked the Miller brothers, both fine dentists, and their upstate heritage, feeling close to them on that account. And he had to chew to live. But Elena was in communication with his doctors. I was not. And she bore the brunt of his care, devoting herself entirely to it when he was with her. After my father's death, Dr. Miller became a follower of Bhagwan Shree Rajneesh, who wound up in a southern jail complaining he didn't like corn grits.

Even before Gladys Morris' death two years before, Father had gone for supper at the Morrises' on several occasions in his bathrobe and pajamas. One night he took off his bathrobe because it was hot. He felt totally at home with Glyn and in his house, always greeting their cat with "How's that old puddy cat." One night when Gladys was alive, he'd gone into raptures over her cooking, her roses and how she never had artificial flowers as some people did. She let him rave on, saying, "Everything in this house is real, Edmund," eventually pointing out that the floral centerpiece was artificial.

My father was always very open about his drinking. No one could ever have called him a secret drinker. Friends of his were not so open. One of them was a severe alcoholic in and out of dry-out centers all the time. My father never suspected. It was part of the mind-on-myself aspect of his character. He couldn't have cared less if someone was or wasn't an alcoholic; it was a strange deception on his pal's part. Strange and sad.

He enjoyed having Glyn say grace and found the whole atmosphere of the Morrises soothing. Glyn had a trained mind and part of the training was to keep it open, which made him a receptive conversationalist and sounding board as far as my father was concerned.

# XXX

W HEN MY FATHER came to Talcottville in late May
1972, Elena said the airlines wouldn't have taken
him if they'd known how sick he was. She also
said Mary Pcolar had encouraged him to come up. But Glyn
and I knew that had nothing to do with it. He pushed himself
to come up. I'd had an emergency telephone with a long line
put in the downstairs room, and an oxygen tank was delivered. Elizabeth Stabb, Bob Stabb's wife and a trained nurse,
and I waited for him to get in, with Elena calling all the time
to see if he'd arrived safely. He had followed his usual routine
of having Mary meet him in Rome and having dinner on the
way over. When he arrived, Liz had to lift his leg out of the
car, but she got him to his bed and stayed with him. He made
his own arrangements with her about when she was to come.
She was also holding down her regular job at the Sunset
Nursing Home and successfully bringing up a family of eight
children. He regarded the Stabbs as old friends.

Ms. Groupie was down before you could say "Jack Robinson" to amuse him the next day, and he led his usual separate life, making his own arrangements and seeing whom he wanted to see. On several occasions, he asked people to tell Ms. Groupie not to come.

He wasn't drinking at all. He'd pour a drink for old times' sake but not drink it. Next day it would still be hanging around with a piece of paper over it. His pulse was very slow. He and I never discussed his condition, except he told me, "I've been told people in my shape go into comas where they seem dead. Be sure I'm not buried alive."

He had me drive him past Dr. Smith's several times. I think he wanted to be sure Smith was selling chestnuts at the same old stand.

Every afternoon Glyn would come and take him out for a drive. My father would throw a trench coat over his pajamas and bathrobe, and wear his bedroom slippers and inevitable brown felt hat. They drove all over. There was no road that Glyn didn't know, dirt or otherwise, and which he didn't travel in his sturdy Volvo. They'd come back and Glyn would settle him in lovingly. My father would thank him again and again for everything, saying, "You're used to caring for sick people." And of course Ms. Groupie would show up pretty regularly to be taken out to dinner.

He and I had dinner out a few times, I usually ordering a double martini, straight up. One night he shook his head over that, fondling his double scotch, which he didn't drink. I kidded him and said he'd never gotten over giving the lecture at Onondaga (an Indian reservation) to the Iroquois Temperance League. He and Olive Fenton had gone over, as Bill was at the American Folklore Society in Indiana in 1962. The occasion was the Peter Doctor Scholarship Award Dinner. Olive Fenton said my father was nervous at first with all those Temperancites but relaxed as he discussed his *Apologies to the Iroquois*. When they eventually got back to Albany, he had a couple of stiff ones at the Fentons and called his tax contact at the IRS whom he referred to as "Boris Karloff." He was worried about his taxes at that point.

Bill Fenton was someone he took very seriously. At one of our last dinners, Father spoke of a letter I'd written him one April Fool's Day claiming to be a woman who had new Jonathan Swift letters and said he'd really been fooled for a while because he wanted to be, and because he wanted to believe there was more Jonathan Swift material around. He remembered the letter almost verbatim. April 1972 was the only April Fool's Day in years we hadn't exchanged jokes. The letter turned up at Yale marked "April Fool's Letter by Rosalind" in his handwriting (see Appendix).

He was leading the life he always led in Talcottville. Mary Crosten came in to see him. Her husband was out at Stanford and she was staying with our friends the Howlands in Boonville, supervising the building of her new house. Charles Helmsing, manager of the Fort Schuyler Club, came up and sent a photographer up a few days before my father's death. Helmsing was one of the people he really enjoyed, as he knew his way around literature, and spoke Russian well, as well as several other languages. I was spending some nights at the stone house with him, Liz, others. One night as I dozed off on the loveseat, he came in and poked me with his cane. "Some watchdog you turned out to be."

He was often very uncomfortable, having a miserable time getting in and out of bed or navigating at all. Once when our old dog Wrecky was dying, we had all been commiserating with him when he had a hard time getting up. "You mustn't watch him in his indignity," my father had admonished us.

# XXXI

I USUALLY WENT OVER to see my father in the evenings for a
few minutes before he retired, and on one of these occasions I told him that the literary executor of a friend of ours
had run into the trouble a lot of literary executors run into in
that the dear departed had been writing letters about the literary executor to people. "Well, everything has to come out always," he said. I think he really meant it. In his own diaries,
everything didn't come out. He certainly had been in love with
Helen Augur at one point in the days when we used to go up
from Red Bank and stay in the apartment building she owned.
She was a very competent nonfiction author and newspaper-
woman. Her book on the Caribbean was a standard. She
loaned us a duplex which was wonderful. There was a spell
when he could talk of nothing else but Helen, how pretty and
intelligent she was, and he didn't know why his mother didn't
like her. Helen wasn't a fast talker like Fern Munn. Fern was a
big wheel in the Republican party in Lewis County. And Helen

was a hypochondriac. People don't always tell all in their diaries.

At one point, Helen had found herself in the stone house taking care of both Phito Thoby-Marcelin and my father, who were on a drinking spree together. One night she'd just run out of the house, called Elena and said she couldn't take it; few people could. My father's reaction was that Helen was neurotic. He would say awful things to me about people and awful things to people about me. But it was really part of the Red Bank habit of thinking out loud. If you were deaf in the period my grandmother was, without modern appliances and training, you often think out loud, and if you're with a deaf person you are likely to do so. The nearest my grandmother could come to natural hearing was when she hooked up a headpiece with wires attached to a box with batteries she set before her. And she did this only when playing bridge. It was an impossible apparatus to assemble for interspersed conversations in day-to-day life.

My father never spoke of Elena in the negative way he did about Mary McCarthy. He always spoke of her loyalty. In the last years, he had studied German with Elena and said she was "formidable" in German. He said when he was thinking of divorcing her that she really should have "married a rich man and led a different sort of a life," and that because of her failure to command the English language, sometimes people thought she wasn't with it. "But the old bean is working all the time."

He never discussed with me the fact that Elena had had eyes for someone younger in the later years, but he must have known it. I think it was over by the time he died.

Ms. Groupie with her big warm car might divert him, but Glyn was the person he relied on for interesting thought and conversation, and Glyn did yeoman duty as a chauffeur, nurse and companion.

I think when he came up to die, his mother and his family

background were much more real to him than Elena and Wellfleet. He had finished with that and his affairs in that part of the world.

Sandy had gone, and he was going. My cousin, Bob Hartshorne, Jr., said when they went to Red Bank for Sandy's funeral and drove through town, my father said wistfully, "Well, there's nothing about me here. Everything's Count Basie," that other celebrity son of the red clay banks. The old movie house was now the Count Basie Theatre, not the Edmund Wilson Theatre, and so on and so on as they drove down Main Street.

Even though the idea was that he was going to meet Elena at Helen and Dorothy's, he didn't speak of it with any reality as he usually did planning what to take them. He didn't talk about it at all. He talked about my grandmother and said he and I had grown up together. But had we ever grown up? Or were we still eating our hot cereal out of our childhood bowls? Two weeks was an odd length of time for him to arrange to stay in Talcottville. I honestly believe the elemental force which had always been part of his character told him he was going to die exactly when he did. One day he got up and went all through the house by himself, managing the two flights of stairs up to the third floor. I had told him that Natalia once told me of a phrase used by Dr. Geoffrey Tooth. The phrase was, "The aging Manolete delivered an acceptable veronica." Geoffrey said it covered a lot of situations if you were an aging gentleman. My father absolutely loved it as he adored a joke Roger Straus told him about an old sculptor who when asked upon receiving a prize late in life how he felt said, "I outlived the sons of bitches."

One day, a few days before he died, my phone rang and Glyn asked me to come over. When I went in, my father was sitting down in a chair he ordinarily didn't use, and he'd put the card table in a place foreign to where it always was. "Elena wants me to have this signed," he said. "She wants Helen to have the Wellfleet house." I said twice, "I don't want to sign this. I don't want to hurt Reuel. Get someone else."

"It won't make any difference." He said, "Don't worry." I scrawled "Rosalind Wilson" in a kind of handwriting I don't usually use. And my legal signature was Rosalind Baker Wilson. He winked at me as I left the room. "Remember when you were a tiny girl and I used to amuse you and Jimmy with the rabbit trick on the train?" I certainly did; it had whiled away the time on the long trip out West.

One of the Minor girls had been placed in his care from Charlottesville to New York when she was about seven. The first hours of the journey, he read silently. Then at noon, he suddenly looked up at her and boomed, "I know what little girls like. Pea soup!" It had been a favorite of mine, not hers. Unfortunately, it was on the menu; but she was compensated by the fact that all through lunch he made his handkerchief into a rabbit he could hardly control and took quarters from her ears, finally giving her a simple mechanical magic trick with a disappearing coin he kept on him for emergencies.

The only time we mentioned Elena's codicil after that was when I said to him later that day, "I signed that document under protest." He said, "Forget it, old dear girl, nothing will come of it. The aging Manolete has delivered an acceptable veronica."

I will never know if they tried to get him around to his lawyers' office in Boston the day before he came up or not.

For more than twenty-six years, the will had provided for at least half of the house to be left to Reuel "because he grew up there first."

# XXXII

A FEW NIGHTS BEFORE HE DIED, my father went to Rome to see *The Godfather* with Mary Pcolar; Glyn and I realized what horrible shape he was in and felt as if we were watching a game of Russian roulette. He didn't think much of the movie but anything was better than sitting at home as evening darkness fell, wondering when the old reaper was going to hit.

One night his dentist, Dr. Edgar Miller, and his wife came in, leaving him a lot of vitamins and a diet he was supposed to follow. After they left, he said to Mabel Hutchins, "That's a lot of nonsense," and had her take them out. He'd stayed on his heart diet for five or six years, except when Ms. Groupie took him out and fed him hot sausage sandwiches. Elena and Mabel Hutchins cooked him the most delicate low-cholesterol meals. Occasionally, he ran rampant at breakfast. But no one was going to take breakfast completely away from him. A lot of waiters in a lot of hotels had been given nervous breakdowns over his breakfasts. One hotel in France produced *le spécialiste de petit déjeuner*, an unshakable Spaniard. The person getting breakfast never knew when it was to be served. Very often you'd have everything ready only to discover your client had retired to bed again and was asleep. One morning in Wellfleet, I was interested to hear Elena say softly, "Oh, get it yourself," when my father's voice heaved out in a mighty cry of, "Where's the lemon for the kippers?" Certainly a far cry from the "Coming right away, dearest-est-est" of the early days, although that's what she still often said out loud, including the added "ests."

After his death, the Edgar Millers came and retrieved the vitamins.

One night before his death, he had a substitute trained nurse for whom he made out a check; she said his pulse was very, very slow. The day before his death, he signed his Social Security check and had me cash it.

On June 11, 1972, Glyn took him out in the afternoon. They drove along the Moose River Road to Port Leyden, passing the prominent cemetery there, large for the Lewis County part of the world. My father seemed fascinated by it, saying, "I'm going to be cremated." They talked of T. S. Eliot. He said Eliot wouldn't talk to anyone who didn't believe in original sin, and he spoke of magic and how the magicians hated Conan Doyle, whose biography he had read recently, and of Ayrshire cows, which they saw and are not usual in that part of the world, which is Holstein country. When they circled back into Talcottville, my father gestured toward the old Grange Hall and said, "My father used to attend the meetings."

That day, after Glyn left, I went over and got Father into bed with his cane beside him. When the Munns came, I got him out of bed, saying, "Goodbye, Father," knowing they'd stay until Liz came on duty. They said they made small talk and had a nice time. There had been the smell of death in the room when I was helping him. I'd left him alone that afternoon to go over to Villa Rosalinda to get *Time* magazine. When I returned, he was furious I'd taken so long and bawled me out. It was all normal as could be. Bob Stabb thought I'd left him alone too much, but perhaps my father and I had some common wavelength, for though I always pack days ahead for a trip, I hadn't yet packed for the approaching trip to Cummington, nor did I ever.

At six-twenty or so the next morning, June 12, Liz called me. I went over in my nightclothes, and she was giving him oxygen, saying "It's going to be all right" again and again. Soon he began to make a terrible noise trying to breathe, and at six-thirty or so it was over. The first thing I said to Liz, who had tears in her eyes, was "My heart goes out to Mrs. Wilson." I called her and she kept saying, "It's not true. It's not true." But it was. I persuaded her with great difficulty to have Reuel sent for. He was in the guesthouse. Ironically, he passed by on the thruway the night of June 6 on his way to the Cape, stopping at Cazenovia to see the Marcelins. Mrs. Stabb kept telling Reuel, "He went easy, very easy." When Dr. Smith came, after he pronounced him dead, he asked, "Why not the heart pacer? It takes over when this happens." I could only say what my father told Glyn. He'd refused it. I had never talked about it with him. He and Liz had been discussing whether he should have a bath or breakfast. He was sitting up in his chair when he died. I sat with him until Mary Crosten, whom I had called, came, holding his hand as it gradually lost its warmth.

Eva called and said, "Phito lost such a big friend." Elizabeth Maguire showed up with two other ladies and sat in true Irish-wake fashion. Glyn arranged to meet Elena's plane. I called the undertaker, who came and did not embalm him but left him in the bed. The oxygen had to be removed. I sat with my father while Liz took some things to be washed. Eventually, I went home and got dressed. No one knew what to do about the funeral service until Elena arrived at about four o'clock. It turned out Glyn was supposed to read the Ninetieth Psalm, which begins, "Lord thou hast been our dwelling place in all generations," and the twelfth chapter of Ecclesiastes. My father had told the Morrises several years before, "I don't want any of these atheistic funerals."

When Elena came in the house, the first thing she did was to walk to the card table and scoop the papers off it, saying, "Where are the diaries? Where are the diaries?" Then she wanted the heat turned up, which I pointed out shouldn't be done, according to the undertaker. Then she went to my father. She behaved with practicality throughout. The Stabbs, the Howlands, Mary Crosten, Glyn, Dr. Edgar Miller, Mary Pcolar and others came to the service at around five-thirty. As Glyn was reading the psalm, Mary Pcolar's voice clanked out metallically, "Where are my flowers? I had placed them right on the table next to the body."

Huldah Loomis had come up before the service with a large ham—a funeral meat—as is the country custom. As she left the room, she blew my father a kiss and said, "Good-bye, old dear."

Elena asked to be left alone with the body as it was being put into the coffin.

After that, she and I went up to the Howlands', and they showed her an article in the paper about her husband's death. For the first time, she burst into tears because that made it really true. She spent the night with me, talking a lot about thank God this was her last visit to the accursed Talcottville, saw the undertaker the next morning, and went off with faithful Glyn to the crematorium to pick up the ashes and then to the plane.

When he came up, my father had called up to have an apple tree branch cut so the car could draw up to the back door of the house. But his coffin was carried out the front door over a board spanning one of the trenches from the road debacle.

Before the service, one of the undertaker's assistants asked me, "What are you going to do with the antiques?" The other undertaker in Boonville had been up to see Huldah Loomis a spell before soliciting her trade, asking her, "What about your antiques?" He also gave her a good new recipe for brandied peaches, but so far as she was concerned that was poor compensation for the fact he coveted not her body so much as her antiques.

Some of the local reactions varied from, "I guess the old boy got what he wanted; he died up here," to the local picture framer Jim Fynmore's "I never read any of his books and I doubt if he did either."

The following night, Elena called me to tell me when the memorial service in Wellfleet would be. Then she said, "We can't find a will. I don't know where the will is." I said, "It probably is at your lawyers', Choate, Hall and Stuart." "What happened?" she said. "Who have you got up there? I don't want Penberthy [my father's lawyer in Utica, who had taken him on for nothing in his tax trouble]."

As far as I was concerned, her tone was such I really didn't want to go to the memorial service and wouldn't have done so except everyone would have thought it strange if I didn't.

When I got to Wellfleet, I burst into tears upon seeing Reuel and apologized about the codicil. He said it had come back unsigned. The first thing Elena said to me as I entered the house was, "Roger Straus' lawyers are going to probate the will," which I didn't pay much attention to at the time. Next thing, people were coming in and out. Sofka Winkelhorn was there, Morley and Barry Callaghan came in. Morley, whom I never met before, was very friendly to me, saying, "I knew your mother." Elena said, "I'm riding to the cemetery with your father," meaning his ashes.

In Article 3 of his will, my father requested that funeral services be held by the Reverend Glyn Morris of Lyons Falls, New York, if he be near and available. In Glyn's mind, he was both, but unfortunately in Elena's, Glyn was part of the hated Talcottville life. So the young Episcopalian minister in Wellfleet read the service, in an uninspired way.

Nina and Paul Chavchavadze greeted me with great affection, and Phyllis and Eben Given and the Walkers. Charlie Walker, who was in the last stages of terminal heart trouble himself, read a little eulogy at the gravesite, saying among other things, "I've known Edmund Wilson fifty-six years; [and then in effect] since the publication of his first great book, *Axel's Castle*, he has never let his standards down."

I left right after the service. I didn't want to leave things unattended too long. Very shortly after, I went down to Boston for the day, where I still had a foothold as far as doctors and lawyers went. At Ropes, Gray they sent over to Choate, Hall for my father's will and codicil. It was the first time I assimilated that extraordinary document, saw who the other signatures were—Glyn Morris and Elizabeth Stabb, and that great empty space at the top with one little signature missing, my father's. It referred to his will drawn up in January 1969 in Wellfleet but beginning, "I, Edmund Wilson, of Talcottville, in the County of Lewis and State of New York . . . " As it referred to his will of 1969, Elena must have known there was a will. Whether she or her lawyers sent up the codicil, I don't know. I think my father must have mailed it back, because if it had been on the table she would have tackled me on the subject when she was here. It must have been awaiting her when she returned to Wellfleet or been sent to her lawyers. Anyway, I believe there's every chance, having known Elena and my father for a long while, she kept asking "Dearest-est-est-est, have you had the little codicil witnessed?" He got bored and said he had, which I guess he had. That's the sort of hairpin my father could be when he felt like it.

At any rate, Elena was upset beyond rhyme or reason. She had no intention of selling the Wellfleet house, as Helen was of age when her father died and was well able to deal with things. Reuel said if they hadn't raised such a fuss he would have let them have it. When the accounting of the estate finally came up, it was in no trouble, and there were still the diaries and books of correspondence to come out. My sister had been left the royalties from her father's work outright, but not the books and not the editorship of them.

Reuel had said to me, "Elena may resort to litigation over the codicil."

Elena Mumm Wilson was a great lady, a fighter, a terrific worker, and probably if she'd decided to paint would have been a much better painter than Mary Meigs. She'd always behaved properly with me and Reuel, being generous and caring with us. She'd created a possible life for herself out of an almost impossible situation. If anyone understood that, that person was myself. The difficulties of living with my father were subtle and incommunicable ones.

Her maternal grandmother had been Russian, Annekov, her maternal grandfather a Russified German, Struve. The Struves were a family of astronomers, physicists, scientists; as one Russian said to me, "You name it." The rest of the way she was German. And her turf was German. Ever since I had known her, she and her family had been fighting over their infinitely complicated property settlements. The champagne business had been taken by the French as war reparations. There were constant negotiations, family quarrels. In 1960 I had met her sister, Olili, in London. We had hardly sat down to dinner when she started in on how strangely Elena had behaved over some property settlement (they later made up). I'd been hearing an obbligato on the same subject from Elena. Occasionally, Elena would get large sums from Germany from the wine business or a false-tooth factory in Switzerland. Eventually, Olili left Elena's daughter an inheritance.

Henry James could have gone to town on Elena Mumm and Edmund Wilson, the European and the American point of view. She read a great deal, was up on current events, and certainly learned a lot in the years with my father. Her field was not American literature.

Once when I had been irritated with Elena over something, Nina had said to me, "There are things you and Sofka and I would think are funny which Elena doesn't. I want you to think about that." I did. I did again and again and again during some of the events which were to follow my father's death.

In the will, Elena was named as executrix and then again in Article 10 as "literary executrix" and then "I direct her to have Leon Edel of Columbia University, New York, or, if he refuses, Daniel Aaron of Smith College, Northampton, Massachusetts, as editor of my journals and other posthumous manuscripts and papers, including correspondence." If Elena ceased to serve as executrix, Jesse R. Fillman or John Dane, Jr., of Choate, Hall were to serve.

Happily, Edel was willing to put aside his own work, which was noble of him. It seemed to me the papers would just be turned over to Edel. I'm sure my father thought that's what would happen and naming Elena "literary executrix" was explained to him as a way of facilitating things. But Elena was much more intimate with Aaron and his family, who had a house in Wellfleet; and she set about tidying up dearest one's remains, literary and otherwise, with terrifying ardor.

She had been through a grueling time during my father's last years, and she had had health problems—pneumonia several times and stomach trouble which her doctor diagnosed as having been brought on "by a little too much Edmund." Certainly, everyone thought she should have the greatest consideration after years behind the mast.

The will, after a hassle, was eventually probated in Lewis County, New York, where it should have been. It would have been out of order for Roger Straus' lawyers to probate it in New York City.

My father had been very generous to me during his lifetime, and I certainly felt I had been treated more than fairly in being left the stone house and its contents, which I didn't know until Boston, as I'd been so testy every time my parent started in on what he was going to leave or not leave.

When I returned to Talcottville, I told Glyn about the codicil's being unsigned. He was totally bemused. "They must think we're awfully dumb," he said. And I suppose whoever the eternal "theys" are in life did. Then he pointed out it would have been illegal for us to have witnessed the signing of the codicil, as we were mentioned in the will. It's the sort of nebulous, pixieish situation my father would have absolutely loved. Good sleight-of-hand artists are always masters of misdirection. A trained nurse, a minister turned assistant superintendent of schools, and a former editor in a publishing house had witnessed a nonexistent signature. But, of course, we had been in the hands of the master, a man who thought nothing of wiping spots off of cards.

There was none of the short, sweet tying up of affairs which had existed when my grandmother died. It took me several years to get the executrix deed for the stone house and the grinding away about the unsigned codicil never seemed to end.

# XXXIII

EBEN GIVEN SAID TO ME when I made my goodbyes to them before leaving Wellfleet, "The house wasn't radioactive with Bunny when we drove by, it was just a house." That's the way I'd felt. With all our fights, difficulties, booby-trapping of doors, and sometimes genuine cruelty, the good vibrations had finally outweighed the bad ones. The superb intellect had left greater waves than the evil temperament that sometimes shook him. "Nothing shows on my radar when I pass Money Hill," Eben said again. It was named Money Hill after the two wealthy sea captains who had built their twin houses there.

In the summer of 1973, my cousin Susan Wilson came to Talcottville to visit me—or really her dog, which I'd taken when she went into the Martha Jefferson Home. She was at her most adorable, the perfect, soft-spoken southern lady. One afternoon we went over to the Foltz Home in Herkimer to visit a friend of hers who had been head of social services in New York State. Members of the Mafia seemed like wimps compared to these ladies. They sat so sweetly in the summer sun cackling: "We outlasted five public health commissioners." I realized those men hadn't had a chance, in spite of their limousines and political connections. The ladies rambled on with delight about some of the methods they'd used to break them or at least whip them into shape.

I gave a dinner party for Susan, and she flattered all the men in her soft-spoken, antebellum way until one of them, John Howland, started telling a story about a lawyer in town using some legal terms. "I'd better clarify these for you," he said, turning to Susan. She said in a rather tough voice, "Listen, honey, my father was a professor of law, my brother was a lawyer, my favorite uncle was a lawyer, and my mother ran a boardinghouse for lawyers. They talk quite a lot about law at the University of Virginia." She then proceeded to clear up the legal point John had been speaking of, ruining his story, and holding up a huge goblet, ending with, "Would you take this glass, Br'er John, fill it almost to the top with bourbon, and slosh a touch of branch water over the top."

Barry Callaghan stopped by from Toronto and drove Susan to the Cape. His family was in Wellfleet for a few weeks.

Susan had a great affection and respect for Elena. But after she left Wellfleet, I got a letter saying, "I tried to tell her a codicil is just the same as a will, and you can't probate an unsigned will, and it made no difference what his intentions were, and she'd be happier to forget it." They'd tried everything by that time, sending up to Penberthy's for old wills, and I had begun to feel they were really enjoying arguing over the patrimony. Eventually, Reuel took the guesthouse as a substitute for half the big house and its contents.

Elena had been a big part of my life, and there were many fine memories, but to go down to Wellfleet would have been madness; so I floated around the Black River, occasionally getting reports from old Cape friends who stopped over, saying Elena was very much Madame l'Executrix and having a happy social time.

I assumed the papers had been turned over *in toto* to Edel, but that turned out not to be the case.

The first indication I got that things weren't running smoothly between Elena and Edel was a phone call from Eben Given. When I was a child in the Dosses' house, Eben had loaned me his kayak, saying, "I'll always have a boat waiting for you." And he always did. Later I used to go over to their island in Maine and there was always a boat with a captain at the dock. We had a special rapport, knowing the words to all the Jimmy Durante records. He loved creating an air of mystery. And we used to hit the after-hour places in Boston when they stayed at the Vendôme, where he created fantastic stories about the occupants. Phyllis was only too glad to be rid of us. He began his call by signing on with the opening stanza of a Durante song, "Who will be with you when I'm far away, far away from you?" then got into the heavy stuff. "Elena's turned into the fastest draw in town, saying Edel's a bad hombre about your pappy's gold mine up in them thar hills." He always put things in Western terms. I was surprised because Elena and the Givens had never been very cozy, but apparently she'd been coming over there, requesting they get their letters from "my pappy" in order and belch them up. Eben said she was rabid on the subject of Edel's misdemeanors. "She's planning to corral your pappy's works herself and run Edel out of town." Read "edit" for "corral." I couldn't believe it. I thought Eben must have misunderstood. But the Welsh seldom misunderstand that sort of thing. I expressed incredulity, sang Durante's "Did you ever have the feeling that you wanted to go and still have the feeling that you wanted to stay?" and turned the conversation elsewhere.

I thought it was all part of Elena's wanting to take a vacuum cleaner and some furniture polish and get dearest one's literary remains in order. Someone had once said, "Of course, Germans have two sides, wanting to bring order out of chaos and a very sentimental side. I must say in working with the Wilsons, she's working with shifting sands."

At that point in my life, I didn't want to read book reviews, my father's diaries, or know anything about the whole affair. I always liked a desultory country life, which is what I was leading, with a few visitors on the scene occasionally. Natalia, who naturally had gotten an earful, came up and said it was all quite incredible. "The Chavchavadzes still love you," she said. Why shouldn't they? What had I done except be a patsy for my father's not wanting to sign the codicil.

"Well," Natalia said, looking back at the stone house as she left for her home in Geneva after one of her visits, "big trees leave big holes."

Other old Cape acquaintances seconded what Natalia had said. One of them said, "Whatever the rights and wrongs of this, Elena feels very aggrieved." Why? She had the house for her lifetime. Another visitor, a prominent woman of letters, liked Elena but nevertheless put it squarely: "Elena's devious and she's out of her depth when it comes to editing your father's works."

"But Edel's dealing with my father's works," I said. "If he'd wanted Elena as editor, he wouldn't have left Edel as editor."

My visitor shook her head. "She has ambitions to be his editor. It's the old German thing: Let's not have part of the world, let's have the whole world."

I cited the fact she hated *Upstate* and my father had told both Glyn and me he considered it the highlight of his career. I wish I'd asked him *why*. With Glyn he hadn't qualified it with "journalistic" career.

My father and I never sat around discussing his work. I did know from comments he made that he thought Edel would take over his papers. I'd met Edel for lunch at Dartmouth really en passant after my father's death and thought again how lucky we were that he was willing to do the job. He was much more in touch with life than a lot of highly accredited experts.

When Barry Callaghan had come up in the spring of 1973, he told me two wonderful anecdotes about our respective fathers. One of Morley's taking out his car, which he seldom did, and driving my parent up the Toronto main drag the wrong way at peak traffic hour, going slowly, pointing out the sights; the other of my father's saying, "I just want to be of use. I want to be of use," in relation to literature. Of course Barry being Canadian, knew about Edel, who naturally had been on the Canadian scene.

The Givens wanted to send their correspondence directly to Edel, but apparently other arrangements were made.

It all seemed unnecessary to have such a fuss, with Elena complaining constantly to everyone about Edel. My family had originally gone to Choate, Hall and Stuart in Boston because of Charley Curtis. He was Houghton Mifflin's lawyer and very knowledgeable about literature. He and Ferris Greenslet had done several books together, one of them *The Practical Cogitator*. By the time my father died, Curtis was either dead or retired. Things might have been different if he had still been on the scene. He was a brilliant man. Occasionally, he would come into the Houghton Mifflin office and he had one of those intelligences you could feel.

Eventually, in 1976, I got a letter from Edel saying he might have to bow out if interference from Wellfleet continued. He'd been planning the letters, literary and political, as a makeweight volume to offset the confessional side of the journals. He said the letters were bunched together without any relation to chronology and that that was the sort of thing my father would have criticized, as he did in *Patriotic Gore* about the editing of those letters of Teddy Roosevelt's that were written before his presidency. The manuscript was apparently totally scrambled. And I was astonished to hear that Elena had established a dual editorship with herself and Edel. Eventually, her volume came out with a great deal of help from other people.

I'd shared an office with Craig Wylie, who was doing Houghton Mifflin's big American history and letters' books. Although we tried to give each other as much privacy as possible and close our ears to the other's affairs, I couldn't help but realize the difference in the sort of work I was capable of doing and the sort he was. I had no deep knowledge of American history. I would have thought it screamingly funny if someone had suggested I was better qualified than Edel to edit my father's papers. What was amazing was that Elena didn't see that she too was less qualified. Nina had been right. A bull's-eye for the old grand duchess.

Elena had had my father dependent on her in many, many ways, but in the end she couldn't grab on to all the written words, all the ideas, all the commentaries, although she tried. The part of her dearest one that soared from his intellect remained elusive. She was such a charming and decent person that she could brainwash people. One woman had said to me, "Of course, Edmund Wilson never really wrote until he married her." There were *Axel's Castle* and *To the Finland Station*. Edel should certainly have been given carte blanche, but Elena was a woman who liked to be in control.

Edel also thanked me for being the only person to send him the article of the will pertaining to his work. It seemed incredible the lawyers who probated the will hadn't.

Elena may have felt aggrieved, but I began to feel irritated. After all, deathbed codicils trying to get the testator to change a bequest he has refused to alter for twenty-six years and more aren't very nice. And making me miserable over it had been unnecessary.

My father would have loved the fuss over the codicil. He

would have been appalled that Edel was on the brink of being "run out of town," as Eben put it.

I think Elena may have actually been unclear as to just what Edel's qualifications were. In one letter to Edel, she said that Edmund had discussed with her everything he wrote. That wasn't quite true. For several of the summers during their marriage, they had had no communication at all during his Talcottville stays. He wasn't even calling her. Until his last years, he was still doing a certain amount of journalistic legwork which she wasn't a part of.

Once my father and I had been discussing Conan Doyle's *The Hound of the Baskervilles* in Talcottville. We'd come home and found some large paw prints by the front door. "The footprints of a giant hound?" I asked.

"Yes, the curse of the Baskervilles is on us," he said.

"You never really knew the Baskervilles," I said. "A seedy county family. One wouldn't want to be seen at the Hulbert House with them."

"Elena doesn't know she doesn't know the Baskervilles," he said absolutely apropos of nowhere, it seemed to me, but perhaps not.

Reuel's attitude was, "Let her have a volume of letters as a memorial to her husband."

I thought Edel should be allowed to function on his own completely. When Elena died, Reuel said he heard there were many people at her funeral. "Sure," he said, "she'd been kind to so many." And I was, on the whole, one of them.

# XXXIV

THE STONE HOUSE STOOD VACANT, with the front lawn cut off by the State of New York in its infinite wisdom. When the house went on the historic register, I got congratulatory letters from two representatives. I wrote back that it was a shame their state had made things so miserable for my father in his last years. The mailman said he couldn't get used to not seeing the portly figure in bathrobe and pajamas and felt hat on the front porch in the summer.

Would-be chroniclers of Edmund Wilson began scrambling up Route 12D. One of them asked me if I'd give him my father's cane if I liked what he wrote. It was like dealing with Uriah Heep. At that point I invited Barry Callaghan to come and stay in the stone house and take the load off me, which he did gallantly. After that I sent people to Barry, who's fairly elusive.

By far the best thing written about Edmund Wilson since his death is the piece by Sir Isaiah Berlin appearing *in toto* in the *Yale Review* about Father's visit to London and Berlin at

Oxford—the best because it's written by a worthy commentator who intuitively knew the score and was in a position to see things from the top. The piece also had humor, unlike some of the gloomy commentary by lesser lights which has appeared.

Berlin describes my father's complaining they wouldn't let him see the prostitutes, that they were trying to keep him away from the prostitutes. It's the old Red Bank communication problem again. Most people would have simply thought, "They won't let me see the prostitutes." If you substitute "peonies" for "prostitutes," you have my grandmother sitting in her Cadillac saying, "Why won't Oscar drive me past Addie's place? They don't want me to see the peonies I gave her. They didn't do what I told them and now they're poorly. Why won't Oscar take me by the peonies? They're probably replacing them with new ones. Isn't that something high, by old Billy Ho, they planted them too shallow and now they won't let me see the peonies."

Talcottville went on being Talcottville. The house was burglarized on the same day the final papers came; I had gone to Boston for two nights. They got in through the back door. Among the things taken were the large oval paintings of the Adirondack lakes, the birdcage tip-top table, a brass bed warmer, a charcoal foot warmer, and many other delightful pieces.

The new road built for safety's sake was soon the scene of accidents involving members of the same families who'd had trouble on the old road. One night I walked over to the stone house across a road literally running in blood. One of the boys thrown out of the car lay like a rag doll. They had to scrape him up.

The judge awarded four hundred dollars for the damage done to the house by the new road. That's the policy of judges, apparently awarding less and less in land takeover cases. Now if a Canadian firm, for example, wants to run a pipeline through your property, they can. No one really owns their land anymore; the state can, if it desires, send people through your house room by room to access it.

Now the farmers are going down like ninepins and the predatory developers will soon be on top of us.

Fort Drum, forty-five miles north, has been injudiciously expanded because of the efforts of a Mephistophelian-looking type, a Representative Martin. There are stories of the waste up there. Great packs of chickens, never used, still in ice, thrown out at the dump. People were going to collect the excess food, but they closed it as the people were also talking. Jerry—built buildings with every third board nailed. When the National Guard goes in up there, they spend as much money as possible or else they won't get a like amount the following year. Contractors are getting enormous grants to build expensive housing in Watertown. A huge salmon hatchery at Altmar costs millions of dollars, but you can't eat the Great Lake salmon because the PCB levels are so high.

The army is trying to take over Tug Hill the same way they tried to take over the Cape Cod National Park. But perhaps this rugged country and its people will fight back.

Mansur Ralfizadeh, who some newspapers have said was connected with Savak, the Shah of Iran's secret service, built a mammoth barn in Boonville, bigger than any barn in New York State. That's gone now. A strange outfit opened a resort in back of Talcottville on Tug Hill and advertised "the nearby St. Lawrence" (eighty miles away) and "nearby Oneida Lake" (twenty miles away), making the old Florida land-deal crooks seem like innocents. All this since my father's death. They have come and gone.

My father's work remains. The stone house remains. What a house for anyone who loves gossip. A great roast beef for a gossip. I sold the house. The beautiful countryside remains, with its romantic quality of being "on the way" everywhere— to the west, to the east, to the vast expanse of Canada.

I think of my father sometimes; of his taking me to Bennington where I had a small scholarship and waited on tables, choosing the furniture for my room, including an awful chair. "You've got to have a chair." Standing by me when I had my wisdom teeth removed, coming to the hospital with a great bottle of Myers' rum—when I woke up drunk from the ether, he was equally so. But the person has receded and cognizance of the work comes rolling in.

In spite of attempted landfills and acid rain, the countryside is still spectacular, with its high western American sky, short lush summers, fantastic autumns, harsh winters with their etched landscapes, and muddy yet tender springs.

Important men of letters should die in houses like the stone house and have their coffins exit through majestic doors. Waldo Frank died in a dark room in a nursing home.

The choice of the twelfth chapter of Ecclesiastes my father asked to be read at his funeral service showed a great self-knowledge, and I find verses twelve and fourteen the most pertinent:

12   And further, by these, my son, be admonished: of making many books there is no end; and much study is a weariness of the flesh.

14   For God shall bring every work into judgment, with every secret thing, whether it be good, or whether it be evil.

Stephen Spender's poem beginning "I think continually of those who were truly great" was etched with a diamond pencil on three windowpanes between my father's room on the second floor and the bathroom. He often stopped in the hall between rooms and gazed at it for a while. You'd see him when you looked up the stairs.

I'd say Edmund Wilson thought "continually of those who were truly great" and was of use to them.

*My father and I always celebrated April Fool's Day. The following
letter, which replicates the original, turned up at Beinecke Library
at Yale and is one of my more successful attempts to fool him.*

April Fool's letter by Rosalind *[in EW's hand]*

April 1, 1949
16 Oak Street
New Haven, Conn.

Dear Mr. Wilson,

I suffered from a slight stroke several months ago, and, as a
result, I have just come to read my New Yorkers. I read your
article on Swift with particular interest; and it led me to take a
step which I have long been vacillating on. I have in my
possession some very interesting and valuable material on
Swift, which was the property of my late husband. The
material consists of a hundred or so letters written by Swift to
an old Dublin lady, an ancestor of my husbands.

I am now seventy five. In 1900, I was married to John
Trefry, master in Greek at the university of Dublin. Trefry was
much interested in Swift and had in his hands the letters of
which I speak, written to Mrs. Mary Ann Trefry. He had
arranged to publish these letters in a pamphlet with an introduction by himself. The pamphlet was titled, *The Dean's
Little Joke.* However, the night before the publication, the
printing house was broken into, the plates destroyed and the
night watchman killed. The next day my husband was visited
by several members of the cloth, who said the pamphlet must
not be published under any circumstances. One of these
dignitaries, a gentleman, rich in his own right, offered to
purchase the letters for a gigantic sum. My husband refused.

Two weeks later he was murdered by a blow on the head on
his way home from the university. Again, the letters were put

aside. I had never been in love with my husband and any project dear to his heart was naturally not dear to mine. Also, as a young woman, it seemed to me there were other sources of excitement than Swift's letters. I dreaded going through my husband's papers. There were a great many unfinished manuscripts and poems, the latter which I was afraid I would find were not exactly odes to me; so the trunk and I travelled around together for years.

I think even now I would have hesitated to do anything, if I were not hard pressed financially. I would naturally like to get as much as possible for these letters. The letters prove without a doubt that it was Swift who wanted to marry Mrs. Johnson that she was of a cold an hysterical temperament and would not marry, that Swift (Biographers and psychologists to the contrary) had a great many affairs, had a mistress, a Mrs. Brady for years and had three children by Mrs. Brady. They also explain the incident with Archbishop King. King was a noted old gossip, who was always spilling secrets told in the confessional. Swift one day went in to him and made himself the remark always quoted as King's, knowing that King would immediately repeat it. It was Swift who had tears in his eyes, tears of suppressed laughter, as he rushed out. As Swift wrote to Mary Ann Trefry, "You may be sure my dear DORMI * (His pet name for her, standing for Dear Old Relic Mine.) King never could or would have contained himself had there been a reason and had he known it."

Swift always got on well in the society of old ladies. In the case of Mary Ann he confided, things he confided to no one else. Am ambitious man with Swift's brains was hardly likely to go around confiding his affairs to every Tom Dick and Harry.

Mrs. Trefry outlived him by two years, being ninty eight when she died. She, like Swift, was subject to spells of deafness and dizziness from a malformation of the inner ear. In many of the letters Swift passes on to her new pills or oils, which he has found helpful.

In one letter Swift complains to her that his poem about Vanessa has been totally misunderstood, that he had always disliked this girl, that in his poem he is complaining bitterly that it is rather unecassary to read Montaigne while cold creaming the face. This was a habit of Vanessa's which had always driven him crazy. As for those who doubt he had an affair with her, they must be fools who think a girl commits suicide just because a man stops making out her reading lists for her.

But enough, you will see the letters for yourself. In closing I will give one more excerpt to show that no one can doubt Mrs. Johnson's temperament, "Dear Dormi, last evening I went to visit the amiable Stella. She said she was suffering a chill. Mrs. Dingley brought in a jug of chamomile. I left soon after; so she could retire." Now, Mr. Wilson, we are not so innocent as to think this is what actually happened. Jug of Chamomile indeed! What occurred was something quite different. Jug probably stands for hug; chamomile, we cannot take at its face value either, chamo, probably cameo without the E. o and exclamation and mile, well, put an s on it and you have smile. "I left soon after." Left what? The room to go into another room of course so they could retire. In other words he is writing to old Mrs. Trefry. "I went to see Stella. She was chilly; but I gave her a hug and a squeeze. Her chameo face O lit up into a smile. I left the room and we retired."

The letters are full of confidences like the above. May I hope to hear from you soon Mr. Wilson. My friend Miss Hasley in the accounts department of the New Yorker has told me of your Stamford residence. It is a lovely place, Stamford, and I hope you find it so.

# Appendix

A small selection of books from Edmund Wilson's boyhood library from the stone house in Talcottville, New York. Many of them have bookplates, which he never used in later life. The plates say at the top, "The Wicked Borroweth and Returneth Not Again," then there is a lion below, and below that, "Edmund Wilson Jr." Many of the books have the authors' names completed by him when only initials were used, or pages recopyedited by him. His handwriting is totally different from his small, perfect mature handwriting. He signs his name in bold large letters, an obvious imitation of his mother's signature.

*Short Cruises*, W. W. Jacobs (Scribner's, New York, 1907). In EW's hand, his signature, then, "Presented to himself by himself with his Christmas money—1908."

*Light Freights*, W. W. Jacobs (Dodd Mead, New York, 1907). In EW's hand, "Christmas 1907."

*Sailors' Knots*, W. W. Jacobs (Scribner's, New York, 1909). In EW's hand, "Hill School, Pottstown, Pennsylvania, then Hillside." In the back of the book, he repeats the same words in Greek.

*A Master of Craft*, W. W. Jacobs (Methuen Co., London, 1906). EW's signature, then, "bought in London, England when staying at The Grand Hotel, Trafalgar Square, presented by his MOTHER."

*Odd Craft*, W. W. Jacobs (Scribner's, New York, 1906). EW's name, then, "Quebec 1907" in EW's mother's hand.

*Mother Goose Stories*, words and music (no publisher). In EW's hand, "My mother used to play and sing me these."

*History and Habits of Animals (and Those Mentioned in the Scriptures)*, Peter Walker (Presbyterian Board of Publication, 1859).

*Tales from Shakespeare*, Charles Lamb (Dutton, 1906).

*Comedies and Legends for Marionettes*, Giorgiana Goddard King (Macmillan, London, 1904). Title page recopyedited by EW, signed by EW, then, "From little Aunt Addie," his mother's sister named after EW's great-aunt.

*The Lady and the Tiger*, Frank Stockton (Scribner's, New York, 1907). Title page recopyedited by EW.

*First Book of Botany*, Youmans (Appleton, 1872). Signed "Candace E. Putnam."

*The Queen's Museum and Other Fanciful Tales*, Frank Stockton, illustrated by Frederick Richardson (Scribner's, New York, 1906).

*An Abridgement of the Sacred History*, Lomand (sterotyped by L. Johnson, 1833; published by Joseph Lewis, Baltimore). Signed "Grace Baker"; floral design by EW.

*Silver Pitchers and Independence*, Louisa May Alcott (Roberts Brothers, Boston, 1876). Signed by EW's mother.

*The Little Minister*, James M. Barrie (Hurst & Co., no date). Front page copyedited "atthew" after the *M*.

*The Virginian*, Owen Wister (Grosset & Dunlap, New York, 1902; printed by Cushing & Smith).

*The Story of Patsy*, Kate Douglas Wiggin (Houghton Mifflin, Boston, 1889).

*Letters of a Japanese Schoolboy*, Wallace Erwin, illustrated by Rollin Kirby (Doubleday, 1909). EW's signature, then, "From his mother. You are the nicest girl I know."

*Stories and Legends from Irving* (Putnam, New York, 1896).

*The Peterkin Papers*, Lucretia P. Hale (Ticknor & Fields, 1880). In EW's hand, "eabody" after the *P.*

*The Railway Children*, E. Nesbitt (Wells, Gardner, Darton & Co.; Surrey postwar ed.). Impression unclear. Reset with new illustrations and format.

*Lorna Doone,* R. D. Blackmore (Crowell & Co., Boston, 1893). Two signatures of Edmund Wilson. One, "Edmund Wilson, Lakewood 1899," must be EW Senior's, then EW's signature and "The Hill School, Pottstown, Pennsylvania."

*Bob, Son of Battle,* Alfred Ollivant (Doubleday, New York, 1900).

*Songs of the Child's World No.* 2, words by C. D. Wiley, music by Jessica Gaynor (John Church Co., Cincinnati, 1904).

*William Henry and His Friends,* Abby Morton Diaz (Lothrop Publishing Co., Boston, 1871). In EW's hand, "Edmund Wilson Jr. from himself."

*The William Henry Letters,* Abby Morton Diaz (Lothrop Publishing Co., Boston, 1870).

*Letters to Beany,* Henry A. Shute (Everett Press, Boston, 1905). EW's inscription is very amusing. He has signed his name with many embellishments, then in his hand, "From his mother." Then in quotes, "It cost me a great deal of money." Obviously, what his mother said when she gave it to him.

*The Dwarf Tailor and Other Tales,* collected by Zoe Dana (Underhill; Harper, New York, 1896).

*The Little Grey Mouse,* no author (Lothrop Publishing Co., Boston, 1885). In EW's hand, "Stolen from the Presbyterian Sunday school."

*Legends of the Rhine,* Wilhelm Rutland (Hoursch & Bechstedt, Cologne, no date). EW's signature, then in his hand, "Going down the Rhine." Obviously read while doing so.

*The Little Shepherd of Kingdom Come,* John Fox, Jr. (Scribner's, New York, 1903). In EW's mother's hand, "Edmund Wilson, Sept. 14, 1903."

*The Thousand and One Nights, or The Arabian Nights' Entertainments* (William X. Allison & Co., New York, no date).

*De Namin' ob de Twins and Other Sketches from the Cotton Land,* Mary Fairfax Childs, illustrated from oil paintings by Edward H. Potthast (J. W. Burke Co., Macon, Georgia; B. W. Dodge & Co., 1908).